THE SKEPTICAL JUROR

AND

THE TRIAL OF BYRON CASE

THE SKEPTICAL JUROR

THE SKEPTICAL JUROR

AND

THE TRIAL OF BYRON CASE

FIRST IN A SERIES

BY

J BENNETT ALLEN

ALLEN & ALLEN SEMIOTICS, INC.

LONG BEACH, CALIFORNIA

First Edition, January 2010

ISBN 978-0-9842716-0-3
Published by Allen & Allen Semiotics, Inc., www.semiotics.com

Cover design by Ed Lewis, www.edlewisdesign.com
Cover design © 2009 Ed Lewis

Printed on acid-free paper in the United States of Americ

I thumbed through the mail, and there it was. Yet another summons for jury duty. What's that make now? Ten? At least ten. I'll treat it as I have every other time. I'll show up and I'll answer all the attorney questions honestly but concisely. If I'm selected, I'll do my duty and fulfill my oath.

The prosecution doesn't realize it, but they better have a darn good case if they accept me as a juror. I have no qualms about sending bad guys off to prison, I've already done so. But I'm absolutely not going to vote guilty if the State doesn't prove its case beyond a reasonable doubt.

Of course I'll serve if called. I'll raise my right hand and take the oath, and I'll stand true to that oath. I am, after all, The Skeptical Juror.

TABLE OF CONTENTS

PRELUDE

The most famous resident of Lincoln Cemetery is jazz musician and Kansas City native Charlie "Bird" Parker. He got his nickname when the band bus hit and killed a chicken. Charlie, recognizing the possibility of a free dinner, convinced the driver to "go back there and pick up that yardbird." The nickname, often shortened to "Bird," stuck fast.

When Charlie died, he left instructions with Chan, his common-law wife, that she was not "to let anyone bury me in Kansas City." Unfortunately, Charlie never bothered divorcing his first wife, and legal issues caused his body to be returned to Missouri for burial. That was in 1955, during the days of segregation. Lincoln Cemetery was where blacks were segregated for eternity.

In a strict sense, though, Charlie's wish was actually granted. He is buried not quite in Kansas City. Lincoln lies just beyond the city limits, in the unincorporated community of Blue Summit, wedged between Kansas City to the west and Independence to the east.

❖

Deputy Sheriff David Epperson probably wasn't thinking about "Bird" when the headlights of his patrol car fell upon a body lying on the solitary road that ran through Lincoln Cemetery. It was 3:44 AM on the 23rd of October, 1997. It was dark and seriously so. The cemetery had no lights, the moon had yet to rise, and the cloud cover was opaque. Epperson's headlights and his flashlight were the only illumination.

She was lying on her back with her arms above her head. Her eyes were open. She was well dressed, her clothing intact. There was no sign of a struggle. Someone had shot her in the face, probably from close range. Anastasia Elizabeth WitbolsFeugen was 18 years and 100 days old when she died.

Justin Bruton's body was discovered two days later. The two of them, Justin and Anastasia, had been lovers. Justin was twenty years old. He had stuck a shotgun in his mouth and pulled the trigger. It was undisputedly a suicide. The fact he took his own life just days after Anastasia's murder only muddied the waters.

For years, the investigation into Anastasia's murder went nowhere.

Justin and Anastasia had been close friends of Byron Case and his girlfriend Kelly Moffett. Byron was 18 years old then, a month short of 19. He had been especially close to Justin.

Kelly was the youngest of the group. She was 15, and just barely that. After Anastasia's death, Kelly's alcohol and drug use spiraled out of control. She dropped out of school. Her parents kicked her out of the house. She stayed in treatment centers or crack houses.

In September of 2000, three years after it happened, Kelly told her rehab counselor that she knew who killed Anastasia WitbolsFeugen.

INTRODUCTION

Good morning. I'm The Skeptical Juror.

It's Monday morning, April 29, 2002. We're at the Jackson County Courthouse in Kansas City, Missouri. It's a beautiful, clear day today. Temperature at the moment is only 52 degrees, but it's supposed to warm to 70 by this afternoon.

Today, Byron Case goes on trial for the murder of Anastasia WitbolsFeugen. He was arrested almost a year ago after his ex-girlfriend accused him of shooting Anastasia in the head with a shotgun.

Within just a few pages, you and I will become players in a three-act drama based on the actual first-degree murder trial of Byron Case. We will assume the role of jurors. Be pleased by that, for it is an honor and privilege to perform as a juror.

In Act I, The Trial, we will hear the same testimony heard by the actual jurors. We will be given the same jury instructions. We will hear the same closing arguments. We will then retire to decide the fate of Byron Case.

In Act II, Deliberations, we will deliberate the evidence. Based on those deliberations, we will each decide our vote. As you ponder how you would have voted, I implore you to consider the weight and solemnity of your oath. A victim awaits justice. A man's life and freedom are at stake.

In Act III, Aftermath, we'll learn of the actual verdict in the trial of Missouri v. Byron Case. I will reveal the story behind the evidence, and share the shocking conclusion.

Only in the last few pages of this book will we be able to decide if we played our roles well.

❖

So who am I? Who is The Skeptical Juror?

To begin with, I am a juror. I've served jury duty more than most. I've been summoned more than ten times. I can't recall how many more precisely, just that there were more than ten. I've been called enough times that I've lost track.

I've been called to the jury box seven times for voir dire. Voir dire is the process by which the attorneys question potential jurors before the trial and attempt to tailor the final jury to their advantage.

I have actually served on a jury four times, all criminal cases, all felonies. I was an alternate during my first trial, a drive-by shooting in which the victim was wounded in the right buttock. I had no role in deciding that case. On the up side, I didn't need to examine photos of the wound.

The charges for the other three cases were murder, spousal battery, and child molestation. The last trial was a life-changing event. It led me to write this literary recreation of an actual trial, the one in which we are now to act as jurors.

I choose to perform my role as juror as a skeptical juror. As such, I will distrust the prosecution and the defense, the judge, and the witnesses. I will also question my own biases. Each may attempt to deceive and manipulate me. With all this in mind, I will scrutinize all testimony and physical evidence for errors, inconsistencies, and logical fallacies. I will attempt to be unmoved by the drama of the courtroom, or by the theatrics of the attorneys. I may be brought to tears by the pain of crimes past or the fear of liberty lost, both of which can be palpable in a courtroom, but I will not allow the pathos to deter me from my solemn duty.

As a skeptical juror, I will truly and without reservation grant the defendant the presumption of innocence. My default vote will be Not Guilty. I will change that to Guilty only if the State proves each and every element of its case beyond a reasonable doubt. Under no circumstance will I relieve the State of its burden of proof.

As the trial progresses, I will advocate for neither the prosecution nor the defense. Instead I will recognize the public's right to be secure in their persons and their homes while defending the defendant's rights as granted by our Constitution.

Most jurors believe they adhere to these precepts. Experience cautions me otherwise.

But I am not simply a skeptical juror. I am The Skeptical Juror, as if there is but one. To be sure, there are many other jurors who apply a high level of skepticism when adjudicating a case. I fear they are too few, but the existence of just one other is sufficient to prove I am not The Only Skeptical Juror. I use the title simply because it is more marketable than A Skeptical Juror. And because it's cooler.

❖

Trials can be tedious. Reading trial transcripts can be even more so. I want to preserve the integrity of the testimony and the arguments presented here, but I want to spare you the tedium. To this end, I have a plan.

I will spare you the voir dire and the judges' introductory comments. There will be no opening or closing statements. They tend to be long and boring, and in theory they should not matter. The jury instructions will tell you that the opening statements are not evidence, and they will not be presented here. If you, my fellow juror, wish to subject yourself to the ungrammatical arm-waving of the attorneys, the opening statements and all other documents associated with this trial are available on The Skeptical Juror website at www.skepticaljuror.com. Otherwise, you will be spared.

Because of my concern for you, the reader and my fellow literary juror, I will skip all that tedium and instead begin with the testimony of the first witness. That will be Detective David Epperson. He found Anastasia's body early that morning in Lincoln Cemetery.

During witness testimony, some parts will be presented in question and answer format, and some in third person narrative. Extended stretches of question and answer format can be painful to follow.

For most of the witness testimony, it will seem as if the witness is simply telling you what happened. Most minor errors of grammar have been corrected, again to ease the reading. For those of you wishing to read the unadulterated transcripts, those too are available on The Skeptical Juror website.

To preserve the integrity of the testimony, I will incorporate the attorney questions into the narrative. The testimony will unfold before you in the same sequence it unfolded before the actual jury.

When the judge or the attorneys speak, their words will be enclosed in quotes.

When my thoughts intrude, as they are now, they will appear in italics. I will manage them best I can, but they are frequently mischievous and sometimes a bit revealing. We all know how difficult it can be to control one's thoughts.

❖

Ready? Okay then. Sit back, take a deep breath, and turn the page. The bailiff is about to call the courtroom to order.

ACT I
TESTIMONY

TESTIMONY OF DEPUTY DAVID EPPERSON

Assistant Prosecutor David Fry conducts the questioning.

"Good morning. Tell the jury your name, please." » David Epperson.

"And how are you employed, sir?" » I'm a sergeant for the Jackson County Sheriff's Department.

"And on October 23, 1997, were you employed by the Jackson County Sheriff's Department then?" » Yes, sir.

"What were your duties on that particular I guess very early morning?" » I was assigned to District Five, which is the Blue Summit Area of Jackson County. That's an unincorporated area between Independence and Kansas City. Because the area is unincorporated, it's patrolled by the Sheriff's Department. My shift was from midnight to eight. It had been a routine patrol until I entered Lincoln Cemetery.

I was patrolling along Blue Ridge Boulevard, which runs north and south between Lincoln Cemetery to the west and Mount Washington Cemetery to the right. I turned west on an access road leading into Lincoln Cemetery. There's no gate there, so I drove right in. It was 3:44 in the morning. The cemetery is very dark. It has no street lights, there are lots of trees, and in October there are lots of leaves on the trees. It's pitch black in there. About the only thing you can see are the lights of Kansas City off in the distance.

Usually I just travel west on the access road until I come to a circle drive, which allows me to turn around and go back as I came, or turn south. I usually turn south, travel past an old abandoned building, and exit the cemetery onto Truman Road. There's no gate at that entrance either.

On that night, I was about two-fifths of a mile into Lincoln Cemetery when I observed a female lying on the ground, on her back. My first thought was that she could be injured, or intoxicated. Obviously, it was unusual.

I notified dispatch that I had a person down in Lincoln Cemetery. I exited my vehicle and I yelled for the person to get up. I approached and shined my flashlight into the person's face. She had a large wound from the bottom portion of her nose down into her mouth. Her eyes were open. Her arms were above her head. There was a puddle of blood underneath her head.

I backed up. I wanted to make sure there wasn't anybody else in the area. I approached her again and checked for signs of life. I looked to see if her chest or stomach was rising. I checked her wrist for a pulse, but she had none. I also noticed that her skin was cold to the touch, and it was turning a bluish gray color.

I returned to my vehicle and requested assistance. Once the detective unit got there, I secured a point on the perimeter up at Blue Ridge Road.

They checked the victim's pockets, and I think all they found was a key chain. They didn't find any identification, at least that's what I was told. The next day, I learned the name of the victim was Anastasia WitbolsFeugen.

Fry has Deputy Epperson identify a photograph of the body as he found it. There's no way we can see it from here. It's entered into evidence. We'll be allowed to see it during our deliberations.

Fry also has Epperson describe the geography of the area for us, using overhead photos and maps. I made a quick sketch in my notebook.

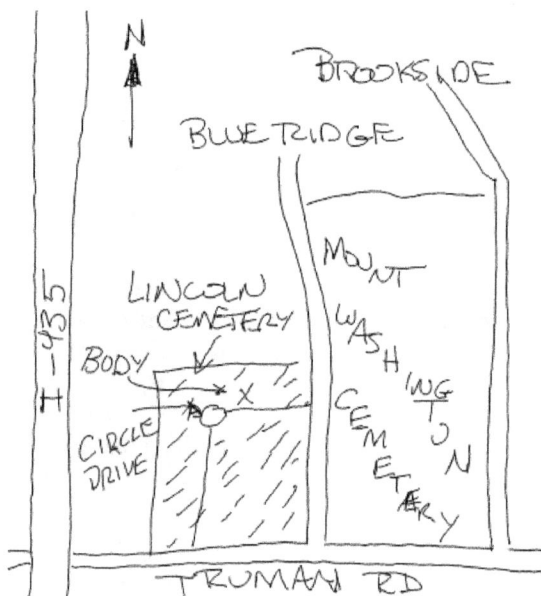

Public Defender Horton Lance conducts the cross-examination.

"Mr. Epperson, from your preliminary observations of the murder scene, can you determine if this act was committed by a stranger or an acquaintance of the victim?" » No, I could not.

That's it! Lance asks that one question and is done. I can think of a dozen questions I'd like to ask right now if I could. Jury duty, though, is an exercise in keeping your mouth shut.

Fry has no more questions, so Judge Atwell excuses Epperson. That wasn't as informative as I would have liked, but there you go.

TESTIMONY OF KELLY MOFFETT: PART 1

Kelly Moffett is examined by Assistant Prosecutor Theresa Crayon who, by the way, is exceptionally pregnant. Wow.

Kelly is 19 now, but still looks very young.

"I know you were just asked by the court reporter your name, but would you introduce yourself to the jury, please." » I'm Kelly Moffett.

"How old are you, Kelly?" » I'm 19.

"Do you know the defendant in this case, Byron Case?" » Yes.

"How do you know him?" » He was my boyfriend for about a year and a half.

"Do you see Byron Case in the courtroom today?" » Yes.

"And where is he sitting?" » He's sitting right there.

"For the record, can you please briefly describe what you see him wearing?" » Black tie, black suit, blue dress shirt.

"Kelly, did you know Justin Bruton?" » Yes. I met him I think spring of '97 in Westport.

"Do you know where he lived at the time that you met him?" » Yeah. He had a condo off the Plaza, and he went to UMKC. I don't think he had a job though. His parents had a lot of money, and they would send him money for school and such.

UMKC stands for University of Missouri, Kansas City. Their most famous graduate is, in my humble opinion, Craig Stevens. He played the title role in the 1959 TV series Peter Gunn. It had one of the best theme songs of all time. The theme song was so cool it was used repeatedly in the Blues Brothers movie, when Jake and Elwood were cruising in the Bluesmobile.

Second most famous student would be Harry Truman. He never had a theme song.

But I digress. Back to Kelly's testimony.

I don't think he had a job though. His parents had a lot of money, and they would send him money for school and such. He was about 19 or 20, I believe, when I met him. Justin and I never dated. We were just friends.

Justin was the one who introduced me to Byron, I would say about May of '97. They were friends, and I met through them. Byron and I started dating almost immediately. I was fourteen then. It was towards the end of my eighth-grade year.

Byron was eighteen. He wasn't in high school. I believe he dropped out earlier. He knew how old I was, because I told him. He also picked me up from my last day of school in eighth grade.

Byron was living with his mom off-and-on, but they didn't get along that well. So most of the time he was at Justin's condo.

We were with Justin and Anastasia a lot. I saw Anastasia just about every day. At first, her relationship with Justin was a mutual thing where they were just totally infatuated with each other. He asked her to marry him. They hadn't even been dating that long when she moved in there. After a while, they started kind of fighting. She would move in then move out of there over and over again.

I think Justin kind of wanted to spend more time with Byron. Anastasia and Byron would fight about that. Justin would be madly in love with her one second, and the next minute would be apathetic towards her.

Byron and Anastasia got along better at the beginning. Later, they became mutually annoyed with each other. Anastasia was jealous because he spent so much time with Justin. Byron was pretty annoyed with her for the most part. Once she started fighting with Justin, she was always paging Byron about their fights. None of us had cell phones then. Byron was the only one who had a pager.

When Anastasia and Justin started fighting really bad, she would leave stuff on his pager. Byron was annoyed by all the pages. I think finally he actually had a pager message that said something like, "Leave a message if this is anybody but Anastasia, because we don't want to talk to you." I remember talking to her about that. She was pretty upset.

Justin and Byron were always looking for some type of get-rich-quick scheme. Justin's family had a whole bunch of money, so they devised some plan to drive down to Tulsa and rob his parents. Justin, Byron, and Anastasia would talk about it in front of me.

In fact, Byron went with them once to rob Justin's parents, but they turned around thirty minutes later and got doughnuts instead. This is what Byron told me. I wasn't with them.

This happened when Justin, Byron, and Anastasia were living in the condo, and I was living at my parent's house in Lenexa, Kansas.

Lenexa, Kansas is southwest of the cemeteries. You can take I-435 most the way there if you wish. It's about a 25 mile drive from Lincoln Cemetery. It will take you around thirty minutes. Wild Bill Hickok once lived there; had a 160-acre claim to the area around Clare Road and 83rd.

They had another scheme where they were going to put plastic explosives in some church in Independence for ransom money. They were also looking for money so they could run off to Europe, but they never did any of it.

Crayon finally gets around to asking about the events leading up to the murder.

"On Wednesday, October 22, 1997, did you go to school that day?" » Yes.

"And did you come home at the normal time?" » Yes.

"What did you do?" » I didn't feel very well so I watched TV and laid down. I ended up falling asleep.

"Did you have any contact with the defendant, Byron Case?" » Yes. He called me.

"What happened after he called you?" » He woke me up from a nap and said that he was with Justin and that they were in the area and wanted to know if I wanted to do anything.

"What happened?" » They came to my house, picked me up.

"Whose car were they driving?" » Justin Bruton's car, a two-door Honda, green blue color. Justin drove. Byron sat in the front passenger seat. I sat in the back seat.

Shortly after I got in the car, Justin said, "You know, I've been upset recently, and Anastasia and I aren't getting along anymore." Then he asked, "Well, who is the biggest problem in my life right now?" I said, "Your parents?" I figured this had something to do with his parents and all these other schemes he came up with. He said, "No. I'm talking about Anastasia." He said, "Wouldn't it just be better, easier, if she was gone?" I thought he was just talking about breaking up with her again.

They told me they had been talking about it all day, plotting to kill her. I said, "That's ridiculous. Why can't you just break up with her?" It just didn't make any sense to me.

Justin said Byron was going to kill her. He said, "Well, I can't do it, so Byron is going to do it."

I said, "Well, if you're the one that wants her dead in the first place, why aren't you going to do it?" He didn't think he would be able to do it. Byron always had a weird fascination with death and wanted to kill somebody anyway.

I said, "How are you going to shoot her? You don't even have a gun." Byron said, "Yeah, it's in the trunk." He told me that he had gotten it from his dad's house, that it was his dad's old hunting gun or something.

They said they were going to do it in a secluded spot in Mount Washington. I said, "This is ridiculous. It's broad daylight. Why are you going to do this in the first place? You don't just pull somebody out into broad daylight and shoot them for no reason."

I didn't think they were really going to do it, because they always had plans like this. Byron even had some plan where he was going to call his dad out in the middle of nowhere and shoot him, because his dad had AIDS. Byron thought it would stop his dad's suffering, but that never happened. It was like they had seen too many movies or something.

I was just, "This is ridiculous. I can't believe you guys are actually going to do this. Why are you even taking me?" They said they wanted me to go to the Phillips 66, the one right off the street from my house, and make a phone call. Anastasia was supposed to meet up with them. I got out and made the call. I didn't have Anastasia's number or anything, so they gave me a number. I think maybe Justin dialed it for me.

Anastasia answered. I recognized her voice. I said, "Hi, I'm with Justin and Byron. You know we're supposed to meet." She said, "Well, yeah, you're running a little bit late, but Dairy Queen." I guess the original plan was to meet at Mount Washington, but it got changed to Dairy Queen.

After the phone call, I started drinking some Jack Daniels. I think it was Byron's, because he was the one that had it, and he offered it to me. I didn't drink very much. I had a mixed drink or so, but I wasn't drunk. They weren't acting drunk either. I wasn't sure if they had been drinking or not.

When we pulled up at Dairy Queen, we could see Anastasia sitting inside. We got out of the car to go get her. I believe Justin and Byron did, because Byron had to get out of the front seat to come around and get in the back seat so Anastasia could be in the front seat to talk to Justin.

Judge Atwell interrupts and calls for a lunch break.

"All right. Ladies and gentlemen, what I would like to do is we'll take a recess and I'll ask that you be back in the jury room, say, about 1:20. We'll try to start between 1:20 and 1:30. The Court reminds you that until you retire to consider your verdict, you must not discuss this case among yourselves or with others or permit anyone to discuss it in your hearing. You should not form or express any opinion about the case until it is finally given to you to decide. Do not read, view, or listen to any newspaper, radio, or television report of the trial. All rise, please."

TESTIMONY OF KELLY MOFFETT: PART 2

Lunch breaks during trials are typically an hour and a half. I usually keep to myself during lunch. I'll find a local restaurant, have a nice lunch, read, and then do some walking. I'm the exception, though. Most jurors tend to lunch with one another. Everyone quickly gets used to talking about anything and everything except the one big subject they have in common. It leads to an uncommon amount of bonding in a short time, particularly for the more gregarious jurors.

Today I had a burger and a diet Coke. Burger was nothing special and they didn't serve diet Mt. Dew, so I won't be returning. I noticed a hot dog cart on my way back to the courthouse. Maybe tomorrow.

The judge is just about to enter. Time to rise.

"Everybody, please be seated. Ms. Moffett, as I'm sure you're aware, the oath I gave you at the beginning of the trial still applies. With that being said, Ms. Crayon, you may resume your direct examination of Ms. Moffett."

Theresa Crayon continues her direct examination of Kelly Moffett.

"Kelly, before we broke for lunch, you talked about how you went to the Dairy Queen and you met up with Anastasia. When you arrived at Dairy Queen and Anastasia got to the car, how would you describe how Anastasia was behaving?" » She was pissed at Justin for being late and such. She was being nice to me, but she and Byron weren't getting along very well. I think she thought he was the reason that Justin was late, and she wasn't too happy about us being there, because she wanted to talk about their relationship, not have us be sitting there.

"By us, you mean you and Byron?" » Yes.

"And just to review, how was everybody sitting in the car at this time that you remember?" » Justin was driving. Anastasia got into the front passenger seat. I was in the back passenger seat and Byron got in behind Justin.

"Once you picked her up at the Dairy Queen and you were seated in Justin's car in that fashion, where do you go?" » We went across the street to Mount Washington Cemetery.

"Had you been there before?" » No, I don't believe so. Maybe once or twice. I knew where it was, but I hadn't been there.

We drove around for a little bit, I guess looking for a spot for Justin and Anastasia to get out and talk. We eventually ended up at a big mausoleum type thing.

Justin and Anastasia got out of the car for a few minutes. They were talking when headlights flashed at us from behind. I thought it must be the groundskeeper trying to get us out of there. So Justin and Anastasia got back in the car.

We left the cemetery the same way we came in, onto a busy street. It was dark enough to where the cars had their headlights on. We drove past the side of the cemetery, and down Truman Road, past Erotic City. Then we saw a little dirt road that went up just into the woods. One of them said "Oh, well, let's see where that leads."

We drove up there past a little stone building of sorts. It looked like a little park, and there was a circle drive. Justin drove up to the circle drive.

It was dark enough that I couldn't tell it was a cemetery. It just looked like a little park to me.

Justin and Anastasia got out of the car to talk about their relationship, I guess. They were bickering back and forth and talking.

They were on the driver's side of the car. Justin was standing pretty close to the driver's door. She was back a little further, probably about the second window on the driver's side.

I was in the back passenger seat. Byron was in the back driver's seat. I was still questioning him why, and how long had they been planning this. Why on earth were they going to do something like this? They seemed so calm about it. It didn't seem really planned, it just seemed ridiculous.

Byron said "We have been talking about it all day, and Justin asked me to do it. And I want to do it, so I'm going to."

We talked for a little bit more, then Byron said "I'll be right back." He got out of the car. I looked over, and I could see Justin standing there kind of waving his arms. He was saying Byron's name, and he was saying something in German. I could see Anastasia, but she wasn't reacting. She was like standing there looking at Justin.

I didn't see where Byron got the gun, but I heard the trunk pop before he lifted it. He stepped towards Anastasia away from the back of the trunk. He raised up the gun and shot her. It was a big loud noise. I screamed and turned away. By the time I looked back, I could see Justin waving his hands. He just completely freaked out.

I looked over and Anastasia's body was back, like blown backwards, and I could see her feet. The whole thing, it was like door shut, bam, and no time at all.

Here's my sketch:

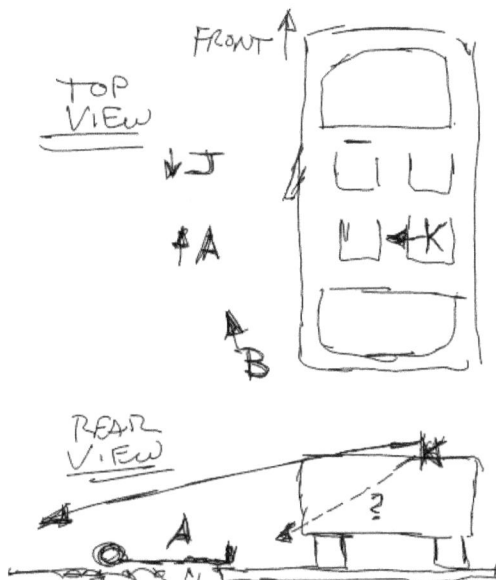

It's crude but I'm pretty rushed here. People are identified by the first letter of their first name. Arrows show which way they were facing. Top view is description before shooting. Rear view is description after shooting. Gotta get back to my note taking.

I started crying. Byron was saying "Justin, get in the car. Come on. We got to go." I heard the trunk close. Justin got in the driver's seat, and Byron went around and got in the front passenger seat, saying "Come on, Justin, drive. We have to get out of here." And Justin was saying "Didn't you hear me? Didn't you hear me saying to stop?" Byron said something like "I already had the gun out. I already had it in her face. What was I supposed to do? You asked me to do this." Justin kept saying "I didn't actually think that you were going to do this. I can't believe you did this."

Byron said they needed to go get rid of the gun. So we drove to some industrial-looking-type park with train tracks and such. Byron got out of the car and threw the gun, and switched places with Justin because Justin was too upset to drive.

When I came forward and told the truth in September of 2000, I was interviewed by Sergeant Kilgore again. He took me on a drive to all these different industrial places right off of Truman Road. He kept asking me if this place looked familiar, that place looked familiar. Basically, it all just looked familiar to me. He wasn't very nice about asking me where it was, either.

All the places looked familiar. He would ask, "Well is this the spot? Is this the spot?" There was one place, he asked if it looked familiar. We had been driving for so long. I wasn't really sure where we were. He said something like "If I brought people back here to search this area, do you think they would find anything?" And I said, "Well, maybe." I didn't know. When Byron disposed of the gun, it was dark, and I stayed in the car. I only had a vague idea of where it was.

After Byron got rid of the gun, we drove back to Justin's condo. Justin just couldn't believe that he had actually done it. He was freaked out about it. Byron was just basically like "Well, you asked me to do it. Now we have to deal with this. What are we going to tell the police?"

Justin kept saying things like, "This isn't right. This isn't right." And Byron said "Well you asked me to do this and, Kelly, you were here too. I wasn't the only one doing this." Basically, it was like stick to this story, and now what's done is done. We have to get past all this.

Byron was saying "We have to have some kind of story to tell the police." Finally Justin kind of, I think feeling really guilty that he was as much a part of it, agreed that it would be believable for Anastasia to have jumped out of the car because they had gotten into fights before where she walked out of their condo. So they asked me if I thought people would believe that she got out of the car, and I said "I guess they would."

The basic story was going to be the same thing that had happened. We picked her up at Dairy Queen so that she could talk to Justin about their relationship. She wasn't happy that Byron and I were there. After fighting for a while, she threw a ring at him and got out at an intersection right by Erotic City. They said it was a bad neighborhood, so the people would believe something might have happened to her.

I'm not sure where we went after the condo. I believe I went back to my parent's house. I recall when I first talked to Sergeant Kilgore about this I told him we made a stop at Abraham Kneisley's house. It's possible. I don't remember. The whole night was such a blur. It's possible we stopped there but I don't remember it. I had to get home by 9 or 9:30 because it was a school night, and it would have looked weird if I was really late.

On the way to my house, we agreed to go in and tell my mom what had happened, in case the police talked to her. We would go in and say "Oh, Mom, you won't believe what happened." Also, Justin was going to use the phone and call Anastasia's house and act concerned about Anastasia getting out of the car.

I got home about 9 or 9:30, somewhere in there. Byron and Justin came in with me. I told my mom the story. Justin called Anastasia's house. I believe he talked to Anastasia's sister. I remember it was really creepy, because right after he got off the phone with her he said, "Oh, great." Her sister said something to the effect of, "Well, thanks a lot. If anything happens to my sister, it's your fault." I remember Justin was really upset about it. It was like she already knew something bad had happened.

After that they left. I never saw or talked to Justin again. I talked to Byron later that night. I think it was pretty late, 11 or 11:30, something like that. I was talking to him about what had happened. He just seemed so calm about it. I was saying I didn't know if I could sleep.

I was supposed to go to my grandparents' house with my mom the next day. I didn't know how I was going to act. I told Byron, "Justin seemed really shaken up. Do you think he's going to be okay?" And Byron said "Well, yeah, he should be okay."

The next day I went down to Lockwood, Missouri, with my mom to see my grandma.

Lockwood, Missouri is 150 miles south of Kelly's house.

I spent the entire day there. When I got home I talked to Byron. I don't remember who called who, but he told me to turn on a news station. I saw the newscast that Anastasia's body had been found. I got really upset and freaked out. Byron said he had talked to Justin earlier that morning. I forget what time it was, but I remember it was weird. He said Justin called him and talked to him and had told him he was having trouble sleeping. I remember Byron had said something like, "Well do you even realize what time it is? I'll talk to you later when I wake up." As far as I know, Byron never talked to him again after that.

Of course, the whole thing was horrible. I don't know if the police were going to try to come talk to me. I was obviously freaked out and I got my mom to give me a ride over to Byron's house in Westport, because I just knew somehow I was never going to see Justin again with how he was acting.

Westport is an historic district in Kansas City, one of the city's entertainment centers. Byron and Justin both lived near Westport. It's northeast of Kelly's house in Lenexa, about a 36 minute drive. It's southwest of Lincoln Cemetery, about a twenty minute drive from there, about half-way between the cemetery and Kelly's house. I made a sketch.

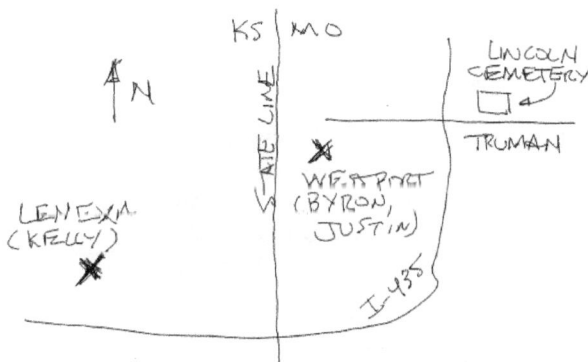

"Okay. So your mother took you over there?" » Yes.

"How long did you stay?" » I spent the night there.

"Was that unusual?" » For my mom to allow me to, yeah.

"And when you spent the night that night, did you talk about the story anymore?" » Yeah.

"Is there anything further unusual that Byron next did in the next 24 hours that sticks out in your mind?" » We basically quit talking about the story after awhile, because Byron said, "Just get over it. Act normal." I remember he had a job interview that night at Crown Center. I couldn't believe he was going to a job interview after all this. I mean, he was worried about going to a job interview and he can't find his supposed best friend, and he's going to a job interview? I asked him why and he said, "Well, we have to make everything look normal."

I talked to the police I believe it was on that Friday, the next morning, after I spent the night at Byron's. My mom picked us up, and we went and talked to the police. That's when I met Sergeant Kilgore.

He talked to us separately. I told him the story we made up, the one that Anastasia had walked out of the car. He asked where she got out. I told him I didn't know the area very well. I said the intersection down by Erotic City.

Erotic City is on Truman Road, south of Lincoln Cemetery. If you were travelling west on Truman, it would be on the left. It's a seedy liquor store type building, not very erotic or exotic from the outside, that's for sure. Erotic City seems, however, to be a common reference point for Blue Summit locals.

The place is notorious for its unregulated video booths and orgy facilities accommodating 15 to 20 people at a time, complete with "buddy buttons" to solicit willing participants. It has "glory" peep holes, floor-to-ceiling mirrors, and wall-to-wall vinyl. Or so I've read.

Here's the kicker. Erotic City was created by one Elvin L. Boone, who died without executing a will. The Probate Court of Jackson County is now running the place, and will be until it can divvy the property among Boone's eight children. That makes Jackson County a smut peddler. I understand business is actually improving under the new management.

Sorry. Back to Crayon's questioning.

"All right. What happened? Did you ever go out there with him to try to show him?" » Yes, I did, but beforehand, I remember Byron took me out there so that everything would be straight, because I said I can't remember where we said she got out of the car, so he drove me out there to show me where we said she got out of the car so it wouldn't be conflicting stories.

"So after Justin was missing and they found him in De Soto, Kansas, did Byron have you add something to the original story that you all had made up with Justin?" » Yeah. The police asked about a gun, about Justin having some type of gun.

"What did you and Byron add to the story?" » He told me that Justin like owned a gun or got some gun at Wal-Mart or something, and that we had seen him with it. That was to make it more believable.

The police were already talking to us like they just assumed Justin did it anyway. I never really saw Justin with a gun, though. I didn't know anything about the purchase of one at Wal-Mart until Byron told me that. I don't remember the exact date, but it was sometime after we talked to the police the first time.

I remember going to Justin's funeral. It was in Tulsa, Oklahoma. My mom drove me and Byron up there.

Tulsa is 270 miles south of Lincoln Cemetery. It's a four and a half-hour drive, without stops. Relative to the Kansas City area, Tulsa is actually "down there" rather than "up there" as Kelly described. J. Paul Getty made his first million there. Garth Brooks, Anita Bryant, Patti Page, Roy Clark, and Leon Russell all hail from Tulsa.

I wanted to go to the funeral because it was just so awful that Justin was dead, because it was just such a situation and that wasn't like him. That wasn't his personality.

We went in, but it was a really creepy, awful situation. I just felt so horrible even just being there. His little sister kept crying. His parents were obviously upset.

I was only in the church for a few minutes before we left, because it wasn't the type of service that seemed like Justin would have wanted. It didn't seem like any of his friends were there. I thought it would help losing him, but it didn't.

I attended Anastasia's funeral too.

The defense objects. "Relevancy." The judge tells the attorneys to "Come on up."

It's called a side bar. The attorneys and the court reporter meet at the end of the judge's bench, the one farthest from us. They huddle and whisper so we can't hear them. We're not supposed to speculate why the defense objected, or what they're talking about. We're just supposed to sit here and ignore what's going on at sidebar, as if it's not really happening.

Jurors are pretty attentive though. Not me so much, but lots of others are. Another juror once informed me that the defense attorney was from out of town. I asked how she knew. "Because he wears the same dress shoes every day." I hadn't noticed. Maybe she was right.

Okay. They're coming back. Crayon is telling Kelly she can continue with what she was saying.

"You can answer the question, Kelly. You said you went to Anastasia's funeral. Tell us why and what it was like." » Well, I didn't even want to go because, I mean, I hadn't known her that long, and it just seemed so disrespectful and horrible. How could you go to a funeral of someone and pretend like you didn't know what had happened? I mean, I saw her get shot and I'm supposed to go there with her friends and family and act like I don't know what happened? Seeing her family and everybody there was really bad, especially her little sister. But Byron said it would look weird not to go, and I guess I kind of agreed with that, because he had known her since high school. So everybody else was going to the funeral, so we should go.

"All right. Kelly, after this happens and after the funerals, tell the jury what happened to you." » Well, what happened to me?

"Yeah." » My life just completely changed. I quit hanging out with like hardly anybody I had been. I quit playing sports. I tried to kill myself. I went from just being, like, you know some normal girl in high school to all I did was do drugs. I tried to talk to Byron several times about what had happened and he's just like, "It's in the past. Let's not talk about it."

My life just got destroyed. My parents always knew something more had happened with this, but I wouldn't talk about it. I had gone from being like an A student honor roll to I quit going to school.

Like an A student?

It got so bad finally my parents wouldn't even allow me back in my house, because they said I wasn't actually dealing with the real problem, that I was just doing drugs. It was awful. I went from living with my family to staying in crack houses. My own friends wouldn't even hang out with me.

I had never been in any type of rehab or anything before that. I had never been in like a Charter type facility or anything. It just got worse and worse, and I kept thinking it would get better, but it just never did. All I did was have nightmares about this. It just completely destroyed my life. I'm sure it destroyed Anastasia's family's life and Justin's family's life too.

I kept seeing Byron for a year or so. He just didn't want to talk about it. He didn't want to hear it. To him it never happened. If I tried to bring it up, he would say "Well, that's in the past. We don't need any more lives to be ruined after this."

One night in particular, I was so upset my parents had to take me to Charter because I was going to kill myself.

I told Byron I wanted to go to the police with what happened, but Byron said, "Nobody else's lives needs to be ruined over this. It will be all right. You were involved with it just as much as I. What are your friends and family going to think? What is your mom going to think?" I asked him, "Well, how can you not feel bad about this? You're a murderer." And he said, "No, a murderer is someone who doesn't feel bad about what they did. I feel bad about what I did, but it's over."

I talked to the police quite a few times. Every time they called me, I would go talk to them. I took a lie detector too or voice stress test.

Uh, oh! Another objection. Kelly said "lie detector" and Lance was up like a shot. "Objection. May counsel approach?" The judge waves them up. Here we go again.

Anyway, another juror once noticed that the prosecutor's zipper wasn't zipped up during his closing argument. When we got back to the jury room, she was demonstrating how her eyes got really big and how she was trying to signal him. Even though it was a serious case, we were laughing so loud at her story that they could hear us out in the courtroom. Sometimes, it doesn't take much to break the stress for just a moment, and then it all spills out.

All right. They're coming back. Looks like the judge wants to talk to us.

"Ladies and gentlemen, we're going to take a recess. During the recess --"

Yeah, yeah. No talking. We get it. Tuning out here.

"With that being said, we'll be in recess. All rise, please."

Darn! He didn't tell us when we had to be back. That pretty much means we go back to the jury room and wait there. It can get pretty old sitting around that room with the same people, day after day, not talking about the only thing we have in common. I prefer to leave the courtroom and wander around the courthouse, or outside.

Maybe next time.

TESTIMONY OF KELLY MOFFETT: PART 3

Okay, we're back. There's the judge. Time to rise.

"Ladies and gentlemen, I have an instruction I would like to give to you, and I would like you to listen to what I have to say very carefully, if you would.

"There is no witness in this case that has ever taken any test with conclusive results regarding their truthfulness or untruthfulness. Furthermore, such tests are deemed inadmissible and incompetent as evidence in state and federal courts throughout this country. To consider any such evidence in this case for or against either side would be horribly unfair. For that reason, you should disregard any testimony regarding such evidence.

"With that being said, you may continue with your direct examination."

Okay. Just forget that Kelly volunteered she took a lie detector test and the defense doesn't want us to know that. Forget it, okay. Disregard it. Unring that bell.

Crayon continues her direct examination.

"Kelly, I think you testified you talked to the police several times after the initial contact with them two days after the homicide; is that right?" » Yes.

"And each time that you were asked to come in and talk to the Sheriff's Department, would you make contact with the defendant, Byron Case?" » Yes, I would.

"And what was his reaction when you would tell him they had called to ask you to come in and talk to them again?" » He would tell me that it wasn't necessary; that they were just harassing us. He told me to say I didn't remember.

"Now, after the two of you stopped seeing each other in a dating relationship, I think you've said in December of '98?" » Yes.

"In December of '98, between then and when you came forward to tell the authorities what really happened that night in September of 2000, did you have any contact with the defendant, Byron Case, in that ensuing almost two years?" » Yes. I had seen him in Westport. I tried to contact him on occasion when I would be real messed up and really upset about what had happened, but it didn't do any good. He didn't want to talk about it.

"Okay. In the summer of 2000, just before you came forward, do you specifically remember any contact with him just before you came forward?" » Yes. I called him to try to talk about what had happened and he wouldn't. He said he didn't want to see me. He didn't want to talk about it. He said it's in the past, that I should just get over it. So I went by his apartment with a friend of mine.

"Was that contact in September of 2000 precipitated by anything that you had heard?" » Yeah. I heard that he was going to move to St. Louis. He was just leaving. I didn't have that option. I was trying to talk to him about everything, because I was thinking about coming forward, and it's like it didn't do any good. He was just running away from the whole situation, leaving me to deal with it.

It's like my life was completely destroyed and he was just fine with it all. He was just going to move, and to him it had never happened, while it had just destroyed everything for me. So I went to see him with a friend of mine named Angie. Some girl was at his apartment. I talked to him in private about the actual murder and everything, but not in front of them.

I asked him why he was leaving. He said he had lots of bad memories and things to get away from. I asked what if the police tried to get in touch with me, but he wouldn't give me a way to get in touch with him.

My dad and my drug counselor never believed that was the actual story, because I had been such a completely different person after that. I was horribly depressed. Either I was going to kill myself or try one last time to get clean.

My dad told me I was never going to get clean and it was never going to get better unless I came to terms with what happened. So I started crying and I told him that Byron had been the one that shot Anastasia and I witnessed it.

That was the night before I went into rehab. It was pretty late at night, and when I went into rehab, I met with Maggie, my drug counselor. Like I said, she knew that whole story about Anastasia getting out of the car was just a bunch of crap, and she knew me well enough to know that was what bothered me.

Finally in one of our sessions, she took me upstairs, and she told me I was going to kill myself with drugs and alcohol if I didn't deal with it. She said I had to come forward, that it wasn't fair to people's families to keep quiet.

So I told her I knew who killed Anastasia. Well, she kind of freaked me out. She said that by law she had to report it. I thought maybe I could just confidentially tell her, but I couldn't. I freaked out. I started crying and I told her that Justin had done it, because he was gone, and that's what everybody seemed to believe anyway. That's what police seemed to believe. So I just kind of blamed it on him, because he wasn't around anymore.

I didn't want to say it was Justin, but I was scared. Byron had told me the whole time that I was just as guilty as he was, that if I said anything it was my ass too.

Maggie called my mom, and my mom came really quickly, within about thirty minutes or so. Maggie told my mom that I said Justin killed Anastasia and that they had gotten in touch with authorities. My mom looked at me and said I told my dad last night that it was Byron. I broke down crying and told her that was the truth, that Byron had killed Anastasia.

I was worried about the police and I was worried what my parents would think. That's why I was scared, because Byron had warned me about what my friends and family would think about me not saying anything for so long. I had already screwed up so much by being a drug addict.

Maggie got me in touch with a friend of hers, John O'Connor. He's a lawyer. I went with him to see Bob Beaird. He's the prosecutor. He said that I wouldn't be charged with anything, that I would get immunity. I wouldn't be charged with lying to the police if I agreed to tell the truth now.

After that, I talked with Sergeant Kilgore. He asked me to give a statement. So I did. And that was when I went and tried to help him locate where the gun was.

Just a couple days ago, I went to a court hearing with Mr. Fry. A different judge granted me immunity again if I told the truth in this case.

Theresa Crayon starts to ask a question about a telephone call Kelly made to Byron and Horton Lance asks to approach the bench. Looks like another delay.

Back to some of the things other jurors notice and I don't. In my last trial, I noticed, as did all the other jurors, that a nun, perhaps a Mother Superior, showed up and sat on the defense side of the courtroom. She was there to show support for the defendant when he took the stand. At some point she disappeared. When we were back in the jury room, one of the jurors said "Oh yeah, she left when he said 'Hell.'" Others nodded their heads in agreement. I'm so busy listening to the testimony and taking notes, I don't see how they have time to be paying attention to anything else.

Looks like we're ready to go. Theresa Crayon continues her direct examination of Kelly Moffett.

"We're going to talk now about some phone contact that you tried to make with Byron Case after coming forward with the information that you have testified to that the defendant was the person who killed Anastasia WitbolsFeugen." » Yes.

"First, you've already testified that he moved to St. Louis. Did you know how to reach him in St. Louis?" » No, I did not.

"And how did you find out how to reach him in St. Louis?" » From law enforcement.

"Okay. So after you came forward, you were given telephone number for him?" » Yes.

"And tell us what happened just before you were trying to make these contacts with him in St. Louis? Who came out to your house? What did they do?" » Sergeant Kilgore came out to my house and installed on his own phone this little recording device where you had to be on that phone to record it.

"It was a phone he provided?" » Yeah. He provided. It was hooked up to, like, a little machine.

"And where was that phone located?" » It was in our downstairs living room.

"Did he show you how to use it?" » Yeah. In order to get an incoming call, you had to be on that specific phone, and to record anything going out, you had to press record to make a tape or in order for it to record it.

"And he left that attached to your telephone; is that correct?" » Yes.

"And after he had done that and after you were provided the telephone number to make contact with Byron Case in St. Louis, did you try to call him?" » Yes.

"What happened when you attempted to do that?" » I never got ahold of him. I talked to some roommate of his or something a couple times, but I never talked to him when he was in St. Louis. I tried a couple of times, but she always told me that either he wasn't there or that he didn't live there. I left messages, but Byron never called me back. It seemed pointless, so I just quit trying for awhile.

After about a year, the police told me that he moved back to Kansas City. They said he was living with his mom, and they gave me her telephone number. I tried to call a couple times until finally I got a hold of him pretty late at night. And I recorded the phone call like they showed me.

Theresa Crayon offers the tape and transcript as exhibits. Judge Atwell doesn't wait for Horton Lance to object again. He just asks him "Do you want to come up, Mr. Lance?" Of course he does. We have another little respite.

This one doesn't last long. Horton Lance loses another one. When they come back, Kelly is allowed to talk about what's on the tape.

"Very briefly, Kelly, I'm going to ask you about the telephone call that we have talked about. Can you tell the jury, generally speaking, what your conversation with the defendant was about?" » I was trying to talk to him about what happened. I had told him that I was still having, like, a really hard time with it. I was telling him that police were trying to get in touch with me, and what should I say to them? And he said tell 'em you don't remember.

"Did you talk about whether or not you should meet?" » Yes.

"Tell us about that." » He didn't want to talk about it on the phone, so I decided it would be a better idea to ask him to meet in person at Loose Park where we could talk about this.

"Did you ever meet him at Loose Park?" » No. I was told not to.

"Why?" » Because the guys just didn't feel like --

Lance cuts her short with an objection. Back to the bench. This one is even quicker than the last one. Theresa Crayon returns and asks for permission to play the tape in court. The judge will allow it. First though, he wants to talk to us.

"Ladies and gentlemen, as you're being passed out these transcripts for this tape, let me give you an instruction if I might. The sole purpose for these transcripts is to aid you in listening to what's on the tape. The transcripts themselves are not evidence. They're only given to you to aid you to listen to what is on the tape. The tape is the evidence. If you feel that there is a conflict between the tape and the transcript, you should rely upon your memory of what the tape said. All right? Everybody got a transcript? Let's play it."

CASE NO: 97-11829

The following is a transcript of a tape-recorded telephone conversation between Byron C. Case and Kelly Moffett. The conversation took place on 06-05-01 at approximately 2330 hrs. The telephone call was placed by Kelly Moffett from her residence.

Byron:	Hello.
Kelly:	Is Byron there?
Byron:	Yes, speaking.
Kelly:	Byron, this is Kelly. Hello. I realize you probably don't want to talk to me. I have to talk to you, I have to talk to you, I absolutely have to fucking talk to you. Okay? Hello? You're listening. Okay. Some extremely bad shit has gone down. Are you listening to me?
Byron:	Yeah.
Kelly:	Okay. I don't know what to do and that's why I called you, because you do realize that I've been a drug addict for some time, my memory is not that good, and they are harassing me for information now, and I don't know what to do about it. Do you know what I'm talking about?
Byron:	Yeah.
Kelly:	Okay. Anastasia's dad has called me, uhm, two or three investigators have called me and I don't know what to do. I don't remember the whole story and I need your information, please, because they're going to call me in, they're going to fucking ask me for a lie detector test again and I have no idea. Okay? I know I'm probably the last person on the earth you want to talk to, but we have to talk about this. Otherwise, we're both fucked.
Byron:	Well, I --
Kelly:	What?
Byron:	Where are you?
Kelly:	I'm at my parents' house.
Byron:	You're still there?
Kelly:	What?
Byron:	Are you still there?
Kelly:	Yes, I'm still there! Why, what?
Byron:	Oh, nothing.

Kelly:	Yes, I'm still living here.
Byron:	That's odd.
Kelly:	What?
Byron:	I said it was just odd.
Kelly:	How is that odd?
Byron:	I don't know.
Kelly:	Where the fuck else am I going to go?
Byron:	I don't know.
Kelly:	Why are you at your parents' house?
Byron:	Oh, don't even ask.
Kelly:	I won't ask. But seriously, this is fucked and we're both going to be fucked. Seriously, I'm not kidding.
Byron:	You know --
Kelly:	What do you mean, "you know?" What?
Byron:	I don't remember.
Kelly:	You don't remember?
Byron:	What?
Kelly:	What?
Byron:	Yeah. Just say you don't remember.
Kelly:	Don't you remember? You don't remember what we said? At all?
Byron:	I do, but --
Kelly:	But what?
Byron:	(unintelligible)
Kelly:	Honey, this is like not a game anymore. And I've like realized that to its like fullest extent and it sucks.
Byron:	I'm sure really surprised they called again.
Kelly:	That they called again. They've called a bunch again. They called while I was in rehab, they showed up out there. Yeah. I don't understand, like seriously, what all went on or whatever, and I seriously, I hate to say this, but why, seriously, why did you have to kill her? What was the whole fucking big deal? Could you explain that to me? Because I don't get it. Seriously, Justin's dead for no reason, she's dead for no reason. It's all just fucked up. And for some reason they're talking to me, because you won't talk. So I'm fucked. And it makes me look horrible because everybody already knows that I'm a fucking crack-head, and that I'm a coke-head, that I'm an alcoholic and I don't remember shit. And if I tried to talk to them, nothing's going to add up. So, I mean, if you could, seriously, explain to me as to why you actually felt the need to kill her, then that would really help me feel better about the whole fucking thing. I mean, was there, seriously, any reason to all of this?
Byron:	We shouldn't talk about this.
Kelly:	Why?
Byron:	Probably because we shouldn't talk about this.

Kelly:	Of course we should.
Byron:	Except, at least, if I need to talk to you.
Kelly:	What do you mean? Yeah, I would love for you to talk to me about it because my, nothing, nothing has been the same since that, okay? And you may have been okay or whatever, but all I did was get more drunk or get more fucked up and that's it. That's it. Okay. I'm not the same person and you know that. I have not been the same person for years, and I hate it. And something seriously has to give or we need to talk or something. Because for some reason, you know, it just seems like you were inaccessible or you were too cold or something, and everybody's coming to me. And I can't talk to Anastasia's dad, and I can't do any of this.
Byron:	(unintelligible)
Kelly:	What?
Byron:	I got, see, I was granted immunity --
Kelly:	What?
Byron:	-- by the lawyer, or by the prosecutor, excuse me.
Kelly:	Uh-huh.
Byron:	Through my lawyer. Because I told them everything about this, you know, I --
Kelly:	You told what?
Byron:	I said I told my lawyer flat out that I didn't, I wasn't going to remember things.
Kelly:	Uh-huh.
Byron:	Told the cops that, too. I was, like I can't remember things. And so, basically, I would, you know, tell them up front before you go in or agree to meet them, just say I'm not going to remember things.
Kelly:	I have.
Byron:	Write something on paper that says that, you know, if I fuck up, you know, because you wouldn't want us to, like slip --
Kelly:	I have! But that doesn't make any fucking difference! What are you talking about they told you this and that, they never told me anything.
Byron:	What?
Kelly:	What?
Byron:	Never told you what?
Kelly:	Did you, what did you say about immunity? What are you talking about?
Byron:	Well, yeah, that basically I was given, which basically means that, like, nothing I said could be used in court against me.
Kelly:	I guess, whatever, but I don't know, okay, I need, I seriously need to talk to you. When is like a time we can talk, please?
Byron:	Tomorrow.
Kelly:	Tomorrow when?
Byron:	When you're free. The earlier the better.
Kelly:	Are you talking about like in person or something?

Byron: Yes.

Kelly: Cause I, yeah, don't like this over the phone bullshit.

Byron: Neither do I.

Kelly: But I can't, seriously, I mean you don't, I was the one that went and took the lie detector test. I was the one that all this shit happened to. And so I'm the one that they're like bothering, and for some reason that dip-shit fucking like police force out there that talked to us, somehow Anastasia's father has my number and you know how disturbing he is.

Byron: Yeah, I know.

Kelly: And he's e-mailing me and he's calling me. I have no idea what to do and I can't remember anything.

Byron: Don't respond to any of these things.

Kelly: I know. But I don't remember anything! This whole thing is like, I thought it would go away and it's not. Okay. Well, so what do you want me to do?

Byron: Uh, do you have a car?

Kelly: Yes, I have a car. Do you have a car?

Byron: Yes.

Kelly: Okay. How about just in, the place that I go to in Loose Park is just the main entrance off of like 63rd, and like the main thing through the Plaza. What time do you want to be there?

Byron: Alright.

Kelly: What time?

Byron: Uh, let's see, how about, well -- What time is it, around midnight?

Kelly: Yeah.

Byron: Uh, to be on the safe side, let's go with 11:00.

Kelly: Okay. Eleven o'clock. I'll be there.

Byron: Okay.

Kelly: Bye.

Telephone conversation concluded.

[signed Sgt. Kilgore]

TESTIMONY OF KELLY MOFFETT: PART 4

I'm pissed. I'm seriously pissed.

In a lot of places, I couldn't hear the tape worth a damn, especially when Byron was talking. I couldn't take notes because I had to read the transcripts to keep track of what the tape was saying. The judge told us we were to rely on the tape and not the transcripts though. What a mess.

The bailiff is collecting our copies of the transcripts. Now I'm even more irritated. I couldn't hear the tape, I couldn't take notes, and now we might not even be able to refer to the transcripts. And they want me to make a big time decision under these circumstances. This bites.

From the looks of a few other jurors, some of them may also feel adrift. Not all of them though, just a few. That bothers me as well.

I don't even have time to jot down any notes now. Crayon just continues her questioning. No one seems to give a rat's ass if we can hear or read or take notes or have any hope of remembering what the hell just happened.

❖

"Just so we're clear, in the very beginning of that tape it sounds like you're having a conversation with someone else in the room." » Yes.

"Can you tell us what's going on there?" » That was my friend, Angie. She was staying the night at my house that night and since I hadn't been able to get in touch with him, I figured nobody would answer, but the second he actually picked up, I made her go down in the basement.

"So she wasn't present for your conversation?" » No.

"She didn't participate in the conversation?" » No.

"And as far as you're aware, Byron Case didn't know that she was present?" » Yeah. He didn't know, huh-uh.

"Just to clear that up, also, you were there by yourself with your friend, Angie, initially and made the tape using the recording device that Sergeant Kilgore had, right?" » Yes.

"And after this conversation that the jury just heard played for them, were you ever able to contact and speak to the defendant again?" » No.

There was one time before the phone call, after we had broken up, around December of '98 or January of '99, that he was flipping out on the phone about everything. He was depressed and crying and kind of hysterical. He was saying he was going to kill himself. He was upset about us breaking up.

I don't know if he had been drinking or not, but he sounded like he had been. He went into great detail how he was going to kill himself. He said he had a weapon, and he wanted me to come over, but I didn't want to. I asked, "So you're really going to kill yourself?" And he said, "Yes." I said, "Okay, if you're really going to kill yourself, I'm going to call the police."

We hung up on each other. And like I warned him, I called 911 and they went over there. Before too long I got a call from Western Missouri Mental Health. They wanted to confirm what I had told the 911 person.

Later I talked to Byron's mom. At first she seemed kind of angry that I had called the police. She goes, "Oh, it was terrible, Kelly. The police came in there and just grabbed him out of his own house and now he can't get out." But I said, "Well, you know how he can get." Then she kind of calmed down after that. And I go, "Well, he told me he's tried to kill himself before. Why would I not believe it now?" And then she kind of calmed down.

"Kelly, I want to ask you regarding Justin Bruton. I know I'm jumping around on you a little bit." » Okay.

"Regarding Justin Bruton, just prior to the homicide, do you know if Justin Bruton was doing any drugs?" » Yes.

"Tell us about that." » Prior to it, I hadn't been with him when he was doing it, but he was telling me he was doing acid and mescaline. He seemed really weird after that. I think he overdosed on mescaline or something, because he was talking about hearing voices and hearing people under the floor and just not feeling right about everything and kind of being scared to leave his house and such.

"How close was that to the homicide?" » Pretty close. Probably within a couple weeks beforehand or so.

"On the night of the homicide that you have described when you were there and saw what you did was anybody doing any drugs that night?" » No. Well, aside from the alcohol that I drank, no.

And with that, Theresa Crayon completes her direct examination of Kelly.

"Your Honor, at this time I don't think I have any further questions for Ms. Moffett."

Judge Atwell calls a quick sidebar then calls for a short recess. I'm still angry.

"Let's take about a ten-minute break before we commence cross examination, ladies and gentlemen. With that being said we're going to be in recess."

Okay. I've calmed down a bit, and no one had to call 911, but I'm still angered by the course of events. I have to go. I need to make some notes of what I remember about the tape, and I need to make them now. We'll talk later.

TESTIMONY OF KELLY MOFFETT: PART 5

This may come as no surprise to you, but I'm still pretty irritated. I wrote down what I could remember, but I'm not sure I got it right. I'm positive I didn't get it all. Crap.

Here we go. Judge Atwell hands the witness over to the defense, to Horton Lance.

"Ms. Moffett, earlier today you described for the jury how you told your father about the evening of Anastasia's murder?" » Yes.

"Do you remember telling the jury about that?" » Yes.

"I wanted to ask you about what you told your mother, because I don't think that's been discussed today, right?" » Yes.

"Now, is it true, when you first told your mother that you witnessed the murder, is it true that you said that Justin Bruton did the murder?" » Yes.

"That was a lie?" » Yes.

"Okay. So when you first described it to your mother, you lied to your mother?" » Yes.

"And you agree that, when the police first interviewed you October of '97, you told the police Anastasia got out of the car and walked away and you don't know who killed her?" » Yes.

"And you're telling the jury today that what you told the police that day was a lie?" » Yes.

"So you agree that you lied to the police?" » Yes, I did. I first talked to Sergeant Kilgore the Friday following the murder. That's the first time I told him that Anastasia got out of the car at Truman Road and I-435 and walked away.

I met with him again a month later. That was our second meeting. That's the one where we drove around Mount Washington cemetery together. I was still telling him the story that Anastasia got out of the car and walked away.

The next time I talked to him was by phone. December 10, 1997 sounds right, but I don't recall the exact date. I talked to him so many different times. Sometimes it was in person. Sometimes it was on the phone. I was still telling him the story where Anastasia got out of the car and walked away and that I didn't know who killed her.

I met with him again in his office, and he took another statement with a tape recorder. Again I'm not certain of the date, but if you say August 22 of '98, that sounds right. And I still told him the story, because that was the story the police already assumed is what actually happened.

I talked to him on the phone again just three days later, I think, and I told him the same thing. So that's at least five times I stuck with that story. I don't recall how many for sure. I met up with him a bunch of times, and we would talk on the phone too. And that went on for three years. I know no one was arrested, and it seemed like there were no suspects.

Yes, I drank some and used drugs before Anastasia died, but it got a lot worse after. I became addicted to crack cocaine, and that got so bad I was basically homeless. My parents kicked me out of the house, so I had to live at crack houses. I moved around a lot. I had friends I would stay with and such, but yeah, I was basically homeless.

The depression and everything just got out of control. I mean, if you know anything about addiction yeah, I was actively addicted to it. But I think it was a symptom of the problem, because I hadn't been like that before. I used drugs before that, but I think there is quite a big difference between experimenting with drugs in high school and living in a crack house.

I don't remember the date I met Sergeant Kilgore at the Mainstream Rehab Center. September 21, 2000 sounds about right. I remember him coming out and us talking, and recording what we said. I told him to the best of my recollection what really happened. Justin and Kelly were fighting all the time. And Justin had been doing acid a little bit before.

I told him that Justin and Anastasia had come up with this wild plan to rob Justin's parents in Oklahoma. I didn't tell him that Byron went with them, but I know for a fact that he left with them to deal with it. The three of them talked about it right in front of me, but I didn't take it seriously. But, yeah, I told Sergeant Kilgore it was Justin and Anastasia's plan.

At the meeting where I first told Sergeant Kilgore the truth, I told him that Justin and Byron needed me as part of the plot to call Anastasia and set up a meeting. I was supposed to be the one to call Anastasia and I was supposed to ask her to meet at Dairy Queen. Well, she already knew they were going to meet up, but they wanted me to ask for her. And I called her from the gas station, and I talked to her on the phone, and when she asked me where to meet, I said Dairy Queen.

I know I said back then that she walked away from the car, and that Justin made the only phone call from the gas station, and that he only talked to Francesca, not Anastasia. But that wasn't true. I believe Justin talked to Anastasia earlier that day. I'm sure he spoke to her, but that's what I had been filled in with later, because I don't recall him using the phone at Phillips 66. I mean the whole story was made up, the story we initially told the police.

As we were on the way out to Dairy Queen, the three of us were drinking Jack Daniels. I don't recall how much I had. Couple drinks. But I wasn't drunk and I don't think they were drunk either.

I might have told Sergeant Kilgore that Byron was acting drunk that night, I don't recall. I don't recall either if I told him that Byron smelled of alcohol when he first picked me up at my house. I guess I said at the deposition he smelled of alcohol, that he was acting drunk.

And I guess I said earlier today that Byron was not drinking that day. I don't recall exactly if he was drinking or not. I'm trying to answer to the best of my knowledge. There was like drinking going on when I got in the car. I know they had alcohol with them and that quite a bit of it was gone.

I don't recall exactly what I said to Sergeant Kilgore about Byron running inside at Dairy Queen to get Anastasia. Somebody got out to go get her, I know that. I told him I thought Byron went in to get her, but I told him I wasn't sure. I didn't say I was positive of it. It didn't seem like that important of a thing. He was just going in to get her. Somebody went in to get her.

After we left the Dairy Queen, all four of us were in the car together. Justin and Anastasia were arguing. Anastasia was yelling at him, and she took off a ring and threw it at him, while we were in the car. She used to get mad and leave the condo sometimes, but I didn't know her well enough to know she was going to get out of the car.

I never saw Byron with a gun. I never knew that he owned any gun. I saw a gun on the wall of his dad's house, but it wasn't Byron's gun; it was his dad's gun. Byron once said that he used to go hunting with his dad, and on the night of the killing he told me it was his dad's gun. I wasn't sure if that was the same one or not. I couldn't be positive.

The first time I talked to Sergeant Kilgore about the shooting, I described the gun that Byron used as an old double-barreled gun, but I don't know for sure exactly what gun was used. I didn't get a real up close look at it or anything.

After the shooting, they threw away the gun not very far from the cemetery. Sergeant Kilgore and I drove around to different places where there were railroads trying to find the spot. We ended up over by Lake Quivira in Kansas. I know that's not close to where Anastasia was killed, but I never said it was the spot. I was just trying to answer, because everywhere we went he kept asking, "Is this the place? Is this the place? Is this familiar?" Well, it all looked familiar.

I wouldn't say he bullied me into agreeing it was the spot, but he wasn't questioning me very nicely. Put it that way. He seemed annoyed with the whole thing. He said, "If I have people come out here and look, will we find anything?" And I said, "Maybe." That was the last spot we went.

I know I told the police that Byron was five feet away from Anastasia when he fired the gun, but that was probably a guesstimate. I think he asked me something like, "Well, do you think it was from here to here?" "Well, how far away would you say that was?" "I don't know, five feet. Something like that." He probably said here to that wall. He showed me an approximation and he said, "Would you say that?" And I said, "Yeah. Maybe that, maybe a little more."

I saw Anastasia fall back and I saw how she landed. I saw her on the ground. She fell on her back. I'm certain of that. I recall telling Sergeant Kilgore "I don't know. I think she was on her back. I looked back and I could see her feet like she was laying on her back." I was trying to remember.

After the shooting, I didn't see any blood on either Justin or Byron. Justin freaked out. He started crying, and I was crying too. We were both crying. After that, he got real calm and like incoherent acting. He was just sitting there like all pale and shaken up. His hands were shaking.

We all had to like pull ourselves together at his condo because I had to go talk to my parents. That's where Byron and Justin started coming up with this story about the car stopping at a stoplight. They asked me if it would be believable and I said yes, because Anastasia was notorious for throwing fits. I never saw her storm out of the car and walk away like that, but I saw her get mad at the apartment and yell at him over the phone and such. She would storm out of the apartment, but she would usually go on a walk and come right back.

After this, we got back in the car and they took me home. I didn't tell my mom what really happened because I was scared. I just talked to her for a little bit and went in my room and tried to go to sleep. The next day, I went down to my grandma's house with my mother. I didn't tell my mom then either, because I was scared. I was scared of how she would deal with me. The whole thing had just shaken me up.

They told me I was going to get in just as much trouble as they were. I mean, the whole thing was just horrible. I didn't want anybody to know about it, much less my mom. I didn't do anything to stop it. I took the whole thing as a big joke and all of a sudden this girl is dead.

I know now that Justin bought shotguns two different times. I never saw him with a shotgun, though. Byron told me about it after the fact, because it would make it more believable that Justin had done it. That was added in later, because it seemed like the police were believing that anyway.

When I finally told the truth to Sergeant Kilgore, I told him the story about Justin buying a shotgun at Wal-Mart was made up. I still don't know for a fact. Byron is the one that told me that. I was just trying to answer the best I could recall, because everything got so confusing.

At some point I went back to Lincoln Cemetery. I went out there and I saw the memorial that had been set up. Anastasia's friends had put up like a wreath or flowers and cards and pictures. That was before I went with Sergeant Kilgore and I pointed to a spot to him. I told him "I think this is the spot where Anastasia was shot dead."

That didn't make it easier for me to point out the spot in the cemetery. I didn't know that's where the memorial was. I didn't know where they would put it. It was just out there. I didn't think that was the exact location.

When I told Sergeant Kilgore that I found out where Anastasia was found, I meant I found out where Lincoln Cemetery was and stuff, that general area. I didn't even know it was a cemetery before that. But I don't remember assuming that the memorial was right exactly the place where her body was found.

Horton Lance asks for a sidebar. It's getting close to the end of the day. I think everyone wants to get through Kelly's testimony before we go home, so it shouldn't be too much longer. Here we go.

"Ms. Moffett, you mentioned today that you have attended drug rehab?" » Yes.

"And is it true that you also have attended some psychiatric counseling?" » Yes.

"In all the time that you attended psychiatric counseling, did you ever tell any psychiatric counselor that you had witnessed a murder?" » No.

"Ms. Moffett, at one point in time you believe that you were in love with Byron Case, true?" » Yes.

"And you told Byron Case that you loved him?" » Yes.

"And even after the death of Anastasia, you continued to tell Byron Case that you loved him?" » Yes.

"And are you aware that, when Byron moved to St. Louis in September of 2000, he attempted to end all contact with you?" » Yes.

"He wouldn't give you his address, his phone number, any of that?" » Yes.

"And for the record, how did that make you feel, the guy you once loved has broken off all contact with you?" » I was upset, but it wasn't for that reason. It was just that he was leaving everything behind, leaving me this mess to deal with, and it didn't affect him whatsoever.

It didn't make me angry that he wasn't in love with me anymore, and it didn't disappoint me that he wouldn't give me his phone number. I already had a new set of friends and a different boyfriend.

I called him in St. Louis, but the only way I got the phone number was through the police. When I finally talked to him on the phone, I was trying to get him to come right out and say he did it. Even though he didn't come out and say it, he certainly didn't deny it. I said it about three times, and he never once denied it. He never said he committed the murder, but like I said, he never denied it.

And it's not because I'm making this up. It's because he doesn't want to talk about it on the phone because he knows he killed her. He already seemed suspicious of me calling him anyway. If you look on that tape, he said, "This is odd" that I was calling him.

As I said before, Justin and Anastasia were standing outside the car arguing. Me and Byron were in the back seat. I can't remember what Justin and

Anastasia were saying right before it happened, but I remember Byron saying "I'll be right back."

I can't tell you exactly what kind of gun he used and I can't tell you the exact spot in the cemetery where it took place, but I know where I saw her body laying. I can't tell you for sure where they threw the gun afterwards, but I don't see how that's something I'm supposed to know. I didn't get out of the car.

With that, Horton Lance completes his cross examination of Kelly Moffett.

TESTIMONY OF KELLY MOFFETT: PART 6

Theresa Crayon has some questions for Kelly on re-direct.

"Mr. Lance asked you about whether or not you described it as a double-barreled gun, and he asked you to just say yes or no, basically. Now I want you to look at your interview where Sergeant Kilgore asked you about the gun. Read what your full answer was to that."

Kelly reads from her prior interview:

> "I don't think he did the little chink chink thing, but I don't know. I don't think he did it. I just saw him messing with it."

Crayon continues:

"And then the follow-up question is: 'What you're describing to me is like a pump shotgun.' That's the question that's posed to you by Detective Kilgore, is it not?" » Yes.

"What is your full answer to that question?"

Kelly reads:

> "No, I'm not sure if he did that. I just kind of saw him fiddling for a couple seconds, but he just grabbed it out and walked on the side of the car. I think it was double-barreled though, because it looked like an old gun."

"So are you sure of what the gun looked like?" » No.

"Was it a little handgun or was it a big gun? Can you tell us that?" » It was a big gun.

"All right. And by using your hand to describe it, can you give the jury an idea of the length of the gun as you remember it?" » Not really. Just like a big long hunting gun.

"Okay. But it's not a small?" » No.

"A small gun?" » No.

"Which leads me to my next question that he asked you about, which is 'How close was he when he shot her?' Tell the jury what your full answer is at that point."

Kelly reads:

> "Pretty Close. Probably here to the wall. He wasn't very far at all. He was close to her."

"And then when Kilgore says, 'Okay, what you showed me is approximately five foot.' I think that's what Mr. Lance referred to in the statement. And what is your complete answer following that?"

Kelly reads:

> "Yeah, maybe that or a little bit over. He was close to her though, really close to her."

At that, Crayon steps around the counsel table and begins to approach the witness.

"Kelly, how far is five feet to you?" » I --

"When you're describing to Detective Kilgore how close Byron Case was to Anastasia when he shot her, I want you to stop me when you have an idea of how close he was to her. Can you do that?" » Yeah.

Crayon starts inching towards Kelly. Wow. Is she pregnant or what?

"If I come this close to you --" » About, you mean from me to you?

"Yes." » Come a little bit closer. I would say probably about -- yeah, about like this.

That's five feet? Really?

"Okay?" » That's five feet.

If that's five feet, Crayon will soon be giving birth to a four-foot-tall baby.

"So you say this is about five feet?" » Yeah.

Interesting. Something's going on here.

"And you have described for the jury how long the gun is; is that correct?" » Yes. But I --

"I know you're not sure. You're giving an estimate. But you're describing a long gun and not a handgun?" » Yes.

"And I want you to show the jury with your own actions, with your testimony, because in here you talk a little bit later, it says: 'How did he hold the shotgun up? At the end of his shoulder? How did he hold it? Do you remember?'" » Yes.

"Tell them what you remember seeing Byron Case do with the long gun." » He lifted it up like that.

Oh my gosh. It's brilliant!

"Did he put it up against his shoulder? Is that what you're showing us?" » Yeah. I'm not sure. It was lifted up like this, but he had on dark clothes, and the gun was dark.

Devious, but absolutely brilliant.

"And Anastasia was about as far as I am right here from you when he did that; is that correct?" » Yes.

Crayon is trying to get us to visualize the shooting in a fashion different than Kelly seemed to describe earlier. Instead of shooting Anastasia from the right-rear quarter from a distance of five feet, Crayon is trying to imprint that Byron shot Anastasia from the front, in the face, from close range.

"He asked you also to look at this statement when he was asking you about the position of the victim's body. Do you remember that question?" » Yes.

I talked to him about seeing Anastasia laying on the ground. I told him she fell back. It was kind of like an explosion. I mean, it just knocked her backwards, the whole thing did. And really quickly Byron just threw the gun in the trunk, you know, like opened it up, threw it in there.

I looked and screamed. I screamed and looked away. Then I looked back, and I think she was on her back just like that. I'm pretty sure it knocked her backwards, because I remember kind of seeing her body on the ground like that. It was dusk when it happened so I was able to see.

I broke up with Byron a little more than a year after it all happened. It was my idea to break up. I remember the day perfectly. We were arguing in his car, and he started yelling and banging on the wheel of his car. And I got out and went to my friend's house.

In December after that, maybe January, that's when I called 911 about him threatening to kill himself. It was in September of 2000 that I found out Byron was going to move to St. Louis. In between, though, I didn't have any desire to get back together with him.

That's it. Finally. Theresa Crayon has no more questions, Horton Lance declines his opportunity to re-cross, and I'm still fuming.

What a day. The other witnesses should go faster, I'm guessing, except maybe the defendant, if he decides to testify. The judge is going to send us home now, I hope.

"Ladies and gentlemen, that concludes the testimony for today. We apologize for the lateness of the hour. We got delayed unavoidably for a little while. In order that we keep pace, I would like to, if at all possible, forewarn you we may well want to go until 5:30 or so tomorrow because, again, our desire is to make sure you get this case no later than Thursday morning.

"With that as a preface, let's get in the jury room shortly before 9, and we may go as late as 5:30. We may even shave lunch a little bit to make sure we're keeping pace. The Court again reminds you --"

Yeah, yeah. Same old stuff. Don't talk, don't read, be on time.

" -- Jury is free to go."

That's what I wanted to hear. See you tomorrow morning.

TESTIMONY OF DEBRA MOFFETT

Here we are, Tuesday morning, just a wee bit after nine. It's a little bit warmer today, by three or four degrees. Although it was bright and sunny when we came in, it's supposed to be pretty cloudy the rest of the day.

My mood's improved somewhat. I don't want to talk about yesterday though.

Day two. They told us it would take four days to get all the testimony in. Yesterday was kind of slow, only two witnesses. We'll see how things go today.

The Judge tells the prosecution they can call their next witness. They call Debra Moffett. David Fry is going to examine her.

"Good morning." » Good morning.

"Now, I'm going to stand way back here by the last juror so you always have to remember to project your voice back this far. All right?" » Okay.

"Would you tell the jury your name, please?" » Debra Moffett.

"Are you related to Kelly?" » I'm her mother.

"As Kelly's mother, did you know Justin?" » Yes.

"Justin Bruton?" » Yes.

"Tell the jurors how you knew him and how well?" » I knew him through Kelly. He was a friend. I didn't know him really well. He called the house quite a bit. I only -- he only came over to the house maybe three times.

"Did you know Anastasia?" » Yes.

"How did you know her and how well?" » The same way. She was a friend of Kelly's. She called our house, you know, usually every other day or so. She was at our house maybe three or four times.

"Did you know the defendant Byron Case?" » Yes.

"And how did you know him and how well?" » He was Kelly's boyfriend for about a year-and-a-half. Spent a lot of time at our house. Ate dinner with us. Knew him pretty well.

"Prior to Kelly, I guess, maybe befriending or becoming the girlfriend of Byron Case, can you describe what her relationships were like with you and the rest of your family?" » Normal, you know. She was 14 when she met Byron, a little rebellious, but normal relationship.

"Fourteen, did you say?" » Right.

"What grade was that that she met him in?" » It would have been eighth grade.

"And you felt like she had a normal relationship with your family?" » Yes.

Now, can you describe how Kelly and Byron started interacting at the very beginning of their relationship for the jury?" » Well, she knew Byron long before we did. He was so much older than her that she really didn't want us to know about him, and I guess she actually had met him that spring of '97. I knew that there was this person calling the house. I didn't know who it was. He had a very deep voice. I thought he was a lot older than her. I questioned her about it. She said "Oh, he's just a friend. No big deal." But I didn't really know Byron at that point. Had never seen him.

She dated him probably a few months, maybe, before we found out about the age difference, and we were concerned about that.

They spent a lot of time at our house. Just activities that kids like that age do. They went to Westport. They spent a lot of time at Borders on the Plaza. They would go out with Justin and Anastasia. Go to the movies. They spent a lot of time at our house.

He would come over when she got out of school. A lot of times he would be sitting on our porch when we got home from school. He would spend the evening with us, eat dinner with us sometimes. When she went out with him, she would always have a curfew. During the week I wanted her home by 8:30 or 9. On the weekends it was 11:30. She was pretty good about it. Most of the time she would be home on time. If she wasn't she would call.

Well, when I first met Byron, I was relieved, because he wasn't what I was expecting. His voice over the phone made him sound like he was 35 years old. When I met him I realized he was much younger than I had thought. And he was intelligent. He was soft spoken. Very mannerly. So my initial impression was better than I had expected. I think he cared a great deal about Kelly. Just the way they were with each other. I think he was very much in love with her actually at the time.

"I want to now direct your attention to October 22nd, 1997. All right? You were working that day; is that right?" » Right.

"About what time did you get off work and what do you do after work?" » I got off about 2:30 and I always picked Kelly up at school. Sometimes Byron would pick her up. But I picked her up that day.

"What do you do for a living?" » I'm a pharmacy technician.

"And that particular day -- I'm sorry, I may have interrupted you. Did you pick Kelly up or was she home already?" » No, I picked her up.

We got home probably about three o'clock. Kelly went upstairs. I know she wasn't downstairs. She went upstairs for awhile. She might have been asleep. I don't remember, but I know she was upstairs for quite awhile. Then she came downstairs, and I was in the kitchen. She came down, and she said that Justin and Byron were going to go pick her up.

I was aware when she actually left because I was in the kitchen and she came in and got her purse. I asked, "Well what are you going to do?" And she said, "Oh, we're just going to drive around and hang out." And I said, "Well, I want you home by 8:30, because it's a school night. No later than 8:30."

I was aware when she came home, because I had told her to be home by 8:30 and I remember looking at my watch and it was 9 or a little after, and she still wasn't there. I was mad. I was waiting for her to get home. She probably got home a little bit later than that, maybe 9:15, 9:20.

I was upstairs. I heard them come in the front door. I could hear them talking. I was mad at Kelly, and I was going to holler for her to come upstairs. I walked to the top of the stairs, and I heard them in the kitchen whispering. This went on for quite awhile and that isn't good when you're a parent to hear a bunch of whispering. I said, "Kelly come up here. I want to talk to you."

She did, and I said, "You know, what's the deal? You were supposed to be here at 8:30. It's after 9 o'clock. What happened? Why are you late?" At that point she told me that they had gone and picked up Anastasia. That they were driving around and Anastasia and Justin had gotten in an argument. At some point Anastasia had said, "I want out of the car. Stop the car. I want out. I want to go call my dad." And she had gotten out of the car at an intersection in Independence and taken off.

Kelly said, "Gosh, you know, that wasn't a very nice area. I hope she's okay." That struck me as odd because Anastasia kind of did things like that all the time. I thought it was kind of unusual that Kelly would be concerned about Anastasia's welfare at that point.

Kelly went back downstairs and I heard Justin make a phone call. I couldn't hear well enough to know what he was saying, but I could tell it was his voice. I heard some more whispering after the phone call, and then the boys left.

I believe Kelly came back upstairs, and I said, "Who was making a phone call?" I was suspicious of this whole situation because of the whispering. And she said Justin had called Anastasia's house to see if she had gotten there. She said that whoever Justin had talked to at Anastasia's house said not only was Anastasia not there, but they had never gotten a phone call from her.

She said Justin at that point said, "Oh, my God. I might as well kill myself right now." I asked, "Why would you say that?" And Kelly said, "Well, you know, it was such a bad area. We're afraid that something happened to her."

My mother is in a nursing home down in Southeast Missouri. She has Alzheimer's. The next morning, Kelly wanted to visit her. I was going to visit her that day so I took Kelly out of school, and we went down that day to see my mom. We left probably 8 o'clock, 7 or 8 o'clock. Kelly slept most of the day. She slept on the way down. We got down there, visited my mom. When we got back in the car to go home she slept all the way home. We got back about 5 o'clock.

The minute we walked in the door the phone rang and Kelly ran upstairs to get the phone. I was down in the kitchen and a few minutes later she came running down the stairs, and she was crying, and she goes, "Mom, turn on the TV. They found Anastasia's body."

After that, they continued to see one another. Byron was there a lot of time. His father died Christmas Eve and I felt really bad for him, because his dad had passed away and Anastasia and Justin were gone. He actually spent Christmas at our house with us.

After the holidays I noticed that Kelly was beginning to complain about Byron. She would get irritated with him. Before, she was infatuated with him. After that was kind of over, that part of it was over. Sometimes she was okay, a lot of times she would be irritated with him. She would pick at him. She would complain to me about him. She was short tempered. That never happened before the murder.

Still they continued seeing each other pretty much daily. She would break up with him occasionally, and they would argue and he would not be around for a day or two. That happened over and over. Right after Christmas she started talking about breaking up with him. Periodically she broke up with him, and then he would be back over. I said, "Kelly, I thought you were going to break up with him?" And she said, "Well, he talked me into staying with him."

She became moodier and harder to deal with. She started telling me she couldn't sleep at night. Actually, at that point, she went into therapy and was in kind of a steady downhill progression from there.

She kind of became more closed off, didn't talk to us as much. When we would have family get-togethers and things, a lot of times she would not be there or would stay in her room. Sometimes she would have periods where she was fine. That would last for a little while. Then she began to have periods where she seemed really depressed and angry.

That following summer she quit softball. She started having panic attacks, really bad ones. I would actually have to go get her from school. She would call me, and she would be crying a lot of times, and she would say, "You're going to have to come get me. I can't be at school."

That spring I began to notice that there was something going on. I suspected it was drug use. It became progressively worse over time. I tried to talk to her. She would just say, "I'm depressed. I don't know what's wrong. I'm really depressed. I can't sleep." She started skipping school.

She broke up with Byron probably in December of '98. I knew she was using drugs prior to that, but after that January, her drug use became really bad. She would disappear. She would be gone for days at a time. We would look for her, but a lot of times we couldn't find her.

She would call me from places I have no idea where she even was. She was skipping school. She finally missed so much school that she lost credit. Physically I saw a change in her. Kelly had always looked very nice. She was very particular about how she looked, but she started looking slovenly, not combing her hair kind of situation. Eventually, she quit school.

She called me probably about 3 or 4 o'clock in the morning in March of that year. I picked up the phone, and she said, "Mom," and she would call me from a drug house occasionally and cry and tell me she was sorry, and, you know, "I'm sorry I'm doing this. Sorry I'm living this way."

That morning when I answered the phone she said, "Mom." And I said, "Yeah." And she said, "I saw Anastasia murdered." And I said, "Oh, my God, Kelly. What happened?" And at that point she said, "I saw her shot in front of me." And I said, "Was it Justin?" And she said, "Yes." And that was the end of the conversation. And at that point I said, "Would you please come home?" And she said, "Okay," And hung up the phone.

She eventually came home. I don't remember if it was the next day or the day after, but she did come home. Her drug use continued. We tried to talk about this situation with her, but after she had laid this bombshell on us she didn't want to talk about it anymore.

June of that year her drug use got so bad we put her in rehab. We grabbed her and put her in the car and put her in rehab. That's where she met Maggie Jenkins, her counselor. We told Maggie about this what Kelly had told us. I said, "My husband and I both feel like she is going to have to talk about this. This is killing her. She is going to have to talk about this at some point." Maggie said she had individual counseling sessions with the residents, and she would try to work on this.

Kelly ran away from rehab two or three times, and we took her back. One of the times that she was home she had come to our door late at night, I don't remember if she asked for my husband or me. But she said I need to talk to somebody and my husband went in and talked to her for several hours. When he came back into bed it was probably 3 or 4 o'clock in the morning, he walked in the room and he said, "Kelly just told me that Byron killed Anastasia."

I believe it was August I got a call at work. It was Maggie and she said, I've been talking to Kelly, and I need you to come right now." I got there in twenty minutes. Kelly and Maggie were upstairs in the counseling room. I went in and sat down. Maggie said, "Kelly, I want you to tell your mom what you just told me."

Kelly said, "Mom, I saw Justin kill Anastasia." I said, "Kelly, you told Dad it was Byron." A few seconds later she kind of slumped back in her chair and said, "It was Byron."

Maggie said, "Stop. Under these circumstances, I'm going to have to contact the police and tell them what's happened." She recommended a lawyer to us, John O'Connor. She called and talked to him. She gave us his card. Dan and I talked to him later that day. Then Kelly went with him to the prosecutor's office.

Debra Moffett is cross-examined by Horton Lance.

"Ms. Moffett, when Kelly first disclosed to you that she claimed she saw Anastasia's murder, was that over the phone or in person?" » It was over the phone.

"And I believe your testimony is in that phone conversation, it was you who asked who did it. She said Justin as a response." » Right.

"And when you met Kelly later in person she wouldn't discuss that aspect of the homicide any further, right?" » No.

"Apparently Kelly, tried to stay with that story for some time?" » Yes.

"That summer. Weeks. Was it weeks or months?" » Months.

"For months you went on with the impression that Justin fired the gun?" » Yes.

"And when Kelly finally disclosed it was somebody else she disclosed it to Kelly's father, your husband?" » Right.

"And you said when you went to see Kelly in rehab later she tried again to tell you that it was Justin who fired the gun?" » Right.

"And you confronted her that she had told a different story?" » Right.

"Did you personally ever receive an explanation from Kelly as why she would say Justin fired the gun?" » Sure. That was the first thing I asked her. She told me that if she said it was Byron, she knew there was going to be police investigation. She was afraid that she was going to be prosecuted.

"And you accepted that explanation?" » Yes.

"Do you remember the dates of the first time Kelly was in rehab?" » I don't remember the exact dates. It was probably beginning of June.

I'm aware that Kelly had been using pot and drugs before she ever met Byron. I'm not claiming that Byron led her into pot or drugs. I am saying, though, that Kelly's drug use got worse and worse to a real serious level. At one point the family was truly unsure of how to deal with Kelly and her drug problem. Eventually, she got kicked out of the house. We told her she couldn't stay at home if she was using drugs, because we could no longer trust her.

Kelly would lie to us about whether she was still using. She was a drug addict. She was lying to me because she needed money. I mean that's what a drug addict does. She couldn't really tell me the truth about any of her activity. I was aware at some point she was living in crack houses.

It was after that that Kelly first admitted to me that she saw the murder. When she first told me, I didn't know what to think. I thought it was really odd after she told us this news, and she came back home that she still didn't want to talk about it. I would have assumed after she told us the truth that it might have been something that she would want to talk about. But then when she came back home she didn't want to talk about it further.

In my opinion, Kelly's inability to talk about the murder ruined her life. I told Officer Kilgore that, and it's still my opinion today. I have a lot of sympathy for her. She is now once again a member of the family.

David Fry asks Debra Moffett only one question during re-direct.

"This welcome back, is it because she has identified Byron as the defendant?" » No, no. That really didn't have anything to do with it. As she began to get better with the drug use, she was welcomed back into the family.

And that's it for Debra Moffett.

TESTIMONY OF DIANE MARSHALL

The Judge tells the prosecution they can call their next witness. They call Diane Marshall. David Fry examines her.

"Good morning." » Good morning.

"Would you tell the jury your name, please." » My name is Diane Marshall.

"And did you know Anastasia?" » Yes. I knew Anastasia. I was her stepmother. I knew her for about five years, since she was 13.

"Would you describe your relationship with her, briefly?" » I was very involved with her life, but we were not close. She didn't confide in me, but, you know, we lived together as a family and, you know, we had a lot of common concerns.

"So she was a 13-year-old when you first came into her life; correct?" » Yes.

"How many stepchildren did you get when you married into the family?" » When I married Robert, I acquired four stepdaughters.

I already had a daughter who was one year older than Anastasia. And later on I had a daughter with Robert, and she was in preschool, beginning preschool at the time of Anastasia's senior year. So I was really wrapped up in the life of a preschooler. It's hard to switch gears from having a very small child to dealing with teenagers. Small children thrive on a calm regular routine and teenagers thrive on excitement. My primary focus was my youngest daughter.

In June of '96, my husband and I bought a much larger house in Independence only a few blocks from my other house, and Anastasia moved in that summer. And she persuaded her sister, Francesca, to come and live with her too. So only Anastasia and Francesca lived with us. The other two girls stayed with their mother.

I knew who Justin Bruton was, but I didn't know him well. I never talked to him on the phone, but I was aware that he called. I don't know how frequently he called, though. I'm not a phone answerer. There are other people in the house that are much quicker to answer the phone than me, so I usually leave it to them.

I didn't know Kelly Moffett. I wouldn't say that I knew Byron Case, either. I think I can recognize him. That's him there.

It was in the springtime of 1997 that Anastasia began a relationship with Justin. I was the chauffeur. That was my primary function in Anastasia's life, was to be the chauffeur, because she went to Lincoln Academy.

And when they came out to Independence, they needed transportation to school. So I worked downtown and, since my hours were fairly flexible, I made the adjustments so that I would take the girls to school in the morning and I would pick them up in the afternoon after school.

Justin didn't go to school with Anastasia. He was a student at UMKC. I don't know of any instance when I ever saw Justin at Lincoln. Anastasia graduated in June of 1997, and Justin attended the graduation. That was a very happy day. We were really proud of her. She was a brilliant girl.

She went to live at Justin's condo on the Plaza. I'm not certain exactly when she moved out. It might have been prior to the graduation. Her mother gave her some pots and pans for graduation, so she may have moved out before the ceremony. But that was her announced goal, that she had made a serious commitment to Justin. There was talk of becoming engaged to be married, and she wanted to go and stay with him.

At some point in the summer of '97, though, she moved back in with us. I think it was when Francesca was having a back-to-school party at our house that we got a call from Anastasia saying that she was breaking up with Justin and that she would be coming home.

She continued having a relationship with Justin after she moved back, but exactly what her relationship was with Justin, I don't know. She didn't confide in me about that.

On October 22nd of 1997, I went to work as usual. On the way home from work, I picked up Francesca and when we came in, Anastasia was in the living room. I see her in my mind's eye. I see her standing in front of the front door and Francesca is standing beside her and Anastasia asks me if I would give her a ride. She wanted a ride, she said her friends were picking her up at Mount Washington and she just wanted a ride. It seemed odd, but, okay.

When she made the request of me, the thought flashed through my head, "Well, the last time Anastasia asked me to use the car I said no." And I thought, "Well, okay, am I going to be the baddie this time? Am I going to be the naysayer?" She was making a polite request. She was asking in a nice way.

I looked at Fran and I thought, "Well, what does Fran want me to say?" And Fran wasn't giving me any clues, because it was an odd request. So I kind of looked at Fran and said, "Well, what does she want me so say?"

So then I said, "Okay. Well, it's not that far away and maybe we can just do it quickly." So that's why I said yes.

I drove her to Mount Washington, to the Truman Road gate.

The only thing I remember definitely was that she was wearing a tan corduroy jacket. In other words, what she was wearing didn't strike me as anything unusual, except I noted that she wore a jacket. It was a beautiful day and normally she didn't dress for the weather. She was somebody who just went out without a coat. I thought, oh, it's good she is wearing a jacket because, you know, it's getting into fall now.

After I dropped her off, I drove away and stopped at a gas station. I have a clear picture in my head of standing at the gas pump with a drink in my hand and looking at my watch, and I did recall that it was twenty minutes after four.

I went to my mother's house and helped her with some work on her insulation. While I was working there, I received a call from Robert, my husband. He was concerned. He had been told that Anastasia had been taken to the cemetery, and he was concerned that she might not be picked up by the friends she was supposed to meet. I think that was about 5 o'clock.

I don't know which friend she was supposed to meet. Anastasia didn't name names. I got the impression it was Justin. Justin usually came to the house, and he usually came with other people. They always did that. They always came and picked her up. It was extremely unusual that she asked me to drop her off to meet them at a cemetery.

After the call from my husband, I received a call from Francesca. She wanted me to take her over to Shirley's, who was the babysitter, to get her hair trimmed.

I realized what I had done, just dropping Anastasia off there, was not a wise thing to do. So I decided to go look for her. The baby sitter's place was in the same direction, so I dropped off Fran and drove around Mount Washington Cemetery. I never saw Anastasia there.

I returned and picked up Fran, dropped her off at the house and went back to my mother's house. I was still working there when Robert, my husband, came over and hollered up the stairs. He said it was time to come home.

When we got back to our house, Fran immediately began talking with Robert about the phone call that she had had.

I took Emma upstairs. Emma is my youngest daughter. I took her upstairs to put her to bed. I have a set bedtime routine for her, and I'm the only one that puts her to bed. So I was away from the living room, from Francesca talking to her father.

Robert got a call from Justin saying that he and Anastasia had an argument, that Anastasia got out of the car and refused to get back in. He just drove off and left her. So Robert went out and tried to find her. He didn't find her though. We had a very sleepless night. As soon as it was light, I woke him up. I said, you know, "It's getting light now. You better go out again." I don't know. It stuck in my head. I kept worrying about it all night.

Diane Marshall is cross-examined by Horton Lance.

"I don't have a lot of questions. Just bear with me. Bottom line is you dropped off Anastasia at Mount Washington Cemetery entrance on the night of the homicide?" » Yes.

And later around 6 o'clock you drove back through Mount Washington looking for Anastasia?" » Yes.

"When you made that trip through there looking around, did you stop at the Dairy Queen?" » No. I didn't even see the Dairy Queen.

"Okay. I'm satisfied with that answer. On that same evening, October 22nd, is it true that your husband, Bob, had worked late that night?" » Yes.

"Do you remember what time he arrived home?" » It was after dark. Might have been around 8, 8:30, something like that. He came by mother's Victorian house, but he didn't actually pick me up. We drove back in separate cars.

I guess there might have been some time when no one was at my house. Let me run through the people. I was putting insulation in. My mother was at a prayer meeting. Bob was working late. Anastasia had been dropped at the cemetery. Francesca went, I'm not sure if she, I don't remember her going to the church meeting, but then she would have been gone from the house when she got her haircut. So there was probably a short period of time when no one was home.

That's it. The prosecution doesn't want to re-direct, and it looks like we're going to get a recess. Time to stretch, as soon as we get the usual warning from the judge.

"All right. We're going to take a midmorning recess for fifteen or twenty minutes-- ."

Blah, blah, blah.

"We'll be in recess for about fifteen or twenty minutes. All rise, please. Jury is free to go to the jury room."

TESTIMONY OF FRANCESCA WITBOLSFEUGEN

The Judge tells the prosecution they can call their next witness. They call Francesca WitbolsFeugen. Theresa Crayon examines her.

"Like the judge said, we need you to keep your voice up so the people in the back row can hear you. State your name for the jury, please." » Francesca WitbolsFeugen. Do I need to spell it?

"No, you don't need to spell it for them. How did you know Anastasia WitbolsFeugen?" » She was my sister.

"How much of an age difference was there between you and Anastasia?" » About three years.

"How old are you now, Francesca?" » Twenty.

"And are you in school?" » Yes.

"Where do you go to school?" » UMKC.

"And did you know Justin Bruton?" » Yes.

"How did you know him?" » He was Anastasia's boyfriend. That's how I met him, a couple times together.

"Did you know Byron Case, the defendant in this case?" » Yes.

"How did you know him?" » He was a friend of Anastasia's and Justin's.

"And did you know Kelly Moffett?" » I didn't know her. I knew of her. She was Byron's girlfriend at the time.

"Did Anastasia ever tell you that they hung out with Byron and Kelly together, her and Justin?" » Yes. I think Byron and Kelly lived in Justin's apartment. For awhile they stayed there.

"Now, I want to take you back to 1996 and '97, that year, that school year. Do you recall who you were living with?" » I was living at my dad's house with him and my stepmother and my younger sister. Her name is Emma. Anastasia was there, on and off. She moved in the summer before I started high school, when she was a senior.

Anastasia met Justin in the spring of '97 before she graduated. I think about a month after they met, she moved into his condo in Westport. I didn't see her very much then. We went out a couple times. She loved him a lot. I think they were planning on getting married. Justin broke off the engagement, though, and she moved out of the condo and moved back into our house.

October 22nd 1997 was a Wednesday. Diane, my stepmother, picked me up from school. It would have been around 3:30, because I have guitar club at school. We went straight home. Anastasia was there waiting by the door, ready to go out. She had her coat on, and she was telling us that she had plans to meet Justin at Mount Washington Cemetery, and that she needed a ride. She was really happy. She was excited to be going out. I don't recall her mentioning meeting anyone else.

Diane took her to the cemetery. That was unusual because Justin had always picked her up before. About 15 or 20 minutes later Justin called. He wanted to speak to Anastasia. I told him that she wasn't there because she went to the cemetery and that she had been there a few minutes already. He said that he was in Lenexa and hadn't planned on picking her up because he thought she didn't have a ride.

A little bit later Diane's mother came over, my step-grandmother. She had received a phone call earlier from Anastasia requesting a ride to the cemetery, but hadn't been able to get there until then. I told her that Anastasia had already left, that Diane had given her a ride. So my grandmother left. Then I called my dad, because I started to get a little worried that Anastasia didn't have a ride home.

Then Diane called. I wanted to go get a haircut. She gave me the phone number to call the lady to get a haircut, and I talked to Diane about going by the cemetery and seeing if Anastasia was there. She finished some work at her mother's house, then came home and took me to get the haircut. Emma's babysitter cuts hair too.

Diane went from there to the cemetery to see if Anastasia was still there. Diane came back a little while later, picked me up, and said she didn't see Anastasia there. We went home, Diane dropped me off there, and headed back over to work on her mother's house.

I worked on some homework, then decided to go to the prayer meeting. I left about 6:45 or so. It's only three or four blocks away from the house, so I walked. I left a voice memo on our answering machine saying that I went to the church and I would be home before 9.

I got home some time after 8:30, probably around 8:45. I checked the answering machine and my memo was still on it. If somebody had come home and checked the memo, it would still be there only if they saved it. Anastasia and I had left memos on there before. It was easier than writing a note and putting it on the refrigerator. There were no messages on the machine.

I had come home with my younger sister, Emma. We had a snack and watched a movie. I was on the computer, when I received a phone call from Justin. He said he had a fight with Anastasia, and she got out of the car. And I heard him talking to someone else in the background. I asked who it was, and he said it was Byron. I don't think he asked for Anastasia. He made it sound like he was letting me know that she would be home soon and that she should call him when she got home.

I asked him where she had gotten out of the car, but I couldn't get an answer out of him. There was a lot of background discussion between him and Byron as to what went on, and I couldn't understand any of what they were talking about. They finally gave me an approximate time around 8:30. I remember that, because the phone call was around 9:30. I said, "You mean she's been out there an hour?"

I was worried. An hour is a long time to be out somewhere alone at night. I believe it was fall, so it was probably really dark. I told Justin if anything happened to her, it was his fault and I kind of hung up on him at that point.

About ten or twenty minutes later, my dad and Diane come home. They were in separate cars, but they come home pretty much back-to-back, one after another. I was on the computer. I thought about telling my dad about the call from Justin, but decided against it because Justin made it sound like she would be home soon. I didn't want to get Anastasia in trouble and let my dad and Diane know that they were having more problems. Anastasia was trying to remain optimistic about the relationship, despite Justin's comments that he didn't love her anymore.

I heard the phone ring and my dad talk to Justin. He sounded upset. After he got off the phone, I told him that Justin had called earlier around 9:30. He told Diane he was going to go out and look for Anastasia. He hadn't come home by the time I went to bed.

I woke up around 7, before 7, and went downstairs. My dad and Diane were in the kitchen talking. I talked to them about what was going on.

During my last class at school, there was an intercom message for me to go to the office. Diane was there and she told me what had happened to Anastasia.

A couple days later, I talked to Sergeant Kilgore. Before that, my dad asked me to remember everything that happened that night and write it all down so that it would be fresh when I went to see Kilgore.

Francesca WitbolsFeugen is cross-examined by Horton Lance.

"On the evening of October 22nd as you described, about what time was it when Justin called the first time?" » It was around 4:30.

"When Justin called that first time around 4:30, did you have the impression that Justin was surprised that Anastasia was not at home when he called?" » Yes.

"And did Justin seem to be further surprised that Anastasia had gone ahead and gone to Mount Washington Cemetery?" » Yes.

"Did Justin come right out and say that he had the impression Anastasia didn't have a ride to get to the cemetery?" » Yes.

"And since he had that impression, he had made other plans over in Kansas?" » He didn't say he made other plans. But he said he was in Lenexa so --

"At that point was it your impression that Justin seemed reluctant to drive over to Independence, Missouri, to meet Anastasia?" » Yes.

"He made general comments like, "Well, I'm over here in Lenexa, and I didn't think we were going to meet after all?" » Yes.

"Now, you said you know who Kelly Moffett is, right?" » Yes.

"On the evening of October 22nd, did you ever speak on the phone with Kelly Moffett?" » No, I did not.

"On the evening of October 22nd, did you ever speak on the phone with Mr. Byron Case?" » I didn't speak with him directly, no.

The only person you spoke with on the phone was Justin, correct?" » Yes.

Theresa Crayon has no re-direct and Francesca steps down. The Judge instructs the prosecution to call their next witness. We are moving along more briskly today than yesterday.

TESTIMONY OF GLEN COLLIVER

Glen Colliver is examined by David Fry.

"Good morning. Would you tell the jury your name, please." » Glen Colliver.

"Mr. Colliver, you've warned me that you have some hearing loss; is that correct?" » That's correct.

"Are you hearing me all right now?" » I am.

"Am I too loud?" » No.

"All right. You're retired now; is that correct?" » That's correct.

"Where did you used to work?" » Mount Washington Cemetery.

"When did you start there?" » I first became associated there in 1943.

"By the time you retired, what was your position with Mount Washington Cemetery?" » I was the general manager there.

"Fair to say you're pretty familiar with the area surrounding Mount Washington?" » That's correct.

"I'm going to try to orient the jury through you with that area. Would it assist you in describing that area to the jury if we used a map?" » Yes.

"Your Honor, can the witness stand over here by the map?"

Judge Atwell says: "Absolutely."

"In this particular map, I'm pointing right here to where it's printed Mount Washington Cemetery?" » Yes. Mt. Washington Cemetery.

"Now, surrounding Mount Washington Cemetery, major roads here, what is this road that's going north and south? » That's Interstate 435 which is our western boundary.

"To the north is Winner Road?" » That's correct.

"And is this Truman Road that goes from 435 on into Independence; is that correct?" » Yes.

"Now, what is the road that is the eastern boundary of your cemetery?" » Brookside Drive.

"And that's this road that goes almost straight from Truman to Winner. Is that correct?" » Yes.

"And a small cemetery located adjacent to Mount Washington, that's Lincoln Cemetery; is that right?" » Yes.

"All right. You can have a seat, sir. I'm going to ask you, sir, to think back with me back to October 22nd of 1997. You were still employed at the cemetery then, right?" » Correct.

On October 22nd of 1997, I was still working at the cemetery. On that particular day, I noticed a young lady sitting near the William Nelson Family Memorial. It's a rather imposing stone building that sits on a tract, about an acre of ground. It's a rather attractive building, located almost in the middle of the cemetery.

The stairs that come from the Nelson actually descend to the street. That's where I saw this young lady for the first time that day. It's not unusual to see people in the cemetery during the day, so nothing really caused me to be suspicious. She was just sitting there, alone. I was close enough, we made eye contact and I smiled and nodded and went on.

I saw her again later, that evening about 9 o'clock, at the same location. This time she wasn't alone. She was standing outside of an automobile with a male. It was after hours, so I drove up behind them and I stopped because I wanted them to move on. There was a male and a female standing outside the car. It was the same young lady I had seen earlier in the day.

I just sat there, and they got back in the car. They understood what I wanted and they left. They drove on to the north and out the gate at Brookside. They didn't speed. They just drove normally.

There are two gate entrances to the cemetery. One is at the northwest corner on Brookside and one is on the south side at Truman. They went out the north gate.

Fry shows Glen a photo and asks if he recognizes the car.

That's the car I saw that night. I can tell by the color, and it's a two-door. I took the license number down, so that, if I had any vandalism or any problems the next day, I would have somebody to start with.

I made a another sketch:

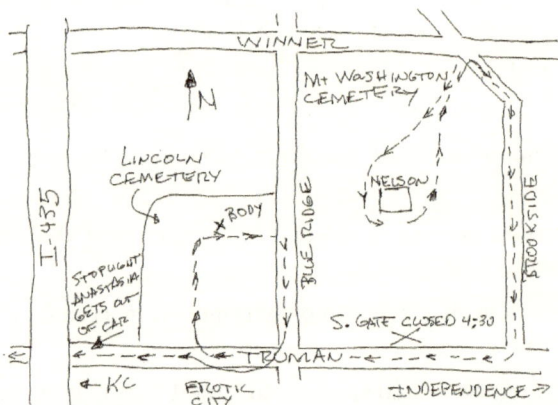

I tried to recreate the route described by Kelly and Glen Colliver. Most of the route is from Kelly's testimony. Glen confirmed what Kelly said about her journey through Mount Washington Cemetery.

The next morning when I went to open up the gates, I noticed a man waiting by the south gate. He told me he was looking for his daughter, that she had not come home that evening. He showed me a photograph. He left me his name and phone number in case I ran onto anything or found out anything.

Fry shows Glen another photo and asks if he recognizes the person.

That's her. I can tell by the face, the shape of it, the face and her hair. That's the girl I saw the day before.

Later that morning, my assistant knew the experiences I had the evening before. I mentioned them to him at 8 o'clock when we opened up. About 9 o'clock he came and told me that he had his car radio on and heard a news report. And he said it sounds strange. He said, "I wonder if it has anything to do with what you saw last night." I said, "I don't know." He said, "I think you ought to go up there." So I went on up to Lincoln Cemetery.

I described the girl that I had seen to the officer there. I gave him the license number, the name I thought might be the victim, the father's name, and the phone number to reach the father.

Glen Colliver is cross-examined by Public Defender Horton Lance.

We close the gate at Truman Road some time between 4:30 and 5:00, and I normally make an inspection trip through the cemetery at that time. The other gate I normally close some time around dark. That night I think I was a little bit later. I went out to dinner, so it was close to 9 o'clock. There is no set time of day that I always close that gate. On that evening, it was between 15 before 9 and 9 o'clock, because I know the time I left my house. I live about five minutes away.

If the police wrote down that I said it was 7 o'clock, they got it wrong. I didn't say that. It was probably closer to 9 or a little after, because coming in contact with the car and following it probably delayed my leaving the cemetery.

Fry has some re-direct.

"Mr. Lance was referring to an officer's report. We have showed you that officer's report previously; is that correct?" » That's correct.

"And the time that the officer wrote down when he wrote the report back in '97, he wrote 1900, which is military time, right?" » Yes.

"You're an old military man, right?" » I'm military, but I didn't use the time fluently.

"But you knew what they were referring to?" » Yes.

"He wrote down 1900?" » That would have been 7 o'clock, but I know it was 9 because I left my house at my wife's instructions because we watch a television show at 9 o'clock. And she said, if you plan on watching that television show, it's a quarter till 9, you'd better get home. So that's why I had the time in my mind, because I know I left the house with ample time to go down, take care of the task and get back.

"All right then. I have no further questions."

TESTIMONY OF JOHN BRUTON

Next witness is John Bruton. He is examined by Theresa Crayon.

"Would you please tell the jury your name?" » John Bruton.

"Mr. Bruton, you're not from Kansas City, are you?" » No, I am not.

"Where are you from?" » Tulsa, Oklahoma.

"But you've come in for the trial this week; is that correct?" » That is true.

"Do you have a son named Justin Bruton?" » I do.

"Would you please explain the nature of your relationship with Justin, how you're related to him?" » I am Justin's adoptive father. Justin was adopted. His mother and I married when he was about 5 years old, and he was adopted one year later.

I met Anastasia on two occasions. They were boyfriend-girlfriend and at one point they had lived together. Justin was a student at UMKC, and we had purchased a condo near the Plaza, close to the university. He lived in that property. He had finished the summer session and was enrolled in the fall session.

There were certain conditions for Justin staying in the condominium. That was Justin's job, being a student. We provided him a car and the insurance. He had no living expenses that he was personally responsible for. We absorbed all of his expenses, but, for that, his job was to go to school and be a student. As far as I knew, up through October of '97, he was doing that.

The weekend prior to October 22nd of 1997, Justin came to Tulsa for a visit. He arrived on Friday and returned to Kansas City on Sunday afternoon.

On Thursday, October 23rd, I received a phone call regarding Justin. The caller had left a message. The essence of the call was that Anastasia had been found murdered, the police would like to talk to Justin, but no one had seen or heard from Justin. The caller was curious to know if we had.

Naturally, hearing that type of a message, we couldn't imagine what to think or not to think. We tried to call Justin's condo. We got no answer, so I got in the car and drove to Kansas City just as quickly as I could. I got there early Friday morning between 2:30 and 3:00 AM.

When I arrived at the condominium, there was a business card from Detective Gary Kilgore on the door of the condo asking Justin, "When you get this, please give me a call." I went in. Nothing was out of order, but he wasn't there. I called Sergeant Kilgore. and promised to let him know if I located Justin.

I stayed at the condo on Friday. In the evening, Byron and Kelly came by. It was a pleasant surprise. I was glad to see them both. I knew they were friends of Justin's. I knew there was a concern for Justin on their part. They came in and we had a conversation. Of course, I was curious to get as much information as I possibly could.

I don't recall Kelly participating in the conversation other than introductions. Of course, I began to ask Byron as many questions as I could possibly think of. Who, why, when, where, what. He explained that they had been on a double date, and were returning Anastasia to her house.

They came to a stop sign. Anastasia turned to Justin and said, "Why don't you love me anymore?" And Justin's response was, "I don't know. I just don't." That answer supposedly infuriated Anastasia, and she got out of the car. Justin rolled down the window and asked her to get back in. She refused, saying that she was going to call her parents. They drove off.

As Byron related this, his demeanor was factual. I wouldn't say he was upset. Everything was just matter-of-fact statements. There was no particular emotion shown whatsoever. It was just as any two people having a conversation about something.

He said that after Anastasia got out of the car, the three of them went to see some friends of theirs. One was named Tara and one was named Abraham. They then returned Kelly to her home. After that Justin took him back to where he was living and Justin supposedly returned home.

I believe Byron said they spoke on the phone the next morning. Justin had called him. It was relatively early, 9:00 or 9:30. Byron told Justin that he was still sleeping and that he would talk to him later.

The next afternoon, about 4 o'clock, the doorbell rang. It was Sergeant Kilgore. He came to let me know that Justin had been found. My first question was, "Is he okay?" He said no, he wasn't, Justin was found dead.

Justin's funeral was the following Tuesday in Tulsa. Byron and Kelly attended. Kelly's mom drove them down. We were glad that they came because they were Justin's friends.

My wife had had a conversation with Justin regarding his relationship with Anastasia just a few weeks before she was killed. Justin said that he and Anastasia had broken up. He felt terrible about it. He once had feelings for Anastasia that were no longer there. Anastasia was having difficulty accepting the fact that he didn't think it was best for them to continue to see each other.

Justin was in a transformation period. He was not a child anymore, but he certainly wasn't an adult either. I explained that if he decided to marry Anastasia, that would be an adult action on his part, and he would be expected to accept the consequences of those actions. Our plan was to equip him with an education so that he could go out and have good earning power for himself and for his family, but in the event he elected to marry, we were going to go with a new program.

If they decided to get married and that was what he wanted to do, then he needed to be prepared financially to be the responsible person in the family. We weren't going to continue to support him.

It was soon after that he decided he was going to stay in school and not marry Anastasia. Anastasia still really was wanting the relationship to continue.

I called the university and had a conversation with them at the time of his death. They informed me that Justin was no longer a student there. Prior to that, Byron told me on that first visit on Friday that Justin had quit going to school.

John Bruton is cross-examined by Horton Lance.

"Mr. Bruton, the events that you described for the jury today and the loss of Justin, is it true that Justin had visited you in Tulsa, Oklahoma, shortly before all these events?" » Yes, it is. The weekend prior to his death.

"So the weekend prior to his death, the weekend prior to Anastasia's death?" » Yes.

"Justin had visited you all down in Tulsa?" » Uh-huh.

"And is it true that Justin had attended a gun show in Tulsa that weekend?" » Yes, it was.

"And did Justin have an interest in guns and attending gun shows?" » Yeah, he did.

"Did you attend the gun show with Justin?" » No, I did not.

"He just mentioned it to you?" » Uh-huh.

"Yes or no?" » Yes.

Theresa Crayon promises a quick re-direct.

"Mr. Lance has asked you about Justin attending a gun show that weekend that he had come down to visit just prior to the week of the homicide?" » Uh-huh.

"And that is something that you did talk to the detectives about; is that correct?" » That is correct.

"And although you weren't with Justin at the gun show, did you talk to him about his attendance?" » Yes, I did.

"And why don't you tell us about that." » I asked him if he had bought anything, and he hadn't. He told me that he had not purchased any guns.

I knew Justin had a pellet rifle. I knew he had a BB gun. The BB gun was in Tulsa. Byron had told me a story about a shotgun that I was not aware of and other than that no, I was not aware of any guns that Justin owned.

Horton Lance declines to re-cross. The judge calls for the lunch recess.

"All right. Thank you very much, Mr. Bruton. We appreciate your testimony.

"Ladies and gentlemen, we're going to take a lunch recess. We're going to try to maybe, if it's all right with you, we're going to try to start about 1:15, if that's all right."

"I will remind you -- "

-- again and again not to talk, look, touch, feel, smell anything about this case."

"With that being said we'll be in recess until approximately 1:15. All rise, please. Jury is free to go to lunch."

I wonder if Atwell realizes how frequently he says "With that being said?" That must have been the fifth or sixth time. Maybe the grammar police will bust him.

TESTIMONY OF JIM DODD

For lunch, I dined alone at the hot dog cart. They served Hebrew National dogs, which are second only to Nathan's. They also had diet Mt. Dew, in cans. I'll be back.

Next witness is Jim Dodd. He's examined by David Fry.

"Good afternoon, Sir. Would you tell the jury your name." » Jim Dodd.

"How are you employed, sir?" » I'm a salesman at The Bullet Hole in Overland Park, Kansas.

Overland Park is about two-thirds of the way between Justin's condo in Westport and Kelly's house in Lenexa. That makes it about 20 minutes from the condo.

The city is the site of the first airplane flight west of the Mississippi. The Wright Brothers demonstrated their Flyer there in 1909. That was more than six years after their first flight in 1903.

"What kind of business is The Bullet Hole?" » It's a gun store and shooting range.

"How long have you been employed there?" » Twenty years.

"So you were definitely employed there back in 1997?" » That's correct.

"I want to then direct your attention back to October the 23rd of 1997. Do you recall some of the events that occurred that day?" » Yes.

"Did a man name Justin Bruton enter your store?" » Yes, that's correct.

"Can you tell the jurors what Mr. Bruton inquired about when he came into your store?" » It was early in the morning, 10:00 or 10:30. I think he was about the first customer. He wanted to purchase a shotgun.

My first thought was he was looking for a hunting shotgun, but he indicated he was looking for something different. We carry a variety of shotguns. The one he pointed out was a Remington H70, which is a law enforcement type gun. It's like a riot gun. It's a shorter barrel. It's mostly for personal protection.

The hunting guns were four, five, six hundred dollars, depending on which one he was looking at. The one he picked out was a Remington H70 which cost $239.

He didn't smell of alcohol. If he did, I wouldn't have been allowed to sell him a gun. If anybody comes in that acts strange, I'll basically talk them out of purchasing something. It's simpler that way.

I asked him if he wanted some ammo. My first choice would have been double-ought buck or something like that. As I recall, he asked for rifled slug. That's a copy of the bill of sale that I gave to him. It's dated 10-23-1997. It shows he bought one box of 12-gauge rifled slugs.

The whole thing took no more than ten minutes. He had his mind made up. Basically I had what he was looking for, and I didn't show him anything else. He picked one out, examined it, and decided that's what he wanted. The price was right, and he had the money. He filled out all the paperwork and that was it.

That's it for Dodd. The defense declines to cross. On to the next witness.

TESTIMONY OF DETECTIVE ALBERT DEVALKENAERE

Next witness is Albert DeValkenaere. He is examined by David Fry.

"Good afternoon. Will you tell the jury your name, please." » My name is Albert DeValkenaere.

"How are you employed, sir?" » I'm a detective with the Kansas City, Missouri Police Department. I've been with them for 18 years. I'm currently assigned to the Kansas City, Missouri Fugitive Apprehension Unit. I've been assigned to that unit for approximately seven years.

On the 11th of June, 2001, I was involved in the arrest of Byron Case. That took place at 1 PM. We arrived in unmarked cars. It was a fairly quiet approach. There were upwards of ten guys dressed in tactical gear, Sheriff's Department logo, police department logo, FBI logo. Everybody has either some type of protective garment, bulletproof vest with either "FBI," "Police," or "Sheriff" on their chest in about four-inch letters.

We surrounded the building to secure the perimeter. I was at the front door. The interior door was open. The screen door was not. It wasn't quite latched. It was slightly ajar like somebody had walked out and had not closed it all the way. I looked through the screen door and I didn't see anybody. I yelled in a loud voice, "Police, anybody inside, come to the door." I yelled at the top of my lungs probably four or five times.

After getting no response, I opened the screen door and moved to a corner between the living room area and the hallway that leads back to the bathroom and a couple of bedrooms. I took a position there to cover the other officers as they cleared the kitchen area.

From that position, I continued to yell, "Police" and "anybody inside come out." About that time, Mr. Case came out of the bedroom door on the north side. He started to turn toward me. He saw me.

As soon as he saw me, he turned and ran back into that bedroom. I gave chase. I got to the door just as he was trying to close it and get it locked, I forced the door open. He used his body weight, I used my body weight to force against it, knocked him backward, and took him into custody.

TESTIMONY OF DR. CHASE BLANCHARD

Up next is Chase Blanchard. She is examined by Theresa Crayon.

"Could you please introduce yourself to the jury?" » I'm Dr. Chase Blanchard.

"Where do you work, Doctor?" » At the Jackson County Medical Examiner's office.

"And how long have you actually worked at that office?" » Since June of last year.

"Now, Can you tell the jury what your education has been to lead you to hold this position?" » Certainly. I completed four years of college and got a B.A. degree. After that I completed four years of medical school in Philadelphia to receive an M.D. degree. After that I did five years of postgraduate training in residency for pathology. And after that I did another year of specialty training in forensic pathology.

"And as part of your duties at the medical examiner's office, what is your position there?" » Deputy Medical Examiner.

"And is there another doctor that works there with you?" » Yes. Dr. Young. He's the Chief Medical Examiner.

"And Dr. Young is actually the one who performed the autopsy in this case; is that correct?" » Correct.

"And he's not in town and available this week; is that right?" » Correct.

"So we've had that instance before, and we have asked you to review, well, tell us what is it that you have reviewed in order to be prepared to come in and testify in his place today?" » I have reviewed the autopsy report that he prepared, as well as the investigator's report from our office, toxicology report, and photographs of the body taken at the time of the autopsy.

The investigative report that I reviewed is a report that one of the investigators from our office completes. We have investigators that will go out to the scene and do an independent investigation of any type of sudden or suspicious death to help us determine the cause and manner of death. So it's a report that the investigator fills out for us.

The autopsy is for an 18-year-old, white female. The report indicates the autopsy was conducted on October 23rd 1997, at 9:30 AM.

The height was measured at 5 feet 2 inches, and the weight 120 pounds. The clothes noted were black Doc Martens brand shoes; dark gray socks; black denim pants with Dungaree label; a size small light brown corduroy jacket with a Brandon Thomas label; a dark gray pullover shirt, size medium, with an Energie label; a black bra and a pair of black panties with a sanitary napkin. She had some small bills and change in her pocket. There is no mention of a purse or billfold. The clothes were not torn or otherwise damaged.

The specific trauma in this case is a gunshot wound. The description of the gunshot wound, according to Dr. Young, is a contact gunshot wound involving the tip of the nose. Contact basically means the muzzle of the gun is right up against the skin of the person. He says the entry wound lies about 4½ inches below the top of the head in the anterior midline involving the tip of the nose.

He says he sees radially-oriented lacerations, which basically means skin tears coming out from the sides of the wound, and these lacerations also are along both sides of the nose here. Then he says, "upon approximating these radial lacerations." All that means is he takes the pieces of skin basically and puts them back together again. And when he puts them back together, kind of like a jigsaw puzzle, he could see that there was a circular defect in the middle. And he says it's a marginally abraded gunshot entry defect that measures about three-eighths of an inch in diameter.

Marginally abraded just means that around the margin, around the outside, there is an abrasion or a scraping of the skin which is one of the important ways to identify an entrance gunshot wound as opposed to an exit wound.

When a bullet is going into the skin, it pushes the skin inwards and leaves a scrape in a circle on the outside. For an exit wound, the bullet is coming the other way. It's going out of your body, so the skin goes outward. The bullet doesn't leave an abrasion. Only when it's going in.

Blanchard is just reading from the autopsy report. What kind of expert testimony is this? I want to hear from Dr. Young, or whoever actually did the autopsy.

Then, let's see. He saw multiple dark particles which he looked at under a dissecting microscope, which is like a big magnifying glass where you can see things closer, that appear to be gunpowder particles adhering to the skin and the face, lips and chin.

He also saw a dark sooty deposit around the face. And the presence of the soot and the gunpowder particles also means a close range shot, because there is soot. To me that means less than six inches. The muzzle must have been less than six inches from the person to the person's skin.

And because of the fact that the wound made those lacerations like a star shape, like this, that to me means not only less than six inches, but probably right up against the skin. And that's what I believe Dr. Young's opinion is, because he calls it a contact.

And the reason that it does that is, if the gun is pressed pretty much right up against the skin, when the projectile comes out, there is also gases, hot gases, that come out at the same time. And if it's tight on the skin, the gases actually go underneath the skin and then kind of burst out. And you wouldn't see that if the gun was farther away, even like this far.

The one thing Dr. Young says, there is no stippling, those dark particles, which are just gunpowder particles. So there was no stippling, but there is soot. Stippling is when you get a piece of partially burned gunpowder that actually tattoos itself into the skin. It makes a red dot. You can see stippling anywhere up to maybe three feet or so away distance, and that's very dependent on the type of gun and the type of ammunition. Usually you don't see stippling closer than six inches either. He doesn't see any stippling, only gunpowder particles.

So based on the absence of stippling, the presence of soot and the star laceration, that led Dr. Young in describing it as a contact wound where the gun used was actually up against her skin.

Wow! That landed like a punch in the gut. You can probably sense my anger, even from there, but I can't talk about it. Not now anyway. Not until deliberation. This is really going to gnaw at me. I am absolutely not a happy juror right now.

Then he followed the wound track. It followed from front to back, and it caused many fractures of the facial bones and then also it caused a large laceration in the scalp in the back of the head where it exited back here. And he fit those lacerations back together. And when he fit them back together, the midpoint of those was about four inches below the top of the head.

And there were fracture lines in the skull associated with that. A distorted lead bullet fragment was recovered from the hair in the back of the head from the scalp. Just a fragment of a bullet.

The only other trauma he mentions are three fine punctate abrasions on the forehead. Punctate abrasions are very superficial almost like circular, just means small or superficial scrapes on the forehead. It's possible those are associated with this gunshot wound.

Other than that, there were no other injuries that were viewed or noted on her body. There were no defensive wounds. Defensive wounds are scrapes or bruises on the person's forearms, generally in this area or on their hands or sometimes even on their feet or legs, and those are caused when the person is attempting to defend themselves.

For instance, if they see somebody coming at them, about to hit them or coming at them with a gun, a lot of times they'll put their hands up to shield themselves, and you might see gunpowder stippling or something on the hands or the arms. Or, if someone is hitting them, you might see bruises where they're trying to shield their body. We did not see any of that on this report.

In my opinion, after conducting a review of the autopsy and considering the information that Dr. Young had received from the investigator at the scene as part of that report, as well as looking at the photographs, I concluded, within a reasonable degree of medical certainty, that Anastasia

WitbolsFeugen died of a gunshot wound to the nose, and that the manner of death was homicide.

A toxicology report is standard for all autopsies. That's routine during all autopsies to take fluid or tissue to test for drugs and alcohol. The findings in this case were negative for alcohol and negative for drugs of abuse.

Also, the investigator notes that a small piece of skull is recovered from the grass near the body. He says it was about eighteen inches to two feet from the head. The significance of that is the weapon would have been a high-powered weapon such as a rifle or a shotgun. If it was a shotgun, it would have been a shotgun slug, because shotguns with pellets, you would have seen multiple small little round pellets inside, and you might have found a plastic wad, and none of those were found. There was a fragment found in the back and that's consistent with a shotgun slug.

That's it for direct. I suspect defense may have a few questions for Dr. Blanchard. Horton Lance conducts the cross.

"Dr. Blanchard, in your expert opinion, is there any way for you to determine if this homicide was committed by a stranger or an acquaintance of the victim?" » No.

"Did Dr. Young reach any such opinion?" » Not that I could determine from reviewing the records.

"Are the autopsy findings in this homicide consistent with a gunshot from a rifle?" » It could be. A rifle or a shotgun slug. I can't tell.

"Are the autopsy findings in this homicide consistent with a gunshot from a handgun?" » Not consistent with a handgun.

"Do you recall being asked that question at a proceeding called a deposition?" » Yes.

"And do you recall whether or not you said at the date of the deposition that it could have been a handgun or pistol?" » I might have said that, if it were a really high-powered handgun.

"Do you think there is any possibility this fatal wound would have come from a pistol such as a .22-caliber pistol?" » I don't think so.

"Do you recall being asked that question on the date of the proceeding called the deposition?" » I don't recall specifically, no.

"Would it help refresh your memory to look at a transcript of what was said the day of the deposition?" » Sure.

"This is a document, Dr. Blanchard. I would ask you to read quietly to yourself. It's not something for you to read out loud." » Okay.

"Dr. Blanchard, you have had a chance to review that document. Do you recall now that I asked you that day if this fatal wound could be consistent with a handgun?" » It said, "This fatal wound could have been from a .22-caliber pistol."

"And your answer was?" » "It's possible."

"So when I interviewed you, obviously preparing for trial, you indicated that this fatal wound could be from a pistol?" » It's possible. I say later it's within the realm of possibility.

"And so going back to I think the question I asked today, are these autopsy findings consistent with a gunshot wound from a handgun? Not consistent. To me that's different than saying is it possible.

"Okay. Do you see I asked a follow-up question? 'Today do you have an opinion whether or not a pistol was used or a rifle?' What was your answer?" » "No. I don't have an opinion."

"All right. If you don't have an opinion if it was a pistol or a rifle, that could be said that the wound could be from a pistol or a rifle?" » You could look at it that way if you wanted to.

"All right. Well, I asked you the direct question. Do you have an opinion if this was a pistol or a rifle. Didn't I ask that question?" » Yes.

"And your answer was: No, that you don't have such an opinion, right?" » Right.

"Is it true that at one point I even tried to ask you the question from today, 'Are the autopsy findings in this homicide consistent with a gunshot wound from a handgun?' And what was your answer under oath?" » "It could be."

"All right. Can you state definitively with any certainty that this homicide was committed with a shotgun?" » It's very difficult to tell, once again, rifle, shotgun slug, or possibly even a high-powered handgun. That's the way I was trying to answer those questions.

"So all three are within the realm of possibilities?" » Yes, you could say that.

"Switching topics. I think this will be my last question about the trajectory of the bullet wound. From your review of the autopsy, when the bullet passed through the victim's head, was the bullet traveling slightly upwards?" » It could have been.

"Okay. And I think you established today the bullet path was front to back?" » Correct.

"And when I asked about traveling slightly upward -- well, let's go back to the measurements. I think the entrance wound was four and a half inches anterior from the top?" » Let's see. Right. Four and a half inches below the top of the head.

"And the exit wound was four inches below the top of the head?" » Correct, four inches inferior to the top of the head.

"And I think the question I was leading up to was, would you agree the bullet path was traveling slightly upward?" » If the person is in the anatomical position, which means standing straight like this with their head like this, then if it entered here, four inches below the top of the head, and you measured the exit, or this is four and a half and this is four, then it would appear that it's going slightly upward. But you have to remember that the person's head in real life isn't going to be just like this, like in a diagram. It might be slightly tilted forward or backward or even side to side.

"So Dr. Blanchard, if I understand your expert opinion correctly, you cannot commit to the statement that the bullet would have been traveling slightly upward?" » Well, you would say with the body in the anatomical position the bullet went slightly upward, but that does not say how the body was at the scene.

"All right. And even an expert such as you, you can't speculate what position she was in at the moment she was victimized and shot?" » No.

"Thank you, Doctor." » Thank you.

Crayon has some re-direct.

"Dr. Blanchard, I want to ask you some questions. Is it a rifle, is it a shotgun, is it a .22? I understand that you said all of these are in the realm of possibility?" » Correct.

"Let's say, from a scale of one to 100, 100 being for certain that it's a .22, and one being it's not, where does the realm of possibility that this is a .22 handgun fit?" » I would say less than ten.

"All right. A .22 rifle, does it move it closer to 100?" » A little closer. There is more velocity there.

"Okay. And a slug shotgun, where does that fit in that realm of possibility?" » That's a good possibility. To me that would be 70, 80, but that would be about the same as a high-powered rifle. I couldn't tell. Either of those two.

"That's my question, is that all of these are in the realm of possibility, because you don't have anything specific that you can say this is what it is; is that right?" » Correct.

"All right. The last thing that Mr. Lance asked you about is the traveling, how the bullet traveled, the wound track?" » Right.

"That it went front to back, no question about that, right?" » Right.

"And that it went slightly upward, correct?" » Right. With the body in the anatomic position.

"Exactly. Let me give you a scenario and you tell me if it's consistent with these findings. That a gunshot I mean a --"

Lance objects. Judge calls a sidebar. We have a few quiet moments here. More than a few, I guess. This sidebar is taking a little longer than usual. Okay. Here we go.

"Dr. Blanchard, if at the time of the shooting, the victim's head was back, would that account for the findings of the upward trajectory, leaning back?" » It could.

"I don't have anything further."

Seems like that's it for re-direct. I'm surprised Lance declined to re-cross. In any case, we're done with Dr. Blanchard.

"Ladies and gentlemen, it's about time for a recess, plus we're waiting on one witness to get here; and there are some productive things to do. So I think it's a good time for us to take a twenty minute recess.

"So with that being said --"

There it is again.

"-- let me again remind you --"

I wonder if he would hold me in contempt if I put my fingers in my ears.

"-- read, view, or listen to any newspaper, radio, or television report of the trial. All rise, please. Jury is free to go to the jury room."

TESTIMONY OF DETECTIVE SCOTT ATWELL

Sorry. I'm still distracted by the last witness' testimony. Next witness is some guy. He's going to be examined by Crayon. Still making notes. Sorry.

"Would you please tell the jury who you are." » My name is Scott Atwell. I'm a detective with the sheriff's office out of Johnson County, Kansas.

Scott Atwell. Same last name as Judge Atwell. There's no mention whether they're related. I presume they're not related. I certainly hope they're not related.

"And how long have you worked at the sheriff's office?" » Twenty-four years.

"And what's your current position here?" » Detective.

"And in October of 1997, you were working there as a detective as well; is that correct?" » Yes, ma'am.

"Do you recall being involved in the investigation of a case involving a Justin Bruton?" » Yes, ma'am.

That investigation commenced on October 25th, 1997, which was a Saturday. I was called out to the scene by our road patrol, at about quarter after one in the afternoon. A two-man unit was patrolling the rural part of our county, and they saw an unoccupied car parked on the north side of an abandoned warehouse-type building. They walked around the west end of the building and found the victim laying there.

He had a wallet in his right rear pocket. In his wallet was his Missouri's driver license. The registration came back to Mr. Bruton. The keys were in his right front pocket.

He was laying behind the building on his back in a east-west position. The building length runs north and south. In the report, I reflected that he looked like he was in a relaxed position. He had one ankle crossed over the other one and, basically, the upper part of his body was up against the building.

There was an 18-inch barrel Remington model H70 shotgun at the scene. I observed the victim to have severe trauma to the head.

I returned and checked the car. I found nothing in the cockpit area. In the trunk I found an empty box that was marked Remington, and on the end label of the box was the make, model and serial number, which was the same as the shotgun found at the scene, and a box of 12-gauge slugs, three of which remained in the trunk. The other two were with the victim.

I also found a receipt in the trunk. It's from where that shotgun was purchased. I collected all those things and turned them over to the Jackson County Sheriff's Department in an effort to assist them in the investigation of this case.

It's typical in situations like this for us to run the license plate in the computer. The computer came back that the person associated with that car was to be held for questioning in a homicide in Jackson County, Missouri. As a result of finding that out, we made contact with Sergeant Kilgore of the Jackson County Sheriff's Department. He volunteered to notify the family of Mr. Bruton's death.

As part of the investigation, I received information from our pathologist, what you call a medical examiner. The pathologist concluded that due to the evidence at the scene and the lack of any other physical trauma, Mr. Bruton died of a self inflicted shotgun wound. The toxicology report was negative. There were no drugs or alcohol found in his system. We ruled the case a suicide.

He was found at approximately one o'clock on Saturday. It had been raining or drizzling for approximately 12 hours. It was dry under the car. When I rolled the body over, I noticed and I also felt that the grass underneath him was dry.

The shotgun was lying parallel to Mr. Bruton's side with the barrel, the muzzle of it, basically up against his left armpit with the, what we call the port side, the ejection side, where the shells eject from, that portion of the shotgun was facing up. That's consistent with a self inflicted gunshot wound to his face.

That's it for direct. No cross by Lance. This might be it for the prosecution. They're huddling by the bench.

Ok. They're back. Theresa Crayon rises and says "Your Honor, at this time the State rests its case."

❖

Here's the deal. The defense could now rest without calling a single witness, and we would still be required to presume Byron Case innocent. The presumption persists unless and until we determine during deliberations that the State has proved its case beyond a reasonable doubt.

That's why, as I mentioned earlier, my default vote is Not Guilty. If I were to be forced to vote right now, I would vote Not Guilty. I've yet to hear from the defense, and we as a jury have yet to deliberate all the evidence. I'm confident, though, that the defense will call more than a few witnesses.

They're at the bench now, discussing things. We'll see what happens.

TESTIMONY OF DAWN WRIGHT

I'll bet dimes to doughnut holes that the defense just asked the judge, during the last sidebar, to acquit the defendant because the prosecution case was too weak to submit to the jury. They almost always do. And I'll double the odds that if asked, the judge declined. They almost always do.

Don't plan on getting out of making the tough decision. We're the jurors. Byron's fate, that of his family, and that of the victim's family rests on our shoulders.

While the defense need not produce a single witness, they will almost always put on an affirmative defense. During his cross examination, Horton Lance attempted to cast doubt on the testimony of each significant prosecution witness. He will now attempt to create further doubt through the testimony of his own witnesses. The prosecution will try to prevent that.

To create doubt, the defense may pursue an alternative theory of the case, sometimes known as soddit. That stands for "some other dude did it." They don't have to prove it, they merely have to make a good enough case that we consider it a viable alternative. If they fail to prove their alternative theory, we as jurors cannot hold it against them. They have no burden to prove anything. We will still be obliged to determine if the State proved its case beyond a reasonable doubt.

So here we go. First defense witness is Dawn Wright. She will be examined by Horton Lance.

"Good afternoon. For the record, please state your name." » Dawn Wright.

"And, Ms. Wright, I'm going to test your memory and ask you to go all the way back to 1997. Okay?" » Okay.

"In 1997, did you work at the Dairy Queen on 24 Highway directly across the entrance to Mount Washington Cemetery?" » Yes.

Highway 24 is Winner Road. That puts the Dairy Queen at the northwest corner of Mount Washington, across the intersection of Winner Road and Brookside Avenue.

"And do you recall the police contacted you and asked you if you had seen any young ladies in the area of Dairy Queen that week, October 22nd, 1997?" » Yes.

"If I told you Officer Kilgore interviewed you on Friday, the 24th, do you have any disagreement with that?" » No.

"All right. Does that make sense? Let me ask it this way: Do recall what night of the week it was you remembered the young lady being in Dairy Queen?" » Not really. In the middle of the week. I read through the papers there.

"Which is your statement?" » Yeah. And in the papers it was Wednesday. So Wednesday night that she came in.

"All right. You understand we allowed you to read the papers to help refresh your memory?" » Yeah.

"Do you remember what shift you worked that night? Did you work until close?" » Yeah.

"And when the police approached you on Friday, did they ask you if there had been any young teen-age girls in the area of Dairy Queen that previous Wednesday?" » He came in and he showed everybody a picture of her in the restaurant. And when he showed me, he asked me if I had seen her. And I said, "Yes, that she was in here a couple of nights ago."

At first I thought that she was missing, but then he said that she was murdered.

I had not seen her before that night, but I didn't have any trouble identifying her from her picture. She had been in there for a little while, and she hadn't bought anything. She was just sitting there. I asked her if there was anything that she needed, if I could get her anything, or if she needed help with anything.

She asked me if I had a pad or a tampon, and I didn't have anything there. But I lived just a couple minutes away, so I called my ex-husband and I had him bring a tampon down for her. She went in the bathroom, and she came back out, and she said thanks. I went to the bathroom shortly after to wash my hands, and there was a wrapper in the trash. It matched the one I gave her, so I assume she used it.

She was just sitting there for awhile. She didn't buy anything. She had a purse with her. It was a big brown purse. She told me she had an argument with her boyfriend, because they had plans that night, and she couldn't get a ride over there to him. So she had gotten to the Dairy Queen, called him and asked if he could come and pick her up. He said that he had already made plans with his best friend, and she was upset. And she asked me, if I was in that position, what I would do, and I told her.

I went out to my car to smoke a cigarette, and she went out to use the pay phone. A few minutes later a car pulled up. I'm pretty sure there was three people in the car: two guys and a girl. I remember they were all wearing dark clothing. They looked gothic, I guess you could say.

I didn't see her talking to anybody but the one guy, and he was in a long trench coat, and that was the only guy that I actually saw her talking to. I saw a lot of hand flailing, and she looked like she was upset.

That started just as soon as they showed up. She walked out the door, and she said a couple of words like, well I don't know what she said. I couldn't hear anything, but I could tell they were arguing. After a few minutes, they left. I didn't see what way they went.

When they picked her up, it was in the 9:00 o'clock vicinity. Whether it was 9:00 or 9:45, I'm not sure, but it was in the 9:00 o'clock vicinity. We were getting ready to close within an hour, and we start our closing procedures an hour early.

She used the pay phone quite a few times that night, yeah. I would estimate four or five times.

Theresa Crayon has a few questions for Dawn.

"Ms. Wright, we just met a few minutes ago in the hallway, didn't we?" » Yes.

"I just want to clarify something. What did you loan the victim?" » It was a tampon.

I'm guessing it wasn't a loan. Let's call it a gift.

"So it was not a feminine napkin?" » No. It was a tampon. And I know I told that guy that I just couldn't think of a polite name.

"I just wanted to make sure I understood. The other thing was, at the time you're talking about, it was dark out, wasn't it?" » Yeah.

And the detective, Sergeant Kilgore I guess, contacted me the next morning too, after that first time on Friday. It was a little before ten in the morning. He asked me for a description of what the girl looked like, what she was wearing, things like that. And I told him what she was wearing, best I could. I said she had on a pair of baggy, light colored jeans that drug on the floor. They were kind of like almost, not really a bell-bottom type pants, but they were bigger at the bottom. They weren't tapered. She was wearing sandals with socks. And I told him about her long brown purse.

She was just wearing a jacket. I mean she had, I don't know if it was a heavy coat or just a jacket, but I never seen a T shirt or a sweater or anything like that. I just seen her coat and her jeans and her shoes and her purse.

Horton Lance has some re-direct.

"Ms. Wright, just a couple more questions. I know you need to get out of here. I know this is a weird topic, but I need to ask you about the tampon, Maxipad thing again. When Detective Kilgore interviewed you in 1997, did you say you gave the young lady a Maxipad?" » Probably.

"Okay. Well, would it help refresh your memory to look at it?" » Yeah, I looked at it out there.

"You understand this was tape recorded?" » Yes.

"So you're on tape saying that. Did you tell Detective Kilgore that what you gave the young lady was, quote, a pad, a maxi pad, feminine napkin?" » I was trying to think of a decent way, I was trying to be polite about it. I guess I should have just said a tampon, but it's a tampon.

"In 1997, on tape, did you say a pad, a Maxipad, a feminine napkin?" » Yes.

"Nothing further."

Now Theresa Crayon has some re-direct. It's like attorney pong.

"Ms. Wright, why is it today that you think it was tampon? What makes you so certain?" » When I first started my period when I was 12, I wore a pad, but since I was about 13 or 14, I've never wore nothing but a tampon. So that's how I know for positive.

"Okay. Thank you."

And of course, Lance has one more question.

"Real quick. Ms. Wright. Would your memory have been better on October 24th 1997 or today, four years later?" » Well, I'm sure it would have been better in 1997, and I probably should have clearly specified more I guess, but I mean --

"Would your memory have been better in 1997?" » Yes.

"That's all I have."

Mercifully, that looks like that's all for Dawn Wright. She's stepping down and the Judge is instructing the defense to call their next witness.

It seems like a lot of thrashing about for very little result, but that's the nature of testimony.

TESTIMONY OF JAMIE LYNN SMITH

Next up is Jamie Lynn Smith. Horton Lance, as always, conducts the questioning for the defense. Of course. He's the only attorney on that side of the room.

"For the record state your name." » My name is Jamie Lynn Smith.

"Where do you currently reside?" » St. Louis, Missouri.

Ah, St. Louis. For fifteen years, home to St. Louis Cardinal shortstop Ozzie Smith, aka the Wizard of Oz. Golden Glove winner 13 years in a row. Hall of Fame inductee on the first round, with 92% of the vote, no less. Nobody before or since has been as good. Sometimes Ozzie did a back flip as he ran out to his shortstop position. That man had some kind of cool. Still does.

"Ms. Smith, do you know the defendant Mr. Byron Case?" » I know Byron Case. I met him in late May, early June of 2000. I was employed at Muddy's Coffee House, 51st Street location. That's over by UMKC, by the university. Byron was a regular customer at the coffee shop. I was early for a shift one day, and he had just got off work and I sat down and started talking to him at the table. We quickly became friends. We never dated, we were just friends.

Our friendship developed quickly and we decided to move to St. Louis and rent an apartment together, as roommates. We decided to move in August of 2000 and, due to some of Byron's circumstances and my own, it ended up that I actually moved early and Byron ended up joining me in St. Louis later. I left on the first of August and secured employment by the 15th and Byron arrived in St. Louis on September 13th.

Prior to knowing Byron, I did not know Kelly Moffett. I met her one time since, in Kansas City. It was directly after we had decided to make the move to St. Louis, and I was still in Kansas City living at the time. I was over at Byron and Kristina's apartment and was playing Monopoly on the kitchen table when Kelly called. It had to have been very early August. I was in Byron's bedroom. Kelly came over. I had known a lot about Kelly before I had ever met her, so it was kind of a big deal to actually meet her. She went into the living room. She had a friend of hers with her. They planted themselves down in the living room, were drinking soda, were smoking cigarettes and attempting to have a conversation with Byron.

Byron expressed to me that he didn't really want her to come over when he had gotten off the phone with her, but she was saying things on the phone to him that I think made him feel sympathetic towards her. And she was complaining a lot about the situation --

Theresa Crayon objects. Hearsay. Sustained.

She seemed distraught that Byron was moving to St. Louis. She was making that kind of a big deal over it. Byron never gave her his new address and phone number where he was going to be. We discussed it on a few occasions, that it was not to be given to people unless we both knew them beforehand and knew it wouldn't get into her hands.

Kelly did call and I did speak to her on a couple of occasions on the telephone. She wanted to speak to Byron. The few times I clearly remember, I essentially lied and told her that he did not live there or he was not able to be contacted at this number.

She called probably a total of three times that I can recall, and each time I thought that I made that pretty clear, but then a few weeks later the phone rang again.

In December of 2000, Byron moved out, but was still living in St. Louis. Even after he moved out, Kelly kept calling trying to find him.

Theresa Crayon will conduct the cross examination.

"Ms. Smith, you and I haven't met before, have we?" » No.

"But we spoke on the phone very briefly a few days ago. I'm going to try not to jump around too much, but you said that you have met Kelly one time and that was in the summer of 2000?" » Yes. I met Kelly just that one time. Though I had moved to St. Louis in the first of August, I was coming back on the weekends. I still had all of my belongings here, and I was trying to secure an apartment there too.

Regarding that one time I met her, when she came over to Byron's house, he tried to in some ways to distance himself from her. But the fact that she was still, she had said on the phone that she needed to take a shower and that she had been living in a very poor situation, and the fact that he was still letting her come in, because that's what her exact request was, to eat something and take a shower. So he was still trying to take care of that for her. When she got there, she didn't look like she needed to take a shower, and she didn't eat anything.

It seemed to me like Kelly wanted to make Byron responsible for her problems. Byron's response was basically I'm not responsible for your problems. You need to dig yourself out of the hole you're in on your own and get it together. She really wasn't saying very much, but she expressed that she was just living through hell. It appeared to me that Kelly was trying to put Byron on a guilt trip.

She was there one or two hours. She just wouldn't leave. Her friend was there also and there were four people in the room. So there was actually a lot of pauses in the conversation where it seemed like there was underlying conversations that would have been if there had not been other people in the room. I think if we had not been there, she would have been talking more.

I visited Byron here three times one weekend. So, yes, I've talked to him before coming to trial here today. And I've talked to his mom, and I've looked through the police reports, yes. His mother is the one who put me in touch with his lawyer. She asked me to come forward and talk to Mr. Lance, based on what I told her about the conversation I had with Kelly.

When Byron and I stopped sharing the apartment, it was actually a mutual agreement. He had met a girl named Bianca and was moving in with her. Also he wasn't contributing financially. It was more of a mutual agreement, but that is one of the reasons.

TESTIMONY OF EVELYN CASE

Next witness is Evelyn Case. She'll be examined by Horton Lance.

"Good afternoon." » Hi.

"Please state your name for the record." » My name is Evelyn Case.

"Where are you currently residing?" » Kansas City, Missouri.

"What is your relationship to the defendant, Byron Case?" » He's my son.

"I want to ask you about the evening of the death of Anastasia WitbolsFeugen. Do you recall that evening?" » Yes.

"All right. Can you recall what day of the week it was?" » No.

"Can you recall whether or not you saw Byron Case that evening, the evening that she disappeared?" » Yes.

"Where did you see Mr. Byron Case?" » In our apartment.

"Do you remember about what time of day it would have been?" » It was in the evening. It was between 10 and 11.

"At night?" » Correct.

That night, Byron behaved just as he always did. I spoke to him when he came home. He didn't smell of alcohol. He wasn't upset. He wasn't acting any different than usual.

He mentioned Anastasia. He said that she didn't even wait for the car to come to a stop before she jumped out. It was just another crazy night with Anastasia and Justin arguing. We sat in the living room a little bit. Then he went to his room to work on his computer, which he always did.

Byron called me in the late afternoon the next day and told me, "Mom, Anastasia is dead." My reaction was, "Oh, my gosh."

After Anastasia died, Byron and Kelly continued to hang around together. Kelly behaved just the same. I didn't notice anything different. She certainly didn't appear to be afraid of Byron.

Dale Case was Byron's father and my ex-husband. We were married ten years. After the divorce we still spoke sometimes. We had joint custody, so we talked about our son.

During the time we were married, we never had any guns in the house. After we were married, I sometimes visited him at his place. I never saw any guns at his place either. Dale never went hunting, Byron never went hunting, and the two of them certainly never went hunting together.

On the week of June 5th in 2001, Byron was sick. I don't remember exactly what he had, but something similar to strep throat. He just wanted to sleep. I would call him from work to make sure he would eat something, but he didn't answer the phone. He was just sleeping. He finally did go to the doctor and got antibiotics. When he was arrested, they had to put him on antibiotics in the detention center.

Okay, that was quick. David Fry will cross-examine her.

"Let's start off with how long had you been divorced from your ex-husband, Dale Case." » The divorce was in 1989.

"So by 1997, you had been divorced about eight years?" » Uh-huh.

"Was Byron primarily living with you during that time?" » No. He was between both of us.

"All right. In 1997, you became aware that Byron started dating Kelly; is that right?" » Yes. He was 18-years-old when he started dating her. I didn't know she was 14-years-old. By looking at her, I didn't know how old she was. She acted like a big girl more or less. She acted very mature.

She was very demanding of him. She wanted him a lot. She was infatuated with him.

Byron must have been infatuated with her. He was very caring with her. Very caring. As a matter of fact, when he introduced her to me, she went to the bathroom and he came up to me in the kitchen and he said, "Mom, Kelly's father is an alcoholic, and he beats her."

Kelly and I weren't close. She was not into me so much, like some of Byron's friends. She never shared her thoughts with me.

They were together a lot because Justin had a nice apartment, and Byron wanted to move out. You know how they want to move out, but they still want the security of their nest. And if they have a friend where they can spend the night, they'll stay there, listen to music all night or whatever. But I guess it was a comfortable place to hang out.

I have no idea how often Byron stayed at Justin's, but it was frequent. I would go to bed early and when I'd wake up, he would be there or he wouldn't be there.

That night Byron got home between 10 and 11. I was up. He always came in and said hello. He was usually in a cheerful mood. That night he was upset because Justin and Anastasia were at it again, which I heard about frequently. Either he didn't see anything of them, because they were such lovebirds, or they were at each other's throats and it was just ridiculous to be around them.

He mentioned that she got angry and had an argument with Justin and that she got out of the car. He thought she didn't even wait for the car to stop when she got out.

With that, Evelyn Case is excused. Looks like that's it for today, day two. Judge is going to give us the speech.

"Okay. Ladies and gentlemen, I believe that's run the gamut for today, does it not, Mr. Lance?

"Okay. The Court again reminds you of what you were told at the first recess of the Court. Until you retire to consider your verdict, you must not discuss this case among yourselves or with others or --"

If you're going to take me anytime soon, Lord, take me now.

"With that being said --"

And again.

"-- have a wonderful evening. We'll be in recess. All rise, please. Jury is free to go.

TESTIMONY OF NANCY NOLKER

Good morning, sort of. Today will be cold and cloudy. It's only going to get up to 59, tops.

Wednesday. Day 3. Possibly the last day of testimony. Looks like we'll get the case later today, or early tomorrow almost for sure. I'm kind of grumpy. I just get grumpy sometimes. Okay, often. Let's get this show on the road.

First witness this morning is Nancy Nolker. Horton Lance will do the questioning.

"For the record, Please state your name." » Nancy Nolker.

"And where do you currently reside?" » Richmond, Missouri.

Richmond is a small town about an hour to the northeast. I don't know of anyone famous born there, but Bob Ford is buried there. Ford was Jesse James' BFF but shot him in the back of the head for the reward money.

"Where are you employed?" » I'm self-employed. We own a couple of dump trucks, Nolker Trucking, and I do the bookkeeping out of our home.

"Ms. Nolker, back in 1997, where were you residing at that time?" » Kearney, Missouri.

Kearney is about a half-hour north of KC. Jesse James was born in Kearney.

"Ms. Nolker, how do you know the defendant, Byron Case?" » He's my nephew.

"And can you describe the relation there?" » His father was my brother.

"What was Byron's father's name?" » Dale Case.

"I need to test your memory a bit and go back to 1997. Okay? During that time frame, would you ever have occasion to sometime visit your brother's home?" » I visited Dale's home on occasion. I never saw any guns in his house. I never knew him to go hunting with Byron. I never knew of him to go hunting at all.

Dale passed away on Christmas Eve in 1997. After he died, I helped take care of his estate. Among other things, I cleaned his home. I never located any guns. I never noticed any areas on the walls where a gun could have been hanging. I never noticed a gun case.

I met Kelly a couple times. The first time she was with Byron visiting when his dad was in the hospital in 1997. I met her again on Christmas day of that year. She accompanied Byron to my home for our family gathering. That was the day after Dale died. I guess that would have been approximately 60 days after Anastasia's murder. Kelly seemed comfortable with Byron. She was a little bit shy because she didn't know the family, and she was by his side the entire time. But she didn't act like she was uncomfortable at all.

That's it for direct. That was quick. David Fry wants to cross.

"Dale Case lived just over here in Kansas, fairly handy over here in Kansas City, Kansas?" » Yes, right.

"And you lived in Kearney; is that right?" » Correct.

"He would visit you probably four or five times a year; is that correct?" » Yes.

"And you would visit him at his house four or five times a year; is that correct?" » Yes.

"In any of your visits that you made to his house during the entire year of 1997, you never saw Kelly there, did you?" » No, I did not.

"So you were never there at the same time?" » No.

"Now, Dale was kind of an outgoing fellow before he got sick, wasn't he?" » Yes, he was.

"In fact, he was a fairly robust fellow, body builder, wasn't he?" » Yes.

"And Dale had lots of friends; is that right?" » Yes, he did.

"And he had lots of male friends, didn't he?" » Yes.

"You have no idea if any of his friends ever asked to keep a gun there in that house for any reason, do you?" » No. I wouldn't know that.

That's it for cross. Wow. That may have been the shortest yet. On to the next witness. Hold on a moment. We seem to have a brief delay. Lance addresses the Judge without going for a sidebar.

"Actually, Judge, before I start with this next witness, we have a stipulation regarding data for the sun on Wednesday 22nd of October, 1997, showing sunrise was at 7:36 AM and sunset was at 6:30 PM.

Fry goes along.

"This is stipulated and no objection, Your Honor."

Judge Atwell accepts the stipulation.

"Okay. So we're stipulating to those facts and we're allowing it into evidence.

A stipulation is an agreement between prosecution and defense to allow some information into evidence without having a witness testify about the information or without requiring some other form of proof. In this case, there's nothing controversial about sunset and sunrise, so the attorneys simply stipulated to the times. As jurors, we're to treat the stipulated matter as fact.

TESTIMONY OF ABRAHAM KNEISLEY

Next witness is Abraham Kneisley. He'll be examined by Horton Lance.

"Sir, for the record, please state your name." » Abraham Kneisley.

"How old are you?" » Twenty-three.

"Where do you currently live at?" » I live in Berkeley, California.

Berkeley? Never heard of it.

"Back in 1997, were you living in Missouri?" » Yes.

"How long have you known the defendant, Mr. Byron Case?" » We met when we were freshmen in high school, 14 years old, and ran into each other again when I was 16 in Westport at a coffee house.

"At that point, did you continue your friendship?" » Yes. We started hanging out more and more from that point to present.

"Did you ever know a girlfriend he dated named Kelly Moffett?" » Yes. I met Kelly from being introduced by Byron. I think the first time I met her was at my apartment in Westport, 1997, probably, around May. I have since seen them together on numerous occasions.

I knew Anastasia WitbolsFeugen. She was also a freshman at Lincoln Prep. I knew her far less than I knew Byron. We had seen each other and hung out intermittently for several months and had seen each other occasionally socially, friends of friends before that.

I know Tara McDowell. She and I dated from October of 1996 until August of 1997, about the same time Justin and Anastasia broke up the first time. I broke up with Tara August 24th, I believe, within a week of Justin and Anastasia breaking up.

And I knew Justin Bruton. I met him before I met Kelly. I met him on the street near a Westport coffee house. He was with Anastasia.

So I had known Anastasia first, before knowing Justin. Not closely or intimately at that point, but certainly as an associate and a classmate in several of my classes at Lincoln. When I met Justin, he was already dating Anastasia for several months at that point. On a couple of occasions I hung out with Justin independently of Byron and Kelly or Tara and several times, probably not more than half a dozen, with Byron, Kelly and / or Tara.

Justin and Anastasia were unlike Tara and I. We broke up and kind of stayed broken up. They got together back and forth intermittently. From the beginning of September until the time of her death, it got to the point where it became a thing of recurring gossip between the circle of friends, whether or not they were back together today, not even this week.

It's fair to say it was on-again-off-again. Anastasia obviously seemed very hurt by it. Justin on the other hand was the most closed-off and emotionally cold person of anybody I ever met. He didn't seem to really like her. So as he started to take that to her, she seemed upset and hurt and would call everyone, Tara, Byron, Kelly, trying to get ahold of him or find out what he had said or whatever, just trying to get a feel of their relationship.

Anastasia was predominantly, but not exclusively, pursuing Justin as opposed to the other way around.

I kind of noticed unusual behavior on the part of Justin from the time that I met him. I mean, his behavior was easier to analyze after he had died, because I guess no one really took him seriously at that point. He had such a fascination or desire to get free from the perceived burden of his parents and their financial hold over his life that, you know, he was always masterminding something, killing someone, kidnapping someone. I guess all of us kind of took it as some humorous quirk and didn't take it seriously. This was a couple years before Columbine or any of the outcry to take all such threats seriously.

As an example, he wanted to go to Oklahoma and rob, kidnap, or kill his parents like, or kill or kidnap the church leader in Independence. And there were a few others that were even more outlandish that I don't even really remember.

When he mentioned these ideas, I never took him seriously. I mean maybe the most serious, at some point he asked me if I could find him a gun. He had been shooting before when he had his shotgun, but I didn't necessarily put the two together even at that point to take him seriously.

It was probably six weeks or so before Anastasia was murdered that he asked me to get him a gun. He didn't know anybody or anything, so he came to me, but I certainly couldn't help him.

When Justin would talk about these wild schemes, Byron was certainly not an active participant. We were an audience, but that would be the participation level that I would attribute. Sometimes laughing, you know. No one really took it seriously. It didn't even seem that Justin did. Apparently he did.

Anastasia and I weren't very close. We hung out a couple of times within two weeks or so of her death, and we seemed to be hanging out more than we had before, but I don't feel like I really got the chance to know her. I certainly liked and respected her, but I wasn't really close to her, because we just hadn't had the time.

I recall the evening of October 22nd 1997. That was the day that Anastasia got out of the car. I was house sitting for a friend of mine in midtown Kansas City. Byron, Kelly and Justin stopped by around 8:30 that evening. I don't recall the exact time. It would be more specific in my original statement.

Tara and I had broken up, I had some of her things, and I had a small list of stuff that she had of mine. I was trying to make a clean break, so I paged Byron and asked him to run it over there for me. It was ten or fifteen minutes before he called back, maybe an hour and forty-five minutes before Byron showed up. Justin and Kelly were with him.

They probably weren't there longer than fifteen minutes. It was mostly casual, just a little bit of gossip on whether or not Anastasia and Justin were together. When I heard that Anastasia had jumped out of the car, I was worried. It was certainly a bad neighborhood. But I mean she had been so emotionally involved for so long that I certainly didn't find it hard to believe.

They seemed normal. I didn't smell alcohol and they didn't seem to be on any drugs. I didn't see any signs of Justin appearing unusually upset. He didn't appear to be pale or shaky. There were no signs that he had been crying.

Like I say, they were probably there not much more than fifteen minutes because of Kelly's curfew. When they left, it was my understanding they were taking Kelly back to her house next.

I heard about Anastasia's death the next day at 5 PM on, I believe, the Channel 5 news. My heart jumped into my throat. I hadn't ever known anyone that was killed like that before. When I heard about it I immediately called Byron. I left a message on his pager, intentionally being vague, not wanting to leave that sort of news on an answering machine.

He called me back relatively quickly, and I was just really blunt with it. Something as, "I just saw on the news Anastasia is dead."

His reaction was first disbelief like me, but you could just hear by his gasps and the way he was breathing that he was certainly shocked by it. And then after probably a series of questions where he asked me if I was serious, I think that was all of our reaction, he then I think attempted to call Justin.

I bumped into Byron at Anastasia's funeral. Went over, you know, said hello, gave my condolences, and we talked a little bit there. We talked several times on the telephone in the days after the murder, over the few days before Justin's body was found. Justin had disappeared and things certainly didn't look good for him, so we were all really worried and just hoping for the best.

During this time, everyone was being interviewed by the police, everyone was going to the funeral, and there was frequent contact in that circle of friends. Tara didn't have a phone at the time, so a mutual friend had to stop by and give her the news. It was certainly very difficult for her. Other than that, I was certainly in touch with Byron who was mostly staying at Kelly and her mom's house during that week because, you know, they kind of needed each other.

We continued to discuss the murder itself for at least over the next two years until Kelly and Byron broke up in 1999. The discussion was not about the details of the murder itself, but it certainly came up. Each of them was asked to give repeated testimony to the police, because there are always misunderstandings about what happened for almost five years.

I was interviewed by the police in October of '97. That's where most of my initial knowledge of the case came from. I was finding out just like everyone else. During the interview, the police dropped some details of the murder. Specifically about Justin purchasing a shotgun the morning after Anastasia was killed, before her body had been identified.

After Anastasia's death, Byron and Kelly were almost joined at the hip for the next two years. I never noticed any unusual behavior on Kelly's part, like was she afraid or suspicious of Byron.

I believe it was June 11th that Byron got arrested for this crime, last year, 2001. At the time, I was living with my father in Kansas City, Missouri. I had seen Byron the week prior to his arrest. I think he moved back from St. Louis in March. He and his new girlfriend had broken up, and I had tried to call him. I hadn't been successful all weekend. I got hold of him either the following Monday or Tuesday which would have been I believe June 4th or 5th.

I reached him on the phone. He seemed delirious and out-of-it from fever. He was really sick. He seemed to be giving unresponsive or non sequitur responses to my questions. I told him he should see a doctor. He said he had a fever. He didn't know how high.

I ran into him later in the week at the coffee house in midtown by UMKC. He still looked pale and sick, but he said he had seen a doctor.

On to cross. Theresa Crayon will conduct the examination.

"Mr. Kneisley, you and I haven't met before, have we?" » Over the phone.

"We spoke on the phone one time just a couple days ago, right?" » Correct.

"And Byron Case is a very good friend of yours; is that fair?" » Yes, we've been close for years.

"And I believe the way you characterized your relationship when we spoke earlier was that he was a very trusted and respected friend?" » Yes.

"You trust and respect him an awful lot; fair?" » Yes.

"And you've testified that you knew Kelly Moffett through him?" » Yes. I met her, I believe, in May of 1997. I didn't know then that she was 14 years-old, but I eventually found out. He was 18. She was 14.

I recall specifically that on the night of October 22nd 1997, Kelly, Byron, and Justin all came by the house where I was house-sitting. They all came in. None of them acted strange. No one acted like they had been drinking or on drugs. No one smelled like they had been drinking. I estimate the time was about 8:30. If I said 8 to 8:15 in my original statement, I would believe that's more accurate. It's been five years. I see also that my statement says they told me Anastasia got out of the car at 7:30.

I mentioned that Justin asked if I could find a gun for him. This was within six weeks, two months. Some time far enough behind I hadn't really thought about it. I've never mentioned it until today.

I wasn't with them in the car on the night of October 22nd, so what I know about what happened came from Justin, Byron, and Kelly herself, even though Kelly didn't say much of anything when they came by that night.

Whew. Finally, done with Abraham. That took a while. My hand is cramping from all the notes. Maybe we'll get a break.

Maybe not.

TESTIMONY OF DON RAND

Here comes the next witness.

"Defense calls Don Rand."

Horton Lance with the questions.

"For the record, please state your name." » Don Rand.

"Can you tell the jury where you were working back in October of 1997?" » Truman Road Amoco, corner of 435 and Truman Road.

"And when you worked there back in 1997, what was your job or job title?" » Mechanic.

"All right. Do you understand we're going to ask you questions about the evening of October 22nd 1997?" » Yes.

"Do you recall if you were working that specific evening?" » Yes, I was.

"Can you recall what shift you worked?" » Two to ten every night.

"On the evening of Wednesday, October 22nd, did you notice anything unusual happening with any vehicles or pedestrians in the area of your job?" » I recall a young lady that had either just gotten out of a car or was in some type of an argument with somebody in a car at the light of Truman Road and 435 eastbound. From that point on she proceeded to walk away from the car before the light had even changed.

I was inside the station about 100 feet from the stoplight maybe. Maybe a little more. It was dusk or just a little bit after dark. I wasn't able to get a really good look at her until she got up close. When she got out of the car, she walked east, towards where I was working. I got a better look at her as she walked by.

There's a pay phone in the area. She didn't stop to use it. She just kept walking east up the hill, right on Truman Road. I didn't speak to her. She was probably about five foot six, five foot seven maybe. One hundred thirty pounds maybe. Dark hair. Not really dark, but brown hair. She was fairly good looking. I remember she was attractive.

I don't know Byron Case. I've never seen him before in my life.

That same week, the police came by. It was like a day or so right after it happened. They showed me a picture of the girl they were asking about. They had two pictures I believe. One of the pictures they showed me looked like the girl that had walked by the previous evening. I told them I had seen this girl get out of the car and walk past.

There's a stoplight where she got out. I remember that it was after dusk, that it was dark outside. I remember that cars were driving with their headlights on.

I can't remember if I actually saw her get out of the car. I think I might have, but I can't be 100 percent certain. Looked like she was arguing with somebody in the car. Because when she came and walked away from the car, she was walking at a faster pace than what she had just walked. It looked like she was angry, upset.

The last time I saw her, she was still walking on the shoulder of Truman Road. I watched her go all the way up to about Erotic City and about there is where I lose sight of people. I never saw her leave the road. I didn't know then that it was going to be important.

Theresa Crayon has some questions.

"Hi, Mr. Rand. I'm Theresa Crayon. You and I spoke on the phone very briefly I think last week, right?" » Yes, we did.

"Amoco is right there on the corner, right?" » Yes, it is.

"And how many businesses, or do you know?" » Amoco, Conoco, Erotic City, a liquor store and then there was another gas station at that time, but it has since disappeared.

"And you can't see anything beyond Erotic City; is that what you're saying?" » Correct.

"And given the nature of those businesses, would they have all been open at the time that you saw this young lady?" » Yes.

"And there is a pay phone at Amoco, right?" » Yes, there is. There is one at Conoco also.

"So those are at least two that you know of?" » Three right there. There are two at the Amoco.

"And the Amoco station is one of those stations that you've got a garage where you were the mechanic, right?" » Correct.

"There is also some cashier who takes the money and has candy and things like that inside there?" » Yes.

"There is a place somebody can go in there and sit and wait for someone if they wanted to, right?" » Yes.

"And you have people show up there to ask to use the phone very often? Would that have been unusual for someone to come in and ask to use the phone?" » No, not really. It wasn't the only time I saw a woman come up from that intersection. It wasn't really sensational or anything. I didn't know anything about it until the police showed up and asked me questions about it.

They showed me two pictures. One was a boy and one was a girl, and I recognized the girl. I told them that I remembered seeing the girl walking east across the drive at about 8:30. Could be about that time. It's pretty dark then, but the Amoco is well lit. Once you get past the businesses, then it's dark, but right in front of the businesses, it's well lit.

I told them that I looked up and saw her walking and thought she was attractive. I guess I told them back then that we couldn't really tell if she was upset or emotional at all. I'm saying today that I thought she was angry or upset because she was walking at a fast pace.

I'm not 100 percent certain that I saw her get out of the car at the stoplight. I didn't tell the police that she did.

I think she might have been having a fight or an argument with somebody in the car. Back then I didn't recall that to the police.

From where I work, I can see the back entrance to the cemetery. That's on the other side of the highway, on the other side of Truman Road, there's a road that winds up and goes up to the old Sysco building. There's another old road that goes in the back way to that cemetery. We watch the sheriffs sit there all the time.

Okay. That's it for Mr. Rand. No re-direct by Lance.

TESTIMONY OF DR. EDWARD FRIEDLANDER

Next up is Professor Edward Robert Friedlander. A professor who uses all three of his names. He's going to be an expert witness. Mark my words.

"Dr. Friedlander, I'm going to ask you to turn and face the jury. For the record, please state your name?" » Edward Robert Friedlander.

"Mr. Friedlander, how old are you?" » Fifty.

"And where is your current employment?" » University of Health Sciences, here in Kansas City, Missouri. I'm Chairman of the Department of Pathology.

"And is it fair to say you basically teach medical students then?" » That's most of what I do.

"What type of education do you have to -- what's your background in pathology?" » M.D. from Northwestern 1977; residency in pathology at Northwestern; board certified anatomical-clinical pathology.

Northwestern University. That's interesting. Northwestern is home to the Center on Wrongful Convictions. The university is pretty well known for having an interest in our justice system.

"All right. And you may have said. How long have you been teaching at the university?" » I taught there on and off for a couple of years before becoming chair.

"And you've been Chairman of the Department of Pathology for ten years?" » I just got my tenure, thank you.

Tenured Professor Edward Robert Friedlander, expert witness, thank you.

"Have you ever been retained as an independent expert in pathology to review case files?" » Yes.

"Have you ever testified in federal or state court as an expert in the field of pathology?" » Yes.

"In the specific case of State of Missouri vs. Byron Case, were you asked to look at the materials in that file?" » Yes, by you.

"So Attorney Lance from the Public Defender's Office contacted you and asked you to look at the file?"

I find it inordinately funny to hear Lance refer to himself in the third person. I fight to suppress a smile. I think of the Seinfeld episode where Jimmy always referred to himself in the third person. "Jimmy really likes Elaine." Now I'm holding back a chortle and the thoughts won't stop. "Jimmy's down!" I cough into my fist and clear my throat. I give everyone the "excuse me" look and I darn near say "Jimmy had to cough." I almost lose it entirely. I cough again, then hold up my palms and bow my head like everything's okay. I try to concentrate. I don't want to get the giggles while sitting as a juror in a murder trial. Darn Jerry Seinfeld anyway.

Friedlander rephrases his answer accordingly.

That's right. I was given what Attorney Lance represented to me to be the entire file. I could really go for a cup of water, please.

Holy cow. This guy teaches college students, and has testified in court before and only makes it about a minute into his testimony before he frogs up. Maybe he's thinking of Seinfeld too.

Judge Atwell says, "Would you get a cup of water, if you would, Greg."

Greg, I assume it's Greg, gets a cup of water from the cooler and delivers it to the witness. Friedlander downs it as only a tenured professor could. He seems to be better now.

I've reviewed the autopsy report. I've been to the medical examiner's office to review the autopsy photos. I've read Dr. Young's findings as far as cause of death, et cetera.

Et cetera? Jimmy thinks that's a bit vague for expert testimony.

I agree the fatal wound in this case was a contact wound. I don't dispute the autopsy findings of Dr. Young in any way. The cause of death was a contact gunshot wound.

You could tell something about what kind of ammunition was used from the wound, but it's not an exact science. I cannot formulate an expert opinion as to whether a shotgun or rifle or handgun was used. It was not a shotgun shell that shot many pellets.

The fatal wound in this case is consistent with the gunshot from a rifle. It is also consistent with a gunshot from a handgun. If there is a way to determine whether one is more likely than the other, it's not something that I know. It would surprise me if that's true.

I don't know if there were ballistics in this case. I've seen no ballistic report. All I saw was the report that a deformed bullet was found in the hair of the deceased. You gave me no copy of a ballistics report.

I guess that means the jury is SOL on ballistics. Amazing. Maybe were supposed to decide this case telepathically.

From the autopsy report alone, there is no way I can formulate an expert opinion as to whether a rifle or handgun would be more likely the weapon.

David Fry will conduct the cross. He promises to be brief. Jimmy will believe it when he sees it.

"Doctor, you came to our office, and we even showed you some more photographs last week. Is that right?" » Right. You showed me the scene photos as well, and I'm glad we got a chance to mention that.

"We made everything we had available to you, is that right?" » You showed me the four pictures that you were going to use.

"You're familiar with a shotgun shell that's a slug shotgun rather than a pellet?" » Yes, I am. I believe I've done two autopsies in which that was the fatal instrument.

"This shotgun shell that you can buy, instead of having normal pellets in it, it has one slug in it, right?" » Right.

"Very powerful slug?" » Right.

"So when Mr. Lance asked you if this injury could have been caused by a rifle, you would say yes, correct?" » Yes.

"And it could have also been caused by a shotgun slug fired from a shotgun?" » Yes. I was waiting for that question from Horton, from Mr. Lance.

"I was too. So now that I am asking if it could have been fired by a shotgun?" » Yes. It would surprise me, because I would expect the entry to be bigger, but I can't tell you that it wasn't.

It's very clear though that it's a contact wound. A shotgun slug in that case would go right through the head, but so would other types of ammunition. I don't know if anything was found. I don't know. I didn't receive a ballistics report.

Looking at the autopsy photo, the wound at the back of the head is consistent with the shotgun slug, a rifle bullet, or a high-powered handgun bullet exiting the head.

That's it for cross. No re-direct, so that's it for Friedlander. Thank goodness that's over. Better yet, it's time for the lunch break. All I have to do now is sit through --

"The Court again reminds you --"

To thine own self be true. Neither a borrower nor a lender be. Never run with scissors. Measure twice, cut once.

"-- television report of the trial.

"With that being said, we'll be in recess until shortly after 1:30. All rise, please. Jury is free to go to lunch."

Jimmy could really go for a dog and a diet Mt. Dew.

TESTIMONY OF BYRON CASE: PART 1

Two more hot dogs from the lady with the cart today, plus two diet Mt. Dews. Not one. Two! Did I mention I have a substance abuse problem?

"The defense calls Byron Case."

So now we know. The defense has decided Byron will testify. It's a tough call. A defendant always wants to testify. A defendant's attorney is frequently less enthusiastic. Defense attorneys know that a seasoned prosecutor can make a defendant look guilty even if he simply kissed a baby, helped birth some kittens, then escorted an old lady across a busy street. "And it's your position today, what you're expecting this jury to believe, is that you touched her only on the elbow. That's not true, is it?"

Byron Case does not have to testify. No one can force him to do so. "No person . . . shall be compelled in any criminal case to be a witness against himself . . ." That's from the Fifth Amendment to the U.S. Constitution. That's why people "take the Fifth."

If a defendant "takes the Fifth," many jurors, though they would deny it, will hold it against him. "If he's innocent, why was he so afraid to get up there and tell his story?" On the other hand, many jurors won't believe a defendant should he decide to testify. "Of course he's lying. He doesn't want to go to prison."

If while on the stand, the defendant doesn't behave according to some unspecified, unspoken standard, some jurors will interpret every non-verbal cue as evidence of guilt.

"Did you see him try to squeeze out that tear?"

"I wanted to slap the smug right off his face."

"Evasive."

"Nervous."

"Cold fish."

"His emotions were just for show."

"He was afraid to look at us."

"You see him glaring at us?"

What we need to do here is listen to Byron's testimony, weigh it just as we will weigh the testimony of all other witnesses. Does it comport with the physical evidence? Is it corroborated? Does it make sense in terms of time and space?

Forget all that other stuff about demeanor and motive. This trial is a show and we're the audience. The defendant is the only amateur here. Both the defense and prosecution are professionals in the Theater of the Court. They're playing to us.

We're nearing the grand finale and it's time for the legal talent to show us what they're made of. If they have the facts behind them, they'll pound on the facts. If they don't have any facts, they'll pound on the table. Either way, there will be some pounding going on.

Ignore the act. Don't allow them to manipulate us. Focus on the evidence.

Deep breath. Here we go.

❖

"Good afternoon. For the record, please state your name." » Byron Case.

"Mr. Case, how old are you?" » I'm 23.

"Did you shoot and kill Anastasia?" » No.

"Were you friends with Anastasia?" » Yes, I was.

"And you attended her funeral?" » Yes, I did.

"You just said you're friends with Anastasia. What about the voice message you once had on your pager?" » At one point in time I had left an outgoing voice message on my pager, which said something to the effect of: This is Byron. Please leave a message unless this is Anastasia, something to the effect of I won't bother returning your call.

"All right. If you tell the jury she was your friend, why would you leave that kind of a message on your pager?" » At the time there was, she and Justin had this relationship that, as you've already heard, had been just on-again-off-again. And every time they broke up, she would always either confide in me or other friends.

And it got to a point where she would call as many as 10, 15 times day, and, to be honest, it was difficult to maintain a friendship with her just because of the fact that she was so obsessed with Justin and keeping their relationship together that, I don't know.

During the last few weeks before her death, I didn't notice any unusual behavior by Justin, not really much more than usual. I guess he had been using a lot of drugs more recently, I suppose. There was one incident where he had taken a very large quantity of LSD, and for probably four days, five days, was just pretty much out of his mind. We were really worried about him. He was hallucinating. Other than that, though, I mean there wasn't really anything that was more unusual than normal.

I heard about his plans to rob his parents. Justin was always coming up with something, and most of the time, I think it was safe to say, it was just joking around. I know that sounds kind of twisted, but we knew he wasn't going to go through with anything. He just had this thing about planning everything.

When he mentioned robbing his parents, I never took that seriously. I never got in the car with him and headed for Oklahoma to rob them. I heard from both him and Anastasia that they had gotten in the car and Justin was seriously considering this. He had the intention, I suppose, of doing this, but Anastasia, from what I heard, talked him out of it.

I don't really remember the specifics about this other plan to put a bomb in a church. He did have a plan about that, but it was ridiculous. I mean, he was talking about plastic explosives. We were all kind of thinking, how's a 20 year old guy living on the Plaza, how is he going to get hold of plastic explosives? It was so outlandish, we never thought anything about it.

Byron is asked about Kelly's recorded phone call.

On the audiotape, yes that was my voice and Kelly's voice. I had been bedridden. I had a fever for about a week before that phone call anyway, and I had been vomiting and just basically sleeping and sweating it off. I went to a doctor.

Lance hands him a document and asks him if he's seen it before.

This is copy of the medical records of when I went to the doctor that week. The date on it is June 6th of 2001. The doctor told me that I had a fever of approximately 103 and I had strep throat. He placed me on antibiotics and painkillers. That was the day after Kelly called just before midnight. I had been sick with strep the entire week.

When she called, I was sleeping. I woke up and went right into the phone call. I didn't deny anything she said because to be honest, I was out of it. I don't really remember most of the conversation, but I would say that I think I may have just misunderstood what she was talking about. She called me many times before upset, and I thought that this was another one of those phone calls where she was calling and she was upset and wanted my input.

On the day she was killed, I had been at Justin's condominium. Justin either received a phone call or made a phone call to Anastasia and she was upset. They were going through another one of their periods where they would break up and then be back together.

My impression was that she was just arguing with him over the relationship as she more or less always did, and she wanted to get together with him to meet and discuss the relationship in person.

Later that afternoon, after that phone call took place, we went out. We went over to Lenexa, Kansas. There's a video game store out there, Funcoland. We'd gone in there to trade in some of his old games that he had brought back from Tulsa that weekend.

Justin didn't have any plans to meet Anastasia. I wasn't entirely clear on what had happened there, but they had attempted to make plans, I believe, and then she had said that she couldn't get a ride, so he basically said, "Okay, well, I'm not going to go pick you up, so let's just do this some other day." It was my impression their plans were cancelled.

While we were at Funcoland, I suggested to Justin that we stop by and pick up Kelly, because it was just essentially on the way back. It was less than I believe five miles from where we were already. So we picked up Kelly up and returned to the condo. I believe there was a message on the answering machine when we returned to the condominium from Anastasia saying that she had already gotten a ride to meet Justin, but obviously we hadn't received that message.

Then Justin got a phone call from Anastasia. That's when he learned that Anastasia was at the Dairy Queen. She wanted him to meet her there. I had no idea where the Diary Queen was. I don't believe Justin knew either. Anastasia gave us the directions.

So we headed for Independence. Justin and I never asked Kelly to make a phone call to the Dairy Queen. Nobody in the car was drinking. Nobody was doing drugs. Nobody was planning on killing Anastasia.

When we got there, I believe we all got out of the car. I vaguely recall having seen her sitting just inside the door. Anastasia saw us walking up. She got up, walked around to the entrance and met us just outside the door. She was very upset with Justin for being late, with everyone. Usually, when Anastasia got upset, if you were in the area, you were kind of in a crossfire.

Everybody got in Justin's car and we went to Mount Washington Cemetery, which is right across the street. We drove into the cemetery, and there was one particular place that she had originally agreed to meet Justin. We drove around to that building. It was already dark, and we knew that most cemeteries close their gates at dusk. So when a car pulled up behind us, I suggested to Justin that we just continue on. I assumed it was the groundskeeper.

Justin was driving. Anastasia was in the front passenger seat. I was behind her. Kelly was behind Justin.

We didn't go to Lincoln Cemetery. I didn't even know where Lincoln Cemetery was. I had no idea. We drove west on Truman Road. Anastasia and Justin had been arguing in the car pretty much since we picked her up at the Dairy Queen. And at that point, Justin made a comment that, I guess made her blow her top, and she got out of the car at the stoplight. Anastasia had asked Justin something to the effect of "Why don't you love me anymore?" And Justin had said "I don't know." That was pretty much it. I think it was more the way he said it. They were looking at each other at the time and I think it just kind of hit home.

When the car stopped at the I-435 stoplight, Anastasia got out of the vehicle, and I presume she started walking. I didn't pay particular attention to where she was walking. I just kind of looked over at Justin and was waiting to see what he was going to do. He didn't turn around and try to get her or anything. We waited briefly at the stoplight and then nobody really said anything. Justin just kind of looked at the road, and we just drove back to his condo.

When we got back to the condo, we just walked in the door when I got a page from my friend, Abraham. I called him back and he had said that he needed a favor. He asked if it was possible for us to take some stuff over to his ex-girlfriend's house, and also pick up some of his belongings as well.

Well, I spoke with Justin just briefly, and he said yeah, that's fine. So the three of us left and drove directly over to the place where he was staying. All three of us went in. We picked up a paper sack. I think it had some pants or something and a letter maybe. I don't know. But we picked it up.

It was getting too late. Kelly had to be home by nine and we were concerned about running late. Justin drives kind of slow. So we headed directly over to Kelly's parents' house and dropped her off at home.

When we were there, I mentioned that Anastasia had jumped out of the car and walked away, but I wouldn't say I made a big show of it. It had never happened before certainly, but I mean, when she would be over at Justin's condominium and they get in an argument, she would get upset and storm out. She would go for a walk on the Plaza for awhile and then eventually she would come back. But getting out of the car, that was something odd.

We dropped Kelly off and then drove to his ex-girlfriend's apartment and dropped off the stuff from Abraham. We were brief, very brief. We handed her the stuff, and talked for a little bit. They had broken up. Since I had known Abraham longer, I was kind of siding more toward him. So we didn't really speak a great deal while I was there. At any rate, we delivered the package.

Justin took me to my mother's apartment, which was where I was living at the time, and we hadn't really discussed anything about plans for the evening. So he just basically drove me into the back lot, and we parked there for a second and he said, "Well, I'll see you tomorrow." I looked at Justin's dashboard clock and it was just a few minutes after 10 o'clock.

I asked him what his plans were for the evening, and he said, "Well, I'm just going to go home and go to sleep." That was unusual. Justin would usually be up until probably two, three, four in the morning. So it was kind of odd that at 10 o'clock he was going to sleep. But I assumed he was upset after the argument with Anastasia. When we were at Kelly's house, he called Anastasia's house, and her sister had said that she hadn't come home yet, and he was concerned about that.

That was the last time I saw Justin alive. I talked to him once more though. He called me the next morning at about nine. I had been up late the night before on the computer and didn't get to sleep until fairly late. So at 9 o'clock I was still asleep and wasn't really up for being on the phone.

From what I can remember it was just, "Hey, how is it going? Do you want to get some breakfast?" I said, "Well, not really. I was asleep. Why are you calling me this early?" He said he had trouble sleeping. I said, "Well, I was sleeping, and I would like to get back to sleep. I'll talk to you later." He said, "Okay, I'll call you this afternoon." I never spoke to him again after that.

I learned about Anastasia being killed in the afternoon. I don't remember the specific time. Probably around five or maybe six. I got a page from Abraham, and it had a "911" extension on the end of it, so I knew that it was pretty urgent. So I called him right back, and he asked me if I had seen the news. I told him no, I hadn't, and he said, "Well, I did, and I just saw that Anastasia is dead."

I was confused. I asked him I think two or three times what he had said just to be sure that I got it right. When it finally sunk in, my immediate response was, "Let me let you go. I'm going to call Justin." So I tried calling Justin, and he wasn't home.

I was interviewed by the police. I went in voluntarily to speak with them. I gave them a full statement. I was interviewed again later. I told them the truth. Absolutely.

I was still dating Kelly at Christmas of 1997. My father had died on Christmas Eve. On Christmas, I went to a family gathering at my aunt's house. Her name is Nancy Nolker. Kelly went with me.

I continued to date Kelly through the holidays and on into 1998. I believe ultimately she broke up with me. There was a period where we kind of went through the same thing as Justin and Anastasia did, where we would break up and get back together. I would say four times, maybe even five. I'm not sure.

We continued to have contact every once in awhile. I had the impression that she was sort of pursuing me, even though she had broken up with me. There was a period where we didn't speak to each other after the breakup. I was upset with her. She was upset with me. We just didn't talk.

I couldn't be specific on when, but she would call me, and would want to get together and just hang out. There were other times when she was more specific. She would say, "Well, you know, we were so good together."

It sounded as though she was trying to get back together with me. I told her I wasn't interested. Either I was seeing someone else or I just didn't want to date anyone at that time. Certainly not her.

There was one instance when we were on the phone, and I couldn't remember the exact conversation if you asked, but I do remember that we were arguing. This was I believe a month after we broke up, I guess. Maybe not even that. I know it was early 1999. I was on the phone with her, and we were arguing about something. At some point, she made reference to getting back together, and I had told her that I wasn't interested. She was kind of rambling about it, and I kind of cut her off and just hung up on her.

She apparently called the police. Maybe 911. I'm not sure. But she called the police and told them that she had just gotten off the phone with her ex-boyfriend who was suicidal and had threatened to kill himself with a knife or something.

I got a knock at the door which I thought was odd, because I wasn't expecting anyone that evening. There were maybe four officers, Kansas City, Missouri Police Department officers, at my door. They pushed their way into the apartment without really saying much. I was confused and a little bit frightened. They instantly started asking me things like, "Are there any sharp objects in the house? Do you own any guns? Do you have any prescription medication?" Things like that. And then they proceeded to explain to me that they had received a phone call. They said, "We got a phone call from your girlfriend who said you were going to try to kill yourself."

They took me to Western Missouri Mental Health. I protested, certainly. I really didn't want to go there. They said there was nothing that they could do, that Kelly had to issue some sort of permission or something like that before I could leave or they had to keep me for observation.

I believe it was 24 hours initially and then they were talking about an additional 24 because Kelly wasn't giving permission to let me go. I don't recall how long I was actually there. It was a disturbing situation.

In 2000 I decided to move to St. Louis. There were quite a few reasons really. One of them was that I was tired of being accessible to Kelly. I didn't like the fact that she was constantly trying to meddle in my life. I wanted to get away from her. She was acting like the traditional psychotic ex-girlfriend, and I didn't want any part of that. I felt I had done everything I could to avoid that. I told friends, "Don't give out my number to anyone unless you know specifically who it is." "Don't give out my address." Things like that.

I had a friend, not someone who I was dating, who happened to be moving to St. Louis, Jamie Smith. We had talked about it, and she was from there originally. We discussed it, and I talked about moving. And she said, "Well, I've been kicking around the idea of moving back to St. Louis."

She moved there a little bit before I did. I think it was two weeks maybe before I did. I moved out there on September 13 in 2000. It was a Friday and the number 13 kind of struck me as odd. I don't know. Lucky number 13. I was thinking, well, this could be a change.

I saw Kelly in person shortly before I moved at my apartment in Kansas City. There was a phone call. I vaguely remember it. Unfortunately, I can't recall specifics. But I had known from a previous phone call that she had made to me, I don't know, maybe a month beforehand that she had either been kicked out of her parents' house or had just left. I'm not really certain.

She expressed that, "the place I'm living now, we got a phone, but we don't have running water, and I haven't eaten anything in like a day or two." She said that I was the only person that ever really cared or that she could turn to really.

Jamie was there. We were at the apartment, just sitting around. Kelly came over with a friend of hers who I had never met before. She was just sort of making nice, if that makes any sense. She was aware I was getting ready to leave for St. Louis. She talked with me briefly about that. It seemed like she couldn't understand why I would be moving. I didn't really come out and say, "I'm moving because of you." I did say I was leaving.

She didn't take it too well. She didn't specifically say, "Don't go," but she was really laying into me, trying to convince me to stay.

When I moved to St. Louis, I didn't think Kelly would have my new address and phone number. She called though, but I never spoke with her. At one point I heard a message from her that she left on the answering machine. She just said, "Byron, give me a call." That's it. I didn't call her back. I was trying to avoid her.

The testimony switches gears.

My dad never owned a gun. He never owned a hunting rifle. I never went out hunting with him. Never. Not even once. I never went hunting with anyone. There was never a gun hanging on the wall at my Dad's place. I never told Kelly that I had taken my dad's hunting rifle. I never at any time said that I wanted to know what it would feel like to kill someone.

I never talked about the idea of shooting my father to put him out of his misery. My dad was in fairly good condition. He had been HIV positive for a few years, but he was always in peak physical condition. He worked out, he took vitamins, and participated in physical fitness competitions. Things like that. So he was in good shape. There wasn't any long period of suffering before the HIV finally got to him.

When he finally died, it was very sudden. He had gone on a trip to New York, and I believe he was supposed to be gone only for a week. I hadn't heard back from him after the initial week, and I found out, I believe it was during the middle of that second week. My aunt phoned me at home and told me that he was in the hospital. I believe he was in there only two weeks before he died.

Byron is asked about prior convictions. I perk up.

I have a prior conviction, for stealing. It was a Class "C" felony. That was in Clay County, in '98. After a Guilty plea, I was sentenced to six months in the County Jail. They suspended the sentence and I ended up with five years probation. Other than that, I don't have any convictions in state or federal court.

That's it for Lance's direct. David Fry is going to cross.

TESTIMONY OF BYRON CASE: PART 2

David Fry will conduct the cross-examination of Byron Case.

"Mr. Case, I'm going to start talking about the relationships that you had with the people involved in this case. Do you understand that?" » Yes.

"First, I'm going to start talking about Justin. At the time of this murder, you had known him for about a year. Isn't that correct?" » Approximately, yes.

"And you met at a coffee house and actually became pretty quick friends. Is that right?" » Yes.

"You had a lot in common. He was a very accepting young man. Is that right?" » Yes.

"Justin's drug abuse and use didn't seem to bother you in that friendship, did it?" » It bothered me when it became, I don't want to say when it became a problem, but certainly when it became excessive.

"What did you do about it?" » I never really did anything about it.

"All right. You frequently spent the night over at his condo. Isn't that correct?" » That's correct.

"Many of your friends thought that you two were inseparable. Is that correct?" » I would say, yes.

Something's up, again.

"Justin's family thought you were a special friend to Justin, didn't they?" » Until yesterday I had never heard that, but obviously.

"Obviously Justin shared that with them, didn't he?" » Yes.

"The Moffetts, they thought that Justin was a special friend, and you were pretty special friends with him, didn't they?" » Yes.

I get it now. This is the same kind of stunt Crayon pulled.

"Your mother knew that the two of you were pretty special friends, didn't she?" » Yes.

They were "special friends." Justin was "accepting." The two of them were "inseparable." These aren't Byron's words. They're Fry's words.

"Did she seem pretty comfortable with you spending the night there routinely, isn't that right?" » Yes.

Fry wants us to believe that Justin and Byron had a homosexual relationship.

"In fact, you spent the night there so routinely, she almost became unaware of that, whether you were with her or with your father or with Justin. Isn't that right?" » Yes.

There's no evidence whatsoever, so Fry is going to sneak the idea in with his "special" questions. It's pretty low.

"All right. There were certain changes that were going on in Justin's life in the year that you knew him, weren't there?" » Quite a few, yes sir.

"One of those changes was Anastasia. Isn't that correct?" » Yeah.

"And that happened in, like, April or May they met, didn't they?" » I really don't recall that. I would say yes.

"Don't say yes to anything that I'm questioning you about if you don't mean it. Okay?" » Okay. I don't recall.

"And it's fair to say that they were quite infatuated with each other?" » For a time, yes.

"At the time that they met and within a month she moved in?" » Oh, yes.

"They even were so happy that they talked about being married, didn't they?" » Yes.

"You heard the other day that Justin was so serious about it, he even mentioned it to his parents, didn't you?" » Yes.

"Were you aware of that?" » Yeah. I remember that he had taken her down with him to Tulsa one weekend, and she had spent the weekend there and met the parents, and they expressed that to them.

"You heard the conversation that the financial support that he was receiving up here in Kansas City was going to end if they got married, didn't you?" » No, I never heard that.

"They never came back and told you that?" » Huh-uh.

"You heard that yesterday, didn't you?" » Yes.

"Was that the first time?" » Yes.

"Your inseparable friend hasn't mentioned that to you at all?" » No.

"Did they ever talk about just living together and not getting married so that they wouldn't lose the financial support or anything like that?" » Like I said, they never talked about anything about their finances. I know Justin was frustrated with the idea of living under his parents' wing, but never really did anything about it.

"Pretty soon there was another change in Justin's life, was that those two started to fight. Is that right?" » Yes.

"She became a burden to Justin, didn't she?" » Yes.

"She became a burden to you, didn't she?" » Yes.

"You heard talk about another change in his life, dropping out of school, didn't you?" » Yes.

"And you were aware of that, weren't you?" » I knew he wasn't going. I didn't know if it was official or --

"Didn't know if he, for instance, withdrew from school and got the money back in his own pocket, did you?" » No.

"He just quit going to classes?" » Sorry?

"You didn't know whether it was just quit going to classes or quit and get the money back and just not tell the parents about it, right?" » No.

"Now, fair to say, you knew about his relationship with his parents and the money and school. Is that correct?" » Yes.

"And at some point in time, you knew that his parents were going to find out that he was not in school, didn't you?" » Yeah.

"And he knew that too, didn't he?" » Yes.

"Did you ever talk about what was going to happen then?" » He had mentioned, I'm trying to remember how he mentioned it or where we were.

"Was this a fairly big thing if the condo wasn't going to be available to you anymore?" » He never said anything about that. All I know is he had mentioned that he had had a desire to try to get a job and, you know, support himself. I know that's something that he said that he wanted to do. But he never specifically said: "My parents are going to stop funding me."

"In the course of your relationship with Justin and his developing a relationship with Anastasia, your relationship with Justin changed a little bit, didn't it?" » I wouldn't say so.

"You heard your mother say that you complained that didn't get to spend as much time with Justin anymore, didn't you?" » Yes, I heard that.

"Did you complain to your mother that way or did she make that up?" » I don't believe she made it up. I don't recall ever having said that, but --

"Okay. You knew there would be less hanging around time between the two of you, didn't you?" » I presume so, yes.

"And there was less spending the night at the condo or, if she was there, you wouldn't spend the night there?" » That was never an issue. I just crashed on the couch in the living room.

"Less spending the night at the condo?" Fry's ramped it up. We're not just supposed to think Byron is gay. We're supposed to think he murdered Anastasia because she came between Byron and his lover.

There's no evidence of it, anymore than there was evidence that Byron walked up and shot Anastasia in the face, as Crayon dramatized during her questioning of Kelly.

It's outrageous. They're making up evidence and disguising it as questioning. It's infuriating.

"Were you jealous of Anastasia's relationship with Justin?" » No, not at all.

"I want to talk with you really quickly, you've had sometimes, it seems, a little difficulty remembering things. You certainly have prepared to come to court today and answer the charges that are before you, haven't you?" » Yes.

"You got all the police reports. I see you have quite a stack there. You've had them the whole time, haven't you?" » Yes.

Fry asks seven more questions about Byron having the police report. Fry wants us to know that Abraham and Byron's own mother have also seen the police reports, and wants us to believe there is something wrong with that. It's an odd segue from the gay implication to the "why so much interest in your own case" questions.

Fry then moves on to asking Byron questions about which he would have no direct knowledge.

"Thursday morning, at 3 o'clock, Anastasia's body is found, and she has been murdered. Is that right?" » Yes.

"The Friday after, the next day after she was found, you're in the deputy's office and you're giving a statement, right?" » Yes.

"Fair to say a little worried about being a suspect in that?"

Lance objects and asks to approach. Looks like he loses. Fry asks the same question when he returns from the sidebar.

"Fair to say you might have been considered a suspect at that time?" » I knew it was a possibility, yes.

"And that's because why?" » Because they were questioning me.

Lance objects again. Judge Atwell asks if he wants to make a record. Lance says "No. Go ahead." Way to hang in there, Lance.

"You were one of the last three people that ever saw her alive, weren't you?" » Yes.

"And that was a close friend of yours, right?" » Yes.

"So you either wanted to help the police for one of two reasons, giving them all accurate information. Is that right? This is the close friend that was killed and you might be considered a suspect, and you wanted to just get rid of any concerns about that right?" » Yes.

"All right. You've been provided a copy of the statement by your attorney. Is that right?" » Yes, I have.

"You certainly read it prior to coming in here today. If I asked you some questions about that statement, you're not going to be surprised, are you?" » No. I don't believe I would.

"I would like to ask you about some of the changes in Justin's life. One of those changes is his thoughts on suicide. He had thoughts about suicide, didn't he?" » Yes, he had.

"He had confided to you that he had attempted suicide in the past and, actually, quite a few attempts. Isn't that right?" » Yes, that's correct.

"Before you even met him, right?" » Right.

"You told Sergeant Kilgore about Justin buying this shotgun, didn't you?" » Yes, I did.

"And you knew he bought it in September, a month before this murder, didn't you?" » I wasn't sure about the exact date, but, yes.

"About three or four weeks is the way you think you described it. Is that fair?" » That's correct.

"Now, there were a couple things, when you told Sergeant Kilgore about this shotgun, that I want to ask you about. One possibility for his buying the shotgun that you gave Sergeant Kilgore was it was for sport. Do you remember telling him that?" » Yeah. I was kind of speculating on why he would have bought it.

"Why would you speculate about Justin using a gun for sport? Did you ever do that with him?" » No.

"In the year you knew him, did he express any interest in that sport?" » No.

"Did he seem like that kind of a young man?" » Justin had so many interests that just kind of popped in and out. He would be interested in something for a week, and then he wouldn't be interested in it anymore.

"Another concern that you expressed to Sergeant Kilgore in that very same statement was some comments that he made that he may just take this gun and shoot himself and get it all over with. Do you remember saying that?" » I don't remember if it was specifically in reference to that gun. But he did say at some point, "Well, I might as well go shoot myself," or something like that.

"All right. You specifically remember Justin saying something about, well, I might just take this shotgun and go shoot myself and get it all over with. You told that to Sergeant Kilgore. Is that right?" » Again, I don't remember specifically saying with that gun but --

"I asked did you remember saying that he made that statement in about the same time that he purchased that shotgun?" » I don't recall, no.

"But when he went right out and bought the gun, were you concerned with him having said that in the past?" » I don't believe I made a connection. Again, it was just, there were so many things that Justin said that we almost didn't even listen to half the time.

"You made the connection in telling Sergeant Kilgore that, didn't you?" » Yes, I did.

"But you didn't make the connection back when it happened?" » No, I hadn't. There was briefly a period before I spoke with Sergeant Kilgore when I had made that connection, and I thought to myself, "Well, should I worry about this?"

Fry is now pounding this point flat. That's maybe the fifteenth question in a row about Justin's suicide and why Byron wasn't more perceptive in seeing it coming. I can't see how it ties in to whether Byron murdered Anastasia. Seems as if Fry is simply trying to paint Byron as uncaring. That now makes the portrayals as gay, too interested in his own case, and uncaring.

"Did you worry about it?" » I spoke with Justin about it and he said that it was nothing so --

"When I asked did you do anything about it and your answer was, "Well, I talked to Justin about it." » Correct.

"When Justin couldn't be found the day after Anastasia was murdered, you called his home, didn't you?" » Yes, I did.

"And he was just missing then, wasn't he?" » Yes.

"You were so concerned that he was just missing that you called his home and told them that he was missing?" » Yeah. I was concerned that he was missing, yes, in light of what had happened and no one knew where he was. I thought it was odd.

"So you called his home and told the parents?" » Oh, his home in Tulsa, yes. I didn't know if he had gone down there or I didn't know what had happened.

"When he bought the shotgun and he said that he was considering shooting himself, did you call then?" » No, I didn't.

"When he was found dead, did that make you very sad?" » Initially, again, it was a shock. At this point I don't even recall how I found out specifically, but I remember that, I do remember that initially it was just kind of, there was too much to deal with and I didn't, I didn't really react immediately.

"Didn't have an emotional reaction?" » My emotional reaction was to shut down.

"I want to now talk to you about Anastasia. Anastasia you knew since the eighth grade in freshman year. Is that correct?" » Yes, that's correct.

"Back then you weren't close friends, right? Just schoolmates?" » Yes.

"Met in coffee houses at Westport and kind of made it easy that you recognized each other and got together, didn't you?" » Well, actually what happened there was I was actually out with Justin one evening. I saw her at a coffee house, and we all, the three of us, started talking. I introduced them.

"And they started dating?" » Uh-huh.

"And then she started staying over with Justin?" » Yes.

"And then she moved in with Justin, right?" » Yes.

"And you've lost track of when they started talking about marriage?" » Yeah. During that time I wasn't paying terribly close attention to, you know, what day what was happening on. So really I would be hard-pressed to pinpoint even a month when they started talking about that.

"Fair to describe that relationship as a good relationship for all three of you for awhile?" » Yes.

"At some point that didn't continue to stay that good, did it?" » No.

"They began to break up, didn't they?" » Yes.

"Now, when she went through this breakup phase, I think you saw a new part of Anastasia, didn't you?" » Yes.

"A very demanding young lady, wasn't she?" » Yes.

"Very needy of Justin, wasn't she?" » Yeah, she was.

"Very determined about Justin, wasn't she?" » Yes.

"She was very stubborn to let Justin just go away, wasn't she?" » She had her moments where she would say, "Well, I don't need him anymore," but for the most part, yes.

"And she would turn right around the next day and call you 10 or 15 times asking about him, wouldn't she?" » Yes.

"She wasn't going to let go of this young man at all, was she?" » No.

"She was fighting every minute, every day to get him, wasn't she?" » I suppose so, yes.

"She was a fighter for him, wasn't she?" » I'm sorry?

"She was a fighter for him, wasn't she?" » Yes.

"And that was consistent with her personality, wasn't it?" » Yes.

"It was very disturbing to you when she was violently murdered, wasn't it?" » Yes.

"She was one of those people that you cared about right?" » Yes, she was.

"She was one of those people that mattered. Is that right?" » Yes.

"Do you remember Kelly describing you as saying well, to you, there were some people that mattered and some people didn't? Do you remember?" » Yes.

"Is that true?" » Yes, but I should offer a qualification that I think that the way that she was referring to it implies some sort of sinister undertones to that. I'm sure that in more than one instance in my life I've said that some people matter and some people don't. But I think in everyone's lives there are people that they care about that they're extremely close to, who matter in their immediate life, and there are those that don't.

"And you categorize them fairly easily, don't you?" » Relatively.

"Yes. Now, I want to talk to you about Kelly. You met Kelly down in the coffee shops, right?" » Yes. Through Justin.

"How long did you know her before you figured out she was in the eighth grade?" » How long?

"How long?" » It had been, I don't know. A month maybe.

"How old were you again?" » When I first met her, I believe I was 18.

"She was 14?" » Yes.

"What grade school or middle school did you go to pick her up when you picked her up with your car?" » Trailridge Middle School.

"No doubt in your mind you had an eighth grader that you were dating. Is that right?" » Yes.

"Did that seem odd to you?" » I was uncomfortable with it yes.

"How long were you dating before you met her parents?" » I would estimate about three weeks. Maybe a month. I'm not sure about that exactly.

"Fair to say you're her big dark secret of dating, right?" » You could say that, yes.

"You were infatuated with her as much as she was with you at that time?" » Initially the relationship started out, when I first met her, I was attracted to her. We had started talking, and she expressed to me that, well, several things that kind of alarmed me and concerned me. And my first thought was, ultimately my first thought was maybe I can save her in a way, and it kind of grew from, there.

"You were going to save her, right?" » Yes.

"From that alcoholic, child-beating father?" » That's what she had told me.

"That's what your mother talked about. Is that what it was about?" » Yes.

"You got to know the Moffett family, did you?" » Yes.

"You were almost a daily fixture in the house, right?" » You could say that, yes.

"And you would either call or come over every day. Is that right?" » Yes.

"Now, at some point in time after October 22nd, the relationship started changing?" » Between myself and Kelly?

"Correct." » Not really, no. If anything we got closer. We were both kind of in shock from everything that had happened and we were just kind of clinging to each other for support.

"Under the circumstances that she described, it would be very important for you to stay close to her, wouldn't it?" » I suppose.

"If you wanted to control her, it would be very important for you to stay close to her, wouldn't it?"

Lance objects.

"Objection, asked and answered."

It's a horrible objection. The problem isn't that Fry asked the same question. The problem is that Fry is once again attempting to introduce, even fabricate evidence by posing a hypothetical. "If you wanted to control her --" There has been no evidence presented of this at all. The judge has to sustain, but Fry has snuck it in anyway. Can't unring the bell.

"Overruled. I guess. I suppose."

Holy cow! A horrible ruling, and namby pamby to boot! I guess it's a namby pamby ruling. I suppose it is. Gimme a break.

Byron answers:

It would be.

"Now, you did stay very close and you went through the holidays and you went through your birthday and you still stayed pretty close through that whole time, didn't you?" » Up until the holidays, yes.

"Then after the holidays you continued to date, didn't you?" » Yes, we did.

"And at some point in time Kelly started becoming verbally abusive to you. Is that right?" » I don't know about that. We were having problems but --

"Her mother described these sessions with you watching you two, as Kelly was being verbally abusive to you. Do you dispute that?" » I can't recall any of that, no.

"You don't recall what Debbie Moffett recalls. Is that right?" » Correct.

"But at some point then, if she is not verbally abusive, you are both arguing with each other?" » Yes.

"And what were you arguing about?" » Really any number of things. There were multiple instances where she would cheat on me, where she would go out and use drugs with friends or something like that, and I would be upset with her for doing that. There were really any number of things.

"She described that for this jury too, that she started seeking other friends away from you, didn't she?" » She had always had other friends. It was just she hung out with them more.

"And she described her drug use and her alcohol use getting worse, didn't she?" » Yeah. It had been escalating ever since we met, though.

"Her arguments with you were that, you know, you guys needed to do something about what happened on October 22nd, weren't they?" » No.

"That's what she said and that's what she told this jury, right? You remember hearing that, right?" » Yes.

"You don't recall that part of the argument?" » No.

"What was the argument then? That she was cheating on you?" » On occasion, yes.

"Why did you want to go back to her if she was cheating on you?" » Well, this could be kind of a long answer, but I was in treatment, or not treatment, but I was seeing a counselor for some time before I met her and continued on throughout the time that I knew her. And when I kind of shared with him details of the relationship, if I would go in and talk about something, eventually my counselor began to express to me that I was probably co-dependent. And for me, it was very difficult to sort of let that go. I felt as though I was constantly supposed to be there for her, to kind of look after her and make sure she didn't get herself deeper into drugs or alcohol and --

"You became like a surrogate father for her?" » You could say that.

"And trying to control that aspect of her life?" » Yes.

"But not controlling her ability to talk about what happened October 22nd?" » Certainly not.

"That's the way she described it though, isn't it?" » Yes, I realize that.

"So you're both describing the same type of relationship, but she says it's because you're trying to control her and stay close to her so she won't talk about October 22nd. And you say no, I'm just trying to save her from drugs, bad friends, bad father and alcohol, right?" » Well, no. At that point it had been established at some point in the middle of our relationship by her mother that Kelly was lying to everyone about how her father beat her or any number of other things. And so it had already been established to me that that was not the case. But everything else, yes.

"I believe, when you were breaking up and she finally broke up with you, was she the one pursuing you or were you the one pursuing her?" » It varied at different times.

"When she finally broke up with you, it was her final breakup, right?" » Yes, that's correct.

"But after the final breakup, you have this sense that you're telling the jury that, you know, for another year she is still pursuing you?" » After awhile she came back, I suppose, or tried to, yes.

"Her pursuit of you is to continue to try to get you to talk about what you're going to do about the events that occurred on October 22nd, aren't they?"

Another objection from Lance.

"Argumentative."

Another overrule from Atwell.

Byron answers.

That was never my understanding.

"That's what she testified. She told this jury under oath that?" » Yes.

"You heard that?" » Yes, I did.

"Her pursuit was only to get you to deal with the events that occurred on October 22nd?"

Another objection.

"Asked and answered."

Atwell sustains this one.

"And you are trying to tell this jury that she is pursuing you, but it's romantically?" » That was, yes.

"That's your perception, right?" » Yes.

"When you're going to St. Louis and she comes over, are you trying to tell this jury that she was begging you to stay here in Kansas City?" » I don't know that begging was really, I don't know that that was really the right term.

"Take the term away. Was she trying to persuade you, influence you, not to leave?" » It seemed that way, yes. She certainly expressed that she didn't want me to go.

"She wanted you to stay here and deal with the events that occurred on October 22nd is what she told this jury. She did want you to stay, didn't she?" » Yes.

"And she did want you to deal with those events, didn't she?" » Apparently. That's what she said, yes.

"But you were clueless as to that?" » Of course.

"Jamie was in the room in that whole conversation. She came in here to testify for this jury. Is that right?" » Yes, she did.

"She didn't describe the meeting in the same way you did at all."

Lance objects again.

"Objection. Commenting on."

Judge sustains the objection. "Just a moment. Sustained. Objection Sustained. It's argumentative."

"I'm going to move on. We have talked about the relationships. I want to talk about these schemes. As I understand your testimony today, they're all Justin's schemes. Is that right?" » Yes.

"Abraham said you would be participative listeners was I think the way he tried to describe it. Is that right?" » Yes.

"You all would just jump into these schemes, start talking and adding to everybody's story. Is that right?" » No.

"You never did that?" » No.

"Kelly told this jury that you did. Did you hear her say that?" » Yes, I did.

"And are you saying that's not right, you didn't involve yourself in these schemes at all?" » Absolutely not.

"Not even, Abraham described, that you were like participative listeners?" » I think Abraham and I are describing the same thing. I think that we were listening, and we didn't really say or do anything about it. So that was the impression that I got. But that was certainly what, I mean, certainly everyone's involvement to the best of my knowledge.

"Were there other schemes that you all came up with to make some money, do anything like that?" » No.

"Anybody scheme to get a job out of any of this time?" » I was working at Kinko's Copies on Johnson Drive. I was employed at least for quite some time. And at one point I quit there but --

"Never had a regular job for the whole year, did you?" » Well, aside from that.

"Aside from that you just lived off your parents and Justin, didn't you?" » After I lost my job there, yeah, I went to go live with my mother.

"So Justin quitting school, losing his finances, might have been a little bit of a concern for you. Is that right?" » Again, I didn't know anything about Justin losing his finances. He never expressed that to me.

"Your inseparable friend never told you anything about that, right?" » That's correct.

Is Fry now suggesting that Byron killed Anastasia because Justin's parents were going to cut off Justin's funds? It makes no sense. This is becoming painful.

"All right. We're going to now talk about October 22nd 1997. All right? Again, I've shown you a page of this document that you gave and it's a statement that you gave Sergeant Kilgore, right?" » Yes.

"You know it exists, right?" » Yes.

What a bizarre question.

"And you've been provided copies of it before coming here today, right?" » Yes, I have.

"Essentially, as I listen to you, you are trying to tell this jury the same thing today that you told Sergeant Kilgore two days after her body was found, or a day after her body was found. Is that right?" » Yes.

"On that day, you had nothing to hide. Is that correct?" » That's correct.

"You told the absolute truth as you knew it. Is that correct?" » Well, I think that, I told the truth, certainly, about everything that I was asked, but I think there were some things which I kind of downplayed, specifically with regards to Justin, but that's really irrelevant I think.

"We might find that or we may not. Fair to say that the night before October 21st you spent the night at Justin's house. Is that right? In his condo?" » I don't recall, but I believe so.

"Did you wake up in his condo the 22nd?" » I'm inclined to believe I did, although I don't specifically recall.

"Two days later, let's see if that refreshes your recollection. 'I think I may have spent the night there before.' Right?" » Yes.

"And when you woke up, do you remember you had no plans, anything to do, either you or Justin. Is that right?" » Yes. That's correct.

"At some point in time the only plan that came forward was that you were going to go to Funcoland. Is that right?" » Yes.

"You spent the entire day with Justin on the 22nd, didn't you?" » Yes. Although I should state that, when you said the entire day, that implies that we got up fairly early. When, in fact, we, as I said before, I mean our sleeping schedules were such that we stayed up very late and didn't wake up until usually early afternoon.

"Needless to say, whenever you woke up, everything Justin did, you did with him?" » Yes, that's correct.

"So when you told Sergeant Kilgore you woke up and you go out to just take care of some things, it was a day just like any other. Is that right?" » Uh-huh.

"Sometime during the day you became aware and you told Sergeant Kilgore that Justin made plans to meet Anastasia at 5:30. Do you remember telling him that?" » Yes.

"And the whole purpose of that meeting was that Anastasia wanted to talk with him about their latest problems. Do you remember telling Sergeant Kilgore that?" » Yes.

"And that's the truth, right?" » Yes.

"Because everything you said then was the truth and everything you're saying today is the truth, right?" » Well, I don't recall the time specifically. I assume that that was accurate, though.

"Do you need to refresh your recollection looking at the statement? If you said 5:30 for that meeting then, was that about as right as you could be?" » Yes.

"Anastasia, for some reason, wanted to meet Justin at Mount Washington Cemetery. Is that right?" » Yes.

"Now, Anastasia you knew had no car, right?" » Correct.

"You knew her family would be at work, right?" » I didn't know her family's schedule.

"Did you know she didn't get along with her parents?" » She had mentioned it in the past, yes.

"Had she shared that it was tough in her mind to ask her parents for help?" » Not really, no.

"She shared with you it was tough moving back home, wasn't it?" » Well, yes.

"Not only because she was away from Justin, but because she had moved back with her parents, right?" » Yes. I think it was more of a burden, or it was more of an inconvenience having to be back there, which is why it was tough. I don't think there was, well, I don't know.

"Help this jury understand why a young lady with no car and no access to a ride makes arrangements with Justin to meet at a cemetery that she can't walk to."

Lance objects.

"Speculation unless the witness knows."

That doesn't stop Fry. He asks Byron if he knows. Judge Atwell tells everyone to hold their horses.

"Hold on. As long as related to personal knowledge, I'll allow the question."

"Do you know why she would have done that?" » No, I don't.

"Does it make sense to you?" » I wasn't clear on where they were supposed to meet originally, so I really can't say. I believe initially she was under the assumption she could get a ride.

"All right." » But they had settled that before, well, earlier in the day, and then plans changed at some point.

"But you knew the plan was, her intent to meet at Mount Washington and that she had to meet Justin there. Why wouldn't Justin just go pick her up and go to Mount Washington? Have you got any idea?" » I remember Justin said he didn't really want to drive all the way out there.

"Well, Mount Washington is less than three miles from her house. What's the difference going to her house or going to Mount Washington?" » I don't know. I would assume that, you know, she got a ride as far as she could or something to that effect, but I don't remember anything about that being said specifically.

"But you became aware, even though she wanted to go to Mount Washington, at some point in time she was having a hard time getting a ride. Is that correct?" » Yes.

"So you take off, and you decide to go to Funcoland with Justin. Is that right?" » Yes.

"Do you remember about what time you take off to go to Funcoland?" » I would estimate some time around three in the afternoon.

"Around three in the afternoon?" » Roughly.

"So before 3 o'clock in the afternoon, she had called and said, 'I'm having a hard time getting a ride.' Is that right?" » Yeah. She had canceled plans.

"Would you have gone to Funcoland if he was still expected to go to Mount Washington Cemetery to meet her at 5:30?" » No.

"So before 3 o'clock, before her parents get home, before she has any chance to get a ride, this little scrapper of a girl, this fighter of a girl, that doesn't want to give up on Justin, is asking to meet Justin that day to talk about their relationship, calls before 3 o'clock and says 'I can't be there.'"

Lance objects to the form of the question. Judge Atwell sustains.

"Do you have any explanation why she would have given up on that meeting so quickly that day?" » Because, as I said, it was my understanding she couldn't get a ride.

"You agreed with me she was very determined, didn't you?" » Yes.

"She was very stubborn, wasn't she?" » She could be.

"About this relationship, she didn't want to let it go and, if she wanted to meet Justin, she would have been stubborn and determined, right?" » Probably, yes.

"Before 3 o'clock, she just gave up on the idea and said, 'I can't get a ride.'" » From my understanding, she had exhausted all the possibilities. She called relatives. I don't know. I never asked about the specifics. It wasn't an important issue at the time.

"She gives up on that and you decide to go to Funcoland, and that's over here in Roeland Park, Kansas. Is that right?" » It was listed as Roeland Park, Kansas, in the phone book. It seemed like Lenexa to me. I'm not sure. I never looked at the map.

"When you drive from The Plaza area where the condo is out to Roeland Park, how long would it take you to get there?" » I would estimate 30 minutes. Maybe a little bit more.

"When you get to Funcoland and you do some trading of these games and stuff like that, how much time did you spend there?" » We were there for a while. I remember Justin kept looking at stuff on the shelves, and I would estimate maybe almost an hour.

"So, if you left at about three, it takes about 3:30 to get there, you're there about an hour, 4:30, and around that time you decide to go over to Kelly's house. Is that correct?" » After we left Funcoland, I suggested to Justin we stop over and see what she was doing.

"It would have been after 4 o'clock, right?" » Yes.

"And you heard Francesca and you heard Diane describe that, about 4 o'clock, Anastasia was getting in the car and driving to Mount Washington, didn't you?" » Yes.

"She didn't know the Mount Washington thing had been called off, do you think?" » There was a breakdown on communication at some point. I don't know. The way that Justin explained it, he had canceled plans.

"She was unaware of that, if she left at that time, wasn't she?" » I guess.

"Well, you heard the evidence today, this week. Did you dispute that?" » I have no reason to.

"You, instead, go over to Kelly's and you get there after 4:30 or around 4:30. Is that correct?" » Yes.

This is more like it. Fry is walking Byron through the timeline for the day. This is testimony that really matters. I'm writing like mad.

"And you decide you're going to go to Justin's condo from Kelly's house. Is that correct?" » Well, that was the original plan and Kelly was just kind of a stop, yes.

"And from Kelly's house, I'm sure you made the trip quite often. How long does it take you to get to Kelly's, from Kelly's house to the condo?" » It takes roughly 25, 30 minutes, depending on traffic and time of day and what route. But we stopped after leaving Kelly's. We stopped at, there was a gas station. I believe there was a Phillips 66.

"A Kicks 66 station?" » Right.

"Kelly remembers making a phone call to Anastasia at that time. Is that right?" » Right.

"We know from the evidence here that Anastasia is at the cemetery about 4:20 and about 4:30 you're at Kelly's house leaving going to a gas station. Is that right?" » Yes.

"And I think you told the jury already by the time you get back to the condo, there is a phone call waiting for you, 'Hey, I'm at the cemetery, I got my ride, meet me down here at Mount Washington.' Is that right?" » She said she was calling from a pay phone, but, yes. She said she had been waiting for some time.

"And, if she didn't get you guys at the condo, it would have been very matter of fact for her to reach you on your pager. Is that correct?" » Yes.

"And, if she had reached you on your pager and given the number, you could have dialed the phone number that Kelly says she dialed and Kelly could have talked to her at the Dairy Queen. Isn't that right?" » If the pay phone allowed incoming calls, yeah.

"And we got this other thing that's very puzzling here, is that Francesca tells the jury that, about ten minutes after Anastasia left with her stepmother to go to Mount Washington, Justin called and said, 'I'm in Lenexa. I can't get there.' Do you remember Fran said that?" » Yes.

"Did Justin make that call?" » Justin called and he was asking for Anastasia. I wasn't listening to the conversation, but I think I was still waiting in the car.

"Were the calls made from Kelly's house or the Phillips, or the gas station?" » No. He made that call from a pay phone at the gas station.

"Okay. And so Justin did call, you're pretty convinced that Justin did call, talked to Francesca, told her, 'I'm in Lenexa.' And Francesca said, 'She's already gone.' Right?" » I don't know what happened during the conversation.

"It makes sense to you, doesn't it?" » Yes.

"You don't dispute it, do you?" » Correct.

"In fact Kelly is right about stopping at the gas station to make a phone call?" » Yes.

"Did you remember getting paged by Anastasia to call at a pay phone?" » No.

"You don't remember that? Even though Justin has confirmed that Anastasia has gone to Mount Washington, she is out there all by herself, she just got dropped off, the three of you decide to come to the condo. Isn't that correct?" » Yes.

"Knowing that she is just out there with no ride and nobody. Is that right?" » Yes.

"Was there any discussion about that?" » I don't really remember. I think there was, Justin may have mentioned something about it after he got off the phone. I don't really recall specifically, but I know that Justin was still adamant about not going out there to pick her up.

"Even after learning she was already there?" » Yes.

"So you remember some discussion in the car driving from the gas station to the condo?" » I don't remember specifically it being in the car. I know, when we got back to the condominium, there was a message on the answering machine from Anastasia saying the same thing, that she was already there and that she was waiting, but we had no phone number to reach her. Obviously, we couldn't get in touch with her.

"All right. You go back to the condo and, of course, you've got this message waiting for you, and Anastasia calls you at the condo again from the Dairy Queen, the pay phone. Is that right?" » Yes.

"And you remember that was after 5 o'clock, maybe closer to 6 o'clock, according to your statement. Do you agree with that?" » Yes.

"And Justin is on the phone probably 20 to 30 minutes is how you estimated it to Sergeant Kilgore. Is that right?" » Sure. I have no reason to dispute that.

"All right. I don't either. And while that conversation is going on, you are just playing Nintendo games. Is that correct?" » Yes. Kelly and I both were.

"About 6:30, Justin tells, you're hearing part of the conversation, I assume. Is that right?" » Yeah.

"Not really paying attention to all of it. Right?" » Right.

"You can't quote all of it, can you?" » No, not at all.

"But at some point, you do know Justin agrees to go out, pick her up at the Dairy Queen. Is that right?" » Yes.

"And the whole point in Anastasia wanting to meet Justin was to talk about their relationship. Is that correct?" » Yes.

"Why didn't Justin just go out there by himself and leave you and Kelly at the condo playing your Nintendo game?" » We had discussed that, and he didn't want to do it, and Kelly didn't want to do it, as I recall, because she had to be back by 9. We didn't know how long they were going to be out there, what was going to happen. And Justin didn't want us kind of bumming around the apartment without him there.

"Knowing she wanted a private conversation with him about the relationship, all three of you pack in the car and drive over to Dairy Queen?" » He told her on the phone, if he came out, all three of us were going to have to come, otherwise he will have to take Kelly home, and it will take longer.

"That has you leaving about 6:30. Is that correct? After a 20, 30 minute call?" » Yeah, sure.

Lance asks to approach the bench. Judge Atwell answers just as Byron did and says "Sure."

The judge calls for a break.

"We're going to take a short break, ladies and gentlemen, and come back in about ten minutes or so, ten or 15. The Court again --"

Take me now, Lord. Wait no longer. Quickly, before he says --

"With that being said --"

TESTIMONY OF BYRON CASE: PART 3

Vivian, juror number 11, says that Lance asked for the break because he had to take a leak. She saw him hot-footing it out of here like he meant business. Given how quick the side bar was, she might be right.

"All rise."

"Everybody please be seated. Mr. Fry, you may resume your cross-examination."

"Mr. Case, I ended by asking the question about all three of you just getting in the car and driving out to the Dairy Queen out on Highway 24. That's correct, isn't it?" » I believe so, yes.

Highway 24 is the same as Winner Road. That's the one that runs across the top of Mount Washington.

"And when you got to the Dairy Queen, I believe you described it that you just drove up. You could see her sitting in there. Was it all three of you got out of the car and approached the Dairy Queen?" » Yes, it was.

"And you heard the woman that worked at Dairy Queen. She remembered seeing one person. That person was dressed in a black trench coat. Do you have a black trench coat?" » Yes, I do.

"Was that you in the black trench coat at the Dairy Queen that night?" » It would have had to have been.

"So it's fair to say, even though she got all the clothes pretty much wrong for Anastasia that night, she remembered this event. She just has a lot of details mixed up. Is that correct?" » I guess.

"Because, if she saw you in the black trench coat, that's what you were wearing that night, right?" » Probably.

"Now, Anastasia immediately began giving you and Justin dirty looks. Is that correct?" » Yes.

"And she immediately began bickering and being very argumentative with Justin and all of you. Isn't that correct?" » Yes. She was upset with having been left out there for so long. She was really angry with everybody.

"It would have been close to three hours sitting out there in the cemetery and Dairy Queen, if her stepmother is correct about dropping her off about 4:20. Isn't that right?" » That's correct.

"She decided to start taking it out on all of you immediately. Is that correct?" » Yeah. She wasn't really upset with all of us for pretty long. She focused in on Justin after that initial encounter, I guess.

"Directing her anger at Justin and forgetting about you?" » Right.

"I have to ask a question. If the whole point of Justin and Anastasia meeting there is to talk about their relationship and she is in such a foul mood, why don't you just stay at Dairy Queen with Kelly and let them go off into the cemetery?" » I don't know. The thought never crossed my mind.

"It made you very uncomfortable to stay with her, I assume?" » Yeah. I don't think anybody likes to be around arguing couples.

"You did drive in Mount Washington and really that's just across the street from the Dairy Queen. Is that right?" » Yes.

"And in Mount Washington, you don't drive around too much, do you?" » We drove around for awhile I think.

"Can you give us an idea for how long you drive around in there?" » Not really. I wasn't paying much attention. I was kind of just daydreaming. So, if I had to estimate, I would say, I don't know, minutes. Maybe fifteen all told.

"Were you pretty focused on just Kelly instead of what was going on there?" » Not really. Like I said, I was just kind of staring up and out into nothing really.

"Mount Washington, about the time you all get there, is closing time. You told the jury you knew about that, right?" » I assumed, yes.

"And it should be pretty empty about that time. Is that correct?" » Yeah.

"You drive in there and you stopped. Do you know if you stopped at this Nelson --" » I didn't know the name of it, but, yes, we did stop there.

"When Mr. Colliver described it in court, did it sound familiar to you?" » Yes.

"And Mr. Colliver described or testified driving up behind the car, people were maybe just getting out or something like that or he either saw them just getting back in, because they saw him drive up. You heard him testify about coming up behind that car. Is that right?" » Yes.

"That was you all, wasn't it?" » Yes.

"Now, you know it wasn't 9 o'clock that night?" » I'm sorry?

"It was not 9 o'clock as he remembers it. Is that correct?" » No. There was no way it could have been.

"He's just mistaken about a small detail, right? But he does see you all there, right?" » Yes.

"And then, as he testified, you all just get in the car and you just drive right out and not in any unusual fashion at all, right?" » That sounded accurate, yes.

"Now, it's after you leave Mount Washington that your version of what happened and Kelly's version of what happened really radically changes. Is that correct?" » Yes.

"That's where you're telling Sergeant Kilgore, as you're telling this jury today, that Justin just pulls out of Mount Washington and just starts driving around. Is that right?" » We pulled out and headed back towards Truman Road. I don't remember if there was anything said about it. I think somebody said something, although I couldn't recall who, about just going back to Justin's condo.

"So that was the discussion, that you all would just go back to Justin's condo?" » Well, I wasn't a part of it, but that's what was said, I believe.

"You came right out of the cemetery right at the intersection of 24 Highway. Is that right?" » Yes.

"And 24 Highway is what you took from 435 to get to the Dairy Queen or are you sure?" » We didn't take 435 to get there.

"What did you do? Take Truman Road?" » Yes. Justin always took Truman whenever he went out to pick Anastasia up, because I remember everyone complained about it. It was a silly way to get there.

"It was a long way to get there, right?" » Yes.

"Long time and long distance?" » Uh-huh.

"So you head back to Truman Road. Fair to say Justin knows Truman Road pretty well then from all his trips out there?" » I guess.

"Anastasia was still bickering, arguing, yelling, and she was ugly to Justin after you left the cemetery?" » Yeah, they were still arguing.

"Why not just take her home?" » I don't know.

"She is three miles away from her house. Why not just take her home? Is there any discussion about that?" » I certainly didn't mention it, and no one else said anything about it, so no.

"So instead you go back to Truman Road, and you're going to drive 40 minutes back into the Plaza?" » Approximately. I don't believe it's quite that long, but it was a fairly long time.

"We would agree there is no fast way to get from Truman Road down to the Plaza. Is that right?" » I would say that's pretty accurate, yes.

"So instead of taking her three miles home, you decide to take her off to the condo, and you're just going along with it, right?" » Yeah. I mean, Kelly and I were just along for the ride from the beginning, so --

"So you get on Truman and you head east and you're headed to Kansas City from Independence. Is that right?" » Yes.

I think Fry goofed on this one, and Byron automatically agreed. Before, Byron and Kelly both described traveling west on Truman Road, not east. And as Fry points out, they were heading to Kansas City from Independence. That's west.

"Nothing for you to stop at between there and the condo. Is that correct?" » That's right.

"Were you going to the condo so Justin and Anastasia could get a little privacy maybe and talk about their relationship? Do you know about that?" » Yeah. I'm trying to remember. I don't remember if someone said something specifically about that, the going back to the condo and Kelly and I taking a walk or something. I really don't remember if that was mentioned or not, but I seem to recall that it was.

"Your statement to Sergeant Kilgore seemed more like you were just going out driving. You really weren't a part of giving directions or having any idea where Justin was headed. Is that right?" » Yeah. That's pretty accurate.

"Fair to say, you just assumed he was going back to the condo. Is that correct?" » Yeah.

"There was no discussions to go back to the condo, was that correct?" » Again, there may have been. I vaguely recall there having been, but I couldn't be sure about that.

"You've had plenty of time to think about that conversation, haven't you?" » Yes.

"Just can't remember it?" » No.

"And you had time two days after her body was found to tell Sergeant Kilgore, yet you had nothing in your statement about that. It was because you couldn't recall it then either?" » Well, a lot of things I said were, for the most part, what happened that was a little out of the ordinary. None of us immediately attributed any special importance to that night. So remembering a lot of things after the fact was kind of difficult. It would be like me asking you what did you do two days ago specifically and breaking it down, conversations that you had. You may or may not remember a lot of things.

"Are you suggesting that, if one of my friends died two days from today, I wouldn't be able to remember what I did with them the last time anybody saw them? Is that what you're suggesting happened to you?" » No. I didn't make myself clear. Again, what I was saying was, because we didn't know at the time that anything really monumental was happening that evening, it was just kind of another day initially. And so I didn't think I'm going to have to remember the conversations as they happened.

"Something monumental, though, does happen on the way down Truman Road when you get to it?" » It was out of the ordinary, yes.

"You wouldn't call it monumental?" » We didn't attribute it as being such, but it became, I guess.

"What you're trying to tell the jury is, when she got out of the car in an area that you described to Sergeant Kilgore as a bad area, two blocks west of the Erotic City and just left, that was not a monumental moment for you?" » At the time it wasn't although I also, at the time, wasn't aware exactly how bad of an area it was.

"By the time you talked to Sergeant Kilgore, you described it as a bad area. Is that right?" » Yes.

"And you knew for sure it was just two blocks west of Erotic City. You made sure you told Sergeant Kilgore about that. Is that correct?" » That was the only landmark I could place, yes.

"I think you told Sergeant Kilgore, when she got out of the car at that time, you just didn't consider anything about it. Is that right?" » I wouldn't say that.

"Do you want me to show you your statement?" » All right.

"Right here it says, 'I mean, we didn't consider anything. She was just going to go call her parents.' Is that your statement?" » Yes.

"She gets out in this area of town. It's about what time?" » Well, somewhere, I would estimate around 7:30.

"And so it's dusk. Is that right?" » No. I think at this point it was pretty dark already.

"Not pitch black?" » I don't recall specifically. I remember it was pretty dark.

"Time of the night and the location didn't cause you to consider anything about this at all?" » Unfortunately, no.

"Now, was Anastasia one of those people you cared about?" » Yes. I was annoyed with her but, yes, ultimately I did care about her.

"Did you do anything about her getting out of that car?" » No, I didn't.

"But you weren't worried about it at all, were you?" » Not at the time, no.

"You expressed no worry at all, did you?" » No.

"What was Justin's reaction?" » He didn't really seem to have too much of a reaction. He was kind of sitting there looking sort of dazed. I remember we sat at the stoplight for a moment after she had gotten out of the car, and we just kind of looked at him and were wondering what was going to happen next and I didn't really know what to say. And obviously Kelly didn't either, because she didn't say anything. We just drove off, and he pretty much drove in silence the whole way. I don't really remember him saying anything until we got back to the condo.

"Did he continue to drive west on Truman Road?" » Yes, he did.

"I'll have to check here. You drove back to the condo and drove directly there. Is that correct?" » Yes, we did.

"And it took you what? About 20 to 30 minutes as a very short estimate of time to get back there?" » Probably closer to 30.

"And when you were there, you stayed there for about a half-hour playing the Nintendo games. Is that correct?" » I believe Abraham paged me just a few minutes after we had exited the car and gone into the condo. So if I was already playing video games with Justin or Kelly, it was just for a few minutes.

"Anybody think to call Anastasia's home?" » No, not at that point.

"You say nobody thought to call Anastasia's home after the half-hour ride home and the half-hour at the condo. Is that correct?" » Not that I recall.

"Did any of the three of you even talk about it?" » No. I didn't want to bring it up, and Kelly was just being quiet also. And Justin, I don't know. He was obviously still upset with what happened. I don't know if he was angry. He didn't really say.

"And then that's when you get your call from Abraham?" » Yes.

"I asked you to remember the drive down Truman Road after she got out. Can I ask you to just stay focused with me on that just a minute?" » Yes.

"I think it's your testimony nobody reacted at all. Is that correct?" » Not that I remember.

"In particular, Justin didn't react to that at all?" » I mean, other than being visibly upset, I don't know. He didn't say anything about it.

"Do you remember, referring to page 21, telling Sergeant Kilgore that Justin said, 'I'm thinking about, you know, tonight I should just kill myself.' Do you remember that?" » Yeah I remember that now. I don't remember those were the exact words he used, but I can't remember specifically what it was that he said.

"That's a strong reaction for you to have forgotten. Don't you agree?" » Yes.

"We talked about his suicide attempts and things that he would do, and you told this jury you were concerned about those things, right?" » At some points, yes.

"At different times in your relationship, right?" » Right.

"Kelly has just gotten out of the car at night --"

Lance objects to the question. Judge Atwell corrects Fry.

"You mean Anastasia just got out of the car?"

Well, at least we know those two are paying attention.

"Dog gone. Anastasia has just gotten out of the car at night in a bad area, startled everybody. Justin drove off, and he said, 'I think I'm just going to go kill myself.' Now, why couldn't you remember that?" » I don't know.

"You remembered that two days later when you talked to Sergeant Kilgore, right? You don't dispute that?" » No, that's right. Although to put that in perspective just a little bit, it wasn't like the second she got out of the car that he said that. It was --

"You told Sergeant Kilgore he said, 'I don't know. All I'm thinking about, you know, tonight, I should just kill myself?' And he said that when you weren't quite halfway back to the condo. That sound about right?" » Yes.

"Okay. Now, with all of this going on, her getting out of the car, him talking about suicide again, getting back to the condo, you do remember you've got Kelly's curfew. Is that correct?" » Yes, that's correct.

"All right. So you get the call from Abraham and then all three of you go over there. Is that correct?" » Yeah. We figured we still had time to go over there and make it back to Kelly's in time.

"And all three of you then leave Abraham's and you go to Kelly's house. Is that correct?" » Yes, it is.

"How much driving time is that?" » Abraham was staying just off maybe a mile, I suppose, from 1-35 and it's approximately a 20 minute drive to Kelly's at that time of night.

"So by the time you get to Kelly's house, that's when somebody finally decides, hey, maybe we better check on Anastasia. And that's the first time. Is that correct?" » Yes. Justin made the phone call.

"When you get to Kelly's house, Kelly is a little late for her curfew, right?" » No. Actually, I think she was early.

"Debbie Moffett didn't think that." » Well, I don't know if it's appropriate for me to say this --

Lance is up like a shot.

"Objection. I object to the form of the question. I don't know that there was even a question there."

Lance was on his toes on this one. Byron was going to say something he probably would have regretted. And the fact of the matter is that Fry didn't actually ask a question. Judge sustains.

"Do you recall Debbie Moffett's testimony?" » Yes.

"Debbie Moffett said that she considered Kelly late. Do you recall it differently?" » Yes I do.

"Now, when you get there, that's why all three of you get into the house, because somebody has thought we better call Anastasia's home. Is that correct?" » No. We were all going to go in anyway and just hang out for just a few minutes.

"All right. You go in just to do some hanging out, and who is it that finally decides we better call Anastasia's house?" » Justin called.

"And when Justin called, were you there in the room?" » Yes, I was.

"When he was having the discussion, did you become aware that he got Francesca on the phone?" » I didn't know who he was talking to, but I assumed it was Anastasia's sister, yes.

"And Francesca started asking Justin some questions, because he stated on the phone the conversation kept going, right?" » Yes.

"And you heard Justin tell the story, right?" » Yes.

"And the story was she got mad, and she got out of the car and just stormed off, right?" » Yes.

"And Francesca has figured it out that it's taken at least an hour, according to the time that Justin finally responds to her, how long she has been out there before anybody thinks to call her home. Is that fair?" » Yes.

"Fair estimate, right?" » Yes.

"And you heard Francesca testify the other day she could hear your voice in the background discussing how to answer what time it happened. You don't dispute that, do you?" » No, I don't.

"And she said you all had a hard time figuring out what time it happened. Is that correct?" » Yes.

"And she asked, 'Where did it happen?' And she heard you two discussing it. Do you remember her testifying that?" » Yes, I do.

"And you had a hard time telling her the location. Do you remember her saying that?" » Yes.

"Did you have a hard time telling her the location?" » I think we were having a discussion over which highway it was, but yes.

"Let me ask you this. Did Justin tell you Francesca said, 'Oh, gosh she just said, if anything happened to her, I'm responsible for it.' Did Justin say that to you too?" » I believe so, yes.

"Is that when you heard Justin say something about committing suicide if something happened to her?" » No.

"It was back on Truman Road that you heard him say that, right?" » Yes.

"Now, Kelly heard it in her house. That's what she said. Do you remember that?" » If she said that, I'm not disputing it.

"Okay. You don't remember Justin saying anything about, 'Fran just said I'm responsible for everything, and I should just go kill myself?' You don't remember that at all?" » No.

"When you left Kelly's house, you considered it still not to be a big deal at all. Is that correct?" » I think at that point it's safe to say we had become more concerned, yes.

"You two did not choose to go back to that area to see if she was still hanging around there, did you?" » No, we didn't.

"Even though you knew she hadn't shown up, and she hadn't called in at all. Is that right?" » Yes, that's correct.

"Were you concerned then about her?" » Like I said, yes, we were starting to get concerned, but it wasn't --

"Did you do anything about it?" » No, we didn't.

"And then you drop the stuff from Abraham at his girlfriend's house?" » Yes.

"And then you just head on to your house. Is that correct?" » Yeah. Justin took me back to my mom's house.

"And when he drops you off, he just says, "See you tomorrow?" » Essentially.

"Had he talked about committing suicide anymore?" » No. And his mood had improved by the time we were over at Abraham's. I think maybe it was just being social that kind of brought it out of him, but he didn't seem all that upset anymore.

"I'm puzzled. Can I ask you a few questions about that? He's thinking about committing suicide as he's driving down Truman Road and an hour later he finds out that the girl he's concerned about and going to commit suicide about has not shown up at her house, has not called her house, and maybe another 40 minutes later, he still doesn't know anything about it, you guys aren't even talking about it, how did he get from suicidal to it was just okay? There was no good news that whole evening about her, Anastasia, and her situation. How did he get better?" » I don't believe he ever was suicidal.

"Why did he say that?" » Again, I mean, I think you may have had to have known Justin to understand that, but I kind of took that as one of the things that he just said.

"But you thought it was significant enough that you told Sergeant Kilgore about it, didn't you?" » After the fact, yes.

"After the fact. The next day, at about 9 o'clock in the morning, Justin calls you. Is that correct?" » Yes.

"And again, I guess at this time you're not concerned about his suicidal nature or what he said about suicide. You just hang up on him because you're sleeping." I didn't hang up on him. He sounded fine over the telephone. He expressed that he had had trouble sleeping and that was really the only thing weird about that, other than the fact it was so early.

"And during the day you, of course, couldn't get hold of him. Is that right?" » Right. Once I had woken up for the day, I actually ended up getting up earlier than usual, but I believe I tried to call him a couple of times, and I wasn't able to get through, so I just went ahead and made other plans.

"You have virtually told this jury what you told Sergeant Kilgore two days after they found Anastasia dead; do you understand that?" » I'm sorry?

"You have virtually today told this jury what you told Sergeant Kilgore two days after Anastasia had been found dead, that Friday. You were out with her Wednesday. That Friday you're giving a statement. You have told this jury virtually the same thing you told Sergeant Kilgore. Is that right?" » Yes.

"And that's what you and your attorney want this jury to believe?" » That's the truth.

"It's hogwash, isn't it? Nobody has believed it from the first time you said it. Isn't that correct?

What the hell kind of question is that?

Lance objects, but without the passion Fry is showing.

"Objection, argumentative."

Court sustains and Fry bears down.

"Your suggestion is that Anastasia gets out of the car in a bad area and walked right past a gas station with a pay phone. Isn't that right? Wouldn't that be a logical conclusion from what you're saying?" » I don't know what happened when she got out of the car, but she didn't use the pay phones, apparently.

"She either walked up nearly a half a mile into Lincoln Cemetery, which was pitch black, or some complete random stranger took her up there. Is that what you would suggest to this jury?" » I don't know what to suggest.

"This young lady that you described as quite a fighter, very determined and very stubborn girl, characterizations of her. Is that correct?" » I believe so.

I'm pretty sure Byron didn't describe Anastasia as a fighter. Those were Fry's words. He said them over and over. He just asked Byron if he agreed. This is all part of the show. This is the hogwash.

"She winds up dead, and she doesn't have a defensive wound on her body, does she?" » Apparently not.

"It's not apparent. You heard the Medical Examiner. There were no defensive wounds. It's true she did not have a defensive wound on her body, did she?" » No.

"And her clothes were not ripped, torn, scraped, in any way; you heard that testimony as well?" » Yes.

"And she wasn't sexually assaulted at all; you heard that testimony too?" » Yes, I did.

"And your suggestion is she just gets up there in Lincoln Cemetery some way without a fight and this just happens to her? The truth is, sir, she went up into that cemetery with three friends, isn't it?" » No.

"And she got out with her boyfriend, and you got out. And you got the shotgun that he bought the month before, and you pointed it at her face, and you shot her, didn't you?" » No, Sir, that's not --

Fry is beginning to cut Byron's answers short. His pace is picking up. He's beginning the crescendo. Answers no longer matter. Just questions and their attendant insinuations. Fry hopes to inflame rather than inform. Hang on.

"You thought this story would work back in 1997, didn't you?" » I'm sorry?

"You thought your explanation of innocence would work back in 1997, didn't you?" » I never made any assumptions. I told the police what I knew.

"At the time you gave that statement, you took Kelly to say the same statement that you had practiced the night before, didn't you?" » No.

"Kelly went with you, didn't she, to give the statement?" » Yes, she did.

"You were both there at the same time, right?" » Yes.

"And that evening you come up with an agreement on what you were going to explain your contact with Anastasia the night before was?" » No.

"You just remarkably told Sergeant Kilgore almost the identical story. Is that correct?" » We told him the truth.

Byron's consistency is portrayed as evidence of deceit. Kelly's inconsistency as evidence of integrity.

"And you thought that Kelly was going to be with you for the rest of your life at that time, didn't you?" » No.

"And you thought you could control Kelly for a long, long time, maybe the rest of your lives, so that the story from Kelly wouldn't come out, didn't you?" » No.

"Once Kelly started getting on drugs, started going to all the psychiatrists, all the counselors, it even occurred to you that she might not even survive to tell the truth, didn't it?" » I never assumed Kelly was suicidal.

"Mr. Case, you don't have the courage to tell this jury that you will accept responsibility for killing Anastasia, do you?" » I don't feel that's a fair question, sir.

"What Justin did was not courageous, was it? Committing suicide was not an act of courage in your mind, was it?" » No.

"But it was his way of accepting responsibility, wasn't it?" » No.

"And you will not accept that responsibility in this courtroom, will you?" » If you're asking me again if I'm guilty, no.

"Your Honor, --

The grand finale.

"-- I have no further questions."

TESTIMONY OF BYRON CASE: PART 4

Lance promises his re-direct will be brief.

"Mr. Case, I want to go back in time to when the prosecutor first started asking you questions. Okay? Think back. Do you remember a question about how Kelly Moffett told you that she had an alcoholic, child-beating father? Do you remember that topic being brought up by the prosecutor?" » Yes.

"Now, all that turned out to not be true, right?" » That's correct.

"That was just another story Kelly told?" » Yes.

"Is that fair?" » Yes.

"All right. Another topic the prosecutor asked you was in October, right after this, you were interviewed by Sergeant Kilgore, correct?" » Yes.

"And you told Kilgore that, when Anastasia got out of the car, quote, 'We didn't think anything about it. She is just going to go call her parents.' End quote. Did you say all that to Sergeant Kilgore?" » I believe so, yes.

"And when you said all that, she is just going to go call her parents, were you aware at that time that no one was home at her house at the time she leaped out of the car?" » No. I assumed somebody was.

"Well, now you have heard the trial testimony, right?" » Yes.

"You have heard now that her mother was not at home, she was at a different house working, and that her dad had been working late. You heard all that, right?" » Yes.

"Sister went to a church meeting. So you know now that no one was at home at that time frame, right?" » Yes.

"But did you know that when you told Kilgore, 'We didn't react. We just thought she was just going to go call her parents?'" » No, we didn't.

"You weren't aware of it, were you?" » No, I wasn't.

"Your Honor, I believe that's all I have."

Really? That's it on cross? There's so much more I want to hear about. So much more I want to learn.

Instead, Atwell asks to see counsel briefly. It's late. It's time to go home. I figure he is going to give us the don't-discuss-it speech. Again.

"Ladies and gentlemen, why don't you be in the jury room shortly after 8:30 tomorrow with the fervent hope that we can begin the closing arguments at that point in time."

Lance jumps in.

"I forgot to say on the record, the defense rests."

Now isn't that a kick in the jurisprudential pants? Byron's own attorney closes the defense case not with a bang, but with a whimper. And even that whimper was an afterthought.

It's all right, though. Judge Atwell says so.

"All right. Come on up."

They huddle again, briefly. Then Atwell gives us the talk.

"The Court again --"

-- will drone on repeating the same warning. I suppose the Court is obliged to do so, again, but have mercy.

"With that being said --"

-- we need to go home, get some rest, and come in tomorrow with our thinking caps on. The judge will read the boring but critical jury instructions, the attorneys will give their dramatic, but irrelevant closing arguments, and the case will be ours. See you bright and early.

INTERLUDE

Missouri is the "Show Me State." It's an informal motto popularized by the otherwise unknown Willard Duncan Vandiver. Willard represented Missouri in the United States Congress from 1897 to 1903. While serving, he uttered a phrase that landed him in Wikipedia a century later. "I come from a state that raises corn and cotton and cockleburs and Democrats, and frothy eloquence neither convinces nor satisfies me. I am from Missouri. You have got to show me."

"Frothy eloquence." I like that. "You have got to show me." I like that too. I figure it wouldn't hurt to have Willard's words of wisdom plastered on the wall of every jury room in America.

The first task for a jury is to select a foreperson. In some jurisdictions, the judge selects the foreperson. I'm not particularly fond of that concept. It feels as if an outsider is making a decision the jury should make for itself.

Usually, the jury selects its own foreperson. In those cases, the initial stage of jury deliberation is usually an extended pregnant pause. Someone might eventually attempt to break the ice and divert attention by saying, "Well, I guess we need to pick a foreman." It might work. It might also result in "I nominate you," followed by nearly unanimous consent.

Out of a group of twelve people, however, it's likely one or two will actually desire the role. Their problem is figuring out how to secure the position without coming across as pushy and overbearing. It would be crude to just say "I'll be the foreperson." A more subtle version, one I used with success during my third trial, is the power grab disguised as reluctant volunteerism. "Well, I guess I would be willing to give it a try if no one else wants to."

For our trial here, no such cunning is necessary. In order to give you, the reader, and my fellow juror, insight into the difficulties and issues involved, I nominate myself as foreperson, and I humbly accept.

On with the deliberations.

ACT II
DELIBERATION

DELIBERATION: INTRODUCTIONS

Good morning. It's Thursday. Day 4.

Yesterday was cold and cloudy, all day. Today it's hot and cloudy, all day. It's already 70 out there, supposed to go over 80, and still be completely overcast. It's an odd start to today's events.

I didn't sleep particularly well again last night. This case is really consuming my thoughts. It's the last thing I'm thinking about before I finally fall asleep, and it's the first thing I'm thinking about when I get up. My wife wanted to know if I would be done today. I told her probably not. I can't see deliberations in this case taking less then a day, even if we stay late.

It's 10:25 AM and we're assembled here in the jury room, ready to begin deliberations. We've already sat through Judge Atwell's reading of the jury instructions. Those instructions are vitally important but Atwell's reading was dreadfully boring. We'll discuss them here, in the jury room, before we deliberate the witness testimony. I'm guessing most juries don't discuss the instructions. If they did, there would be no 20 minute verdicts.

This jury also sat through the closing arguments. Crayon went first. She told us that Anastasia and Justin were speaking to us from the grave, telling us that Byron is guilty. She said Kelly had no motive to lie, and Byron had the best motive of all: he doesn't want to go to prison.

She pointed out that Justin killed himself, Kelly descended into drugs, and Byron refused to take any responsibility. It was a repeat of Fry's soliloquy-like questioning of Byron Case.

Crayon concluded by asking us to tell Byron the gig is up.

Lance closed for the defense. He began by stating as fact that:

> "Anastasia WitbolsFeugen was the victim of a random act of violence committed by some unknown stranger who has never been caught. ... Little did she know there was some stranger up there, maybe a drug addict also desperate for money with a gun looking for easy prey."

Perhaps I was making a sketch or my mind was wandering, because I don't remember that testimony.

Lance then explained that a Not Guilty verdict would mean the case is unsolved, and that might be difficult for us to deal with.

> "To vote Not Guilty, you have to get over that hurdle."

As a skeptical juror, I call that hogwash. There's no hurdle between me and a Not Guilty vote. None. Not Guilty is my default vote. I'll change it to Guilty if and only if these deliberations lead me to believe the State has proved its case beyond a reasonable doubt.

At one point, Lance actually used the oratorical flourish "Blah, blah, blah."

Once Lance was done, Fry closed for the prosecution. Now, I know what you're thinking: Crayon already closed for the prosecution. Well, tough. That's just the way it is, and the way it has always been, at least in this lifetime. The prosecution always goes first, and it always goes last.

Ask prosecutors why they get to go last, and they'll do a little song. They'll do a little dance. They'll squirt a little seltzer down your pants. "We must shoulder the burden of proof, so it's only fair we go last." Or, "We need a chance to rebut the misleading statements defense attorneys are bound to make." Bottom line is that the State writes the rules and the State goes last.

So Crayon presented the opening-closing argument, and Fry presented the closing-closing argument.

Fry began the closing-closing argument in spectacular fashion. He told us Kelly is a liar. Let me check my notes; I tried to get it down verbatim. Here it is.

> "Labeling Kelly Moffett a liar here today isn't a hard thing for you to do. It's when she lied. When she lied, not if she lied. Let me tell you, she lied. She lied to Sergeant Kilgore and she started that lie right after the shooting occurred."

Fry ended by telling us that that Byron is also a liar. I have that one as well.

> "He's a liar. You have to come back and say, "There is a liar." You have to do that. The liar is Byron Case."

Somewhere in between, Fry explained to us how Byron came to be a liar.

> "You know, when you were a kid or when you had kids and they lied to you, they get in trouble many, many more times about the lie than what they did. You know that? I know my dad taught me that way. Caught in a lie. And I know I've done my son the same way.

> "When you lie to a parent, that's where you start. That's where you start. And a parent doesn't care enough to say you're lying and to teach you it's more important not to lie but take responsibility for what you have done, a child begins to think he's a good liar. If nobody ever confronts somebody with that lie, they continue to lie. That's what's happened."

We will not decide this case on such drivel. We will decide this case by carefully deliberating the testimony, in accordance with our instructions.

❖

I guess I should get things going.

"Let's take some of the paper they've left us and make nameplates so we can make sure we all know each other's names. Just put down your first name, or your nickname, or whatever you would like to be called. It'll help during discussions."

So far, so good. No one said it's a stupid idea. The juror names will become familiar as the deliberation continues. Right now, I'll give a quick rundown as people write out their names. Down the long side of the table to your right there's Vivian, Jade, Terry, Chad, and Tony. Down the long side of the table to your left there's George, Liza, Chris, yours truly, and Sondra. Directly across the table at the far end is Christina the bell-ringer.

As juror 6, Christina sat closest to the Judge: front row, right side of the box as we sat in the courtroom. The judge assigned her on day one to be the person who pushes the buzzer button in the jury room when we're all assembled first thing in the morning, or after lunch, or after break. She takes her job seriously.

"I want to say something important up front. I strongly advise, in fact I implore you to withhold, at least for now, any opinion or conclusion regarding the guilt or innocence of Byron Case. Nothing more surely and more quickly leads to a hung jury than jurors staking hard claims early on. If you have an opinion which you've so far wisely kept to yourself, you can change your mind later without losing face. But if you make a bold pronouncement now before we've even started deliberating, it's going to be tough later to change your public declaration.

"During my first trial, a drive by shooting, I served as an alternate. I didn't deliberate, but I talked to the other jurors afterwards. I wanted to find out why everything went so badly in the jury room. Turns out one juror jumped in early with 'I work with those people and that's exactly the kind of thing they do.' That was followed immediately by a juror who saw things somewhat differently. She came back with 'I don't care what anyone says, I'm not voting guilty.' The jury ended up compromising on a relatively minor count of evading arrest."

What struck me wasn't the verdict, it was the breakdown of the jury process. I decided then that if I ever deliberated, I would cleverly maneuver my way into the lofty position of foreperson, caution my fellow jurors against such rash behavior, and lead them to the promised land of a unanimous verdict. In my second trial, that's exactly what happened. It was a thing of beauty. My third trial, though, had a few blemishes. My fourth needed CPR. Hopefully I've learned from my mistakes and I can take advantage of that experience here.

"Let's talk about the jury instructions first."

I can sense the disappointment. We've been waiting patiently all this time to talk about the case, and everyone wants to get on with the juicy stuff.

"I know you all have opinions you want to share. I do too. Although it may not seem like it, this is really the best way to ensure we all get to talk without violating our oath. Jury instructions give us an outline of how we're to do our job. Talking about the instructions first will also help us learn about each other and get a consensus on a relatively low-stress subject before we get into the more controversial testimony."

Vivian, Jade, Terry, Sondra. Now Chad, Tony, George, Liza, and Chris. I'm losing them. I can see it in their faces. Everyone except you, me, and the bell ringer.

"I propose further, for the same reason, that we deliberate the testimony of Kelly and Byron last, after we've discussed the testimony of all other witnesses."

That didn't help. I might be the first foreperson impeached within the first half-hour of deliberations.

"This will give us the best chance of fairly assessing the testimony of these two critical witnesses. In between the instructions and Kelly's testimony, we'll discuss the witnesses in the order they testified.

"We won't take any preliminary votes. Our first vote will come after we've discussed the jury instructions and the testimony of all the witnesses."

Most of them seem okay with that. I guess I'm over the rough patch. Wait until they hear the next part.

"I think we should take this deliberation slowly and methodically. As a rule of thumb, a disciplined jury deliberation takes about one day for each day of trial, at least for short trials such as this one."

Wow. Vivian looks shocked. A few others are visibly restless.

"If we're going to review all the evidence before we reach our verdict, we need to go over the testimony of each witness. With twelve of us having an opportunity to talk about each of the witnesses, I don't see how the process can go much faster. How can we justify a short cut when so much is at stake? So I'd plan on being here tomorrow, and Monday. We'll just have to see how it goes.

"Any questions?"

Vivian's hand is up like a shot.

"Vivian."

Her six-year-old grandson has asthma and he's scheduled to see a specialist on Monday. They've been waiting for months to get in, and she absolutely, positively cannot be here as late as Monday. I ask if someone else can take him. That's a mistake. The boy's parents aren't around, her husband is dead, she's the only one, it's none of my business anyway, and she doesn't want to talk about it. She just can't be here Monday and that's final. She's being very nice about it, but I feel like I've been hit with a brick.

I almost mention that she should have had herself excused from jury duty rather than cut things so close, but I catch myself.

She has an idea. Why don't we just take a preliminary vote to see where we all stand? If we all plan on voting the same way, there won't be any need for three days of deliberation. Chad and George jump in and agree with her. Chad, it turns out has a vacation day scheduled for Monday, and he doesn't want to spend it in here. I'm not sure what George's issue is.

"Well, Vivian, I'm pretty concerned about the idea of a preliminary vote. It'll short circuit what's supposed to be a deliberative process. It will encourage people to stake positions early on and it'll therefore make it harder to come to unanimous consent later.

"I know that's not of any comfort for you, so here's what I propose. Let's prepare a note for the judge and let him decide how to handle it. Maybe he'll excuse us for the day."

Fat chance. But I've shifted the bad guy onus onto the judge.

"Maybe he'll replace you with an alternate. While we're waiting for a response, we'll proceed as we planned.

"And he'll figure something out. That work for you?"

She's willing to give it a shot. She writes out a note, Christina rings the bell. Smooth as silk.

DELIBERATION: JURY INSTRUCTIONS

"There's only one set of instructions. I think we each should have a set. So when the bailiff arrives, I'm going to ask him for eleven more copies."

I give everyone a big smile, like I'm going to get each of them something nice for Christmas.

"He'll relay that request to the judge along with Vivian's note. Then we'll each have a copy. Not only that, we'll give them something to talk about out there. As long as deliberations last, both the prosecution and the defense will be reading tea leaves trying to figure out what's going on in here. Our request for additional jury instructions will stir up some tea."

I give another smile. Some smile back. I think they like the idea of messing with the heads outside this room. It empowers them a little. That's good. We are in fact empowered and we need to realize that.

"Until we get the additional copies, assuming we ever get them, we'll proceed with just the one."

The bailiff arrives. We hand him Vivian's note, I ask for eleven more copies of the instructions, and he leaves without any visible reaction.

"We have seven instructions we must follow. I would like to start with Instruction 5. It specifies the elements the State must prove beyond a reasonable doubt before we can vote Guilty on murder in the first degree. I think we should focus on that instruction first."

It's like talking to air. This isn't what they signed up for. Most were ready to have a rip-roaring discussion of the case. They've been thinking about it since day one, keeping silent about it, as is proper. They figured if they could just get to the deliberations, they could finally vent all their thoughts.

"Instruction 5 tells us that we must find Byron Case Not Guilty of murder in the first degree unless we determine that the State has proved beyond a reasonable doubt each and every one of the following elements."

As I read each element, I write it on the left side of the marker board hanging from the wall behind me.

- On October 22, 1997
- In the county of Jackson, State of Missouri,
- Byron Case killed Anastasia WitbolsFeugen by shooting her
- After deliberation for any length of time
- While knowing that shooting her would probably kill her

"One of the elements the State must prove beyond a reasonable doubt, for example, is that Byron killed Anastasia by shooting her. If we conclude that Byron killed her, but did so by stabbing her, our oath would require us to vote Not Guilty. Does that make sense?"

Heads are nodding, because it's an easy scenario. Nothing to worry about here. It's pretty obvious she was shot.

"Some other odd scenarios are more likely but still unusual. If we decide, for example, the State failed to prove Anastasia was killed in Jackson County, we must vote Not Guilty. If we conclude that Anastasia was killed elsewhere, but we're not sure where, we must vote Not Guilty. If we conclude that the State never established that Lincoln Cemetery was located in Jackson County, we must vote Not Guilty."

Terry, Juror 10, wants me to wait a minute. He wants to know if I would vote Not Guilty even if I thought Byron killed Anastasia but the prosecution forgot to mention that it happened in Jackson County. And I respond "Absolutely!"

In my head.

To Terry, I say:

"I don't think I'd have any choice. The instruction seems pretty clear. If they don't prove each and every element of the count beyond a reasonable doubt, I'm bound by my oath and by the Constitution to vote Not Guilty. I wouldn't be happy about it, that's for sure. And I'd be pretty pissed off at the prosecution for screwing up so badly. But I assure you it would be bad strategy on their part to think I'll clean up their mess by violating my oath.

"So I understand how you feel, and I can't tell you what you should do if it ever came to something like that. It would be between you and your conscience.

Terry informs me that the room temperature in hell might be somewhat below average before he would set free someone he knows to be guilty. All I can do at this point is plant a seed.

"Fair enough. It's something we might all think about. The shooting and county elements aren't going to be controversial, I don't think. A more likely issue might be related to the date of Anastasia's death. Perhaps she wasn't killed on October 22. Her body was found on October 23. No one other than Kelly bothered to tell us a single thing about the time of death.

"One possible scenario is that Kelly is fabricating her story, but that Byron went back after midnight and killed Anastasia."

This has occurred to a number of them. The head nodding begins anew.

"Assuming, just assuming, we reject Kelly's version of events, we would then have no idea when Anastasia was killed. For that reason alone, we would be obliged to vote Not Guilty, even if we thought Byron went back later and killed her.

"What do you think, Terry?"

He doesn't have enough information right now to make a decision on my hypothetical scenario. Maybe he would, maybe he wouldn't. Depends.

Vivian is slouching in her chair. She's not really into this right now. There's a knock on the door. It opens, and there's the bailiff with a stack of paper. It's eleven more copies of the jury instructions. They're still slightly warm from the copying machine. He tells us the judge would like to speak to Vivian. We're supposed to put our deliberations on hold while she's out of the jury room. George makes a break for the bathroom.

I pass out the nice warm jury instructions. Having nothing else to do, people begin thumbing through them. I notice several people turn to Instruction 5, the one dealing with murder in the first degree.

The buzzer rings. That's our cue to head for the courtroom.

When we arrive, I see Vivian sitting in her usual chair, alone in the jury box. Juror 11, back row, second from the right as we sit. The alternates are sitting in their not so good chairs just to right of the jury box. They don't look happy. I don't blame them. Alternates get all the drudgery of jury duty and none of the glamour.

The prosecutors are here, as is Byron Case and his attorney. They're all staring at us as we walk in and take our customary seats.

The judge tells us that he has no guidance or input into how long we might deliberate. That's entirely up to us. As long as we are in deliberation, however, we must show up on time, every day court is scheduled, unless he so directs us otherwise. If our deliberations continue into Monday, and he's not telling us whether they should or should not, he wants to make that clear, but if they continue into Monday then we will start Monday at 10:30 AM rather than 9:30 AM. Our lunch break will be reduced from 90 minutes to 60 minutes, and we will leave at 6 PM, a half hour later than usual.

He asks us if we understand. We nod. A few say "Yes, Your Honor." He excuses us to continue our deliberations.

I take a quick glance at the public seating. Friends and family are waiting on each side of the aisle. I'm guessing that's who they are. They see me glance at them, pleading with their eyes. I look away. At least one side is going to be terribly, terribly disappointed. It reinforces for me that this is serious business.

❖

Vivian is beaming. Judge Atwell called her doctor and kindly asked if he could reschedule her appointment for earlier in the morning. The doctor was very accommodating. Imagine that.

The other jurors congratulate her. She took on the system, stood her ground, and won. It doesn't happen often.

I'm guessing the Judge elected not to use an alternate because it's early and he's already wary of this jury. He's going to save the alternates just in case we continue to behave strangely.

I'm glad he didn't replace Vivian with one of the alternates. We would have had to start deliberations from scratch. True, we haven't progressed very far, but there's already a certain rhythm that would be disrupted by losing one of our own, even at this early stage. That's what happens when an alternate shows up. That makes him an automatic pariah. Being an alternate really sucks.

"I'm glad that's taken care of, Vivian. Congratulations. Now back to the jury instructions."

Did I hear a low moan?

"The remaining six instructions spell out rules and give guidance on how we're supposed to determine if the prosecution proved its case. We'll consider each instruction, briefly."

A mock cheer rises from the far corner of the room, and everyone smiles. I smile back, hoping I'm unifying the jury in spite of themselves.

"Instruction 1 tells us that we must follow the instructions. It instructs us to determine the facts of the case, and determine them only from the evidence and reasonable inferences drawn from the evidence. We are to be fair and impartial, and act without fear or prejudice.

"We're to decide which witnesses are believable and which are not. In making our decision, we may take into consideration: the witness' manner while testifying; their ability and opportunity to observe and remember; any interest, bias or prejudice they may have; and the reasonableness of their testimony in light of all of the evidence.

Sounds reasonable, right?"

Heads nod.

"Well, I have a problem with two of the four items we can consider."

Shoulders slump.

"I'm not a big fan of discerning truth from demeanor. I think people tend to interpret the demeanor of others with a bias that simply reinforces pre-conceived notions. The prosecution tried to convince us we should believe Kelly because she answered well, and disbelieve Byron because he answered badly. I call that hogwash."

A couple of smiles. I've pilfered Fry's word. Anyway, it's an inherently funny word.

"I much prefer relying on evidence. That's why I'm a big fan of items two and four, the ability to know and remember, and the reasonableness in light of other testimony. Could Kelly really have observed what she claimed to see? Was her testimony consistent with the other evidence? Was Byron's inconsistent? I'll take evidence any day. I'll pass on demeanor."

I'm pretty sure they don't all agree, but no one seems willing to take up the challenge.

"That leaves the interest, bias, or prejudice the witness might have. In other words, this instruction tells us we can consider the motive each witness has for lying. This will sound strange at first, but I hope I'll be able to defend my position successfully. I think we should consider everyone's motive to lie, except for the defendant."

"What!?" It's Terry again. Juror 10. He thinks I must be kidding him. There's an adverb before kidding, but I'm pretending I didn't hear it. George agrees with Terry. So does Tony, and Sondra, and Chad. Terry speaks for the group.

"Of course he's got a motive to lie. We all heard the prosecution. He has the biggest motive of all. He doesn't want to go to jail. And it's right there."

He turns to page two of his copy of the jury instructions, stands up, holds the instruction for all to see, and puts his finger smack dab on Instruction 1.

After showing it to everyone, panning first left then right, he reads it aloud, slightly edited, underlining the salient portions with volume.

"In determining the believability of a witness and the weight to be given to the testimony of a witness, you may take into consideration . . . any interest, bias or prejudice the witness may have."

It's right there in the first instruction, and I've been telling them they must follow the instructions, and now I'm telling them not to follow the instructions.

He sits down. Everyone turns towards me.

"I agree with Terry that Byron has a motive to lie. All defendants do. I assume none of them want to go to jail. However, and this is a monstrously gigantic however, we're supposed to presume Byron Case to be innocent. It seems to me that if we refuse to believe him simply because he's the defendant, then we're not granting him the presumption of innocence.

"Instruction 4 covers that issue. I'll discuss it now and come back to the others. Instruction 4 tells us we must not consider the charges against Byron Case to be evidence. We must presume him innocent. We must not vote Guilty unless we determine the prosecution has proved its case beyond a reasonable doubt."

Almost everyone is thumbing through their copy of the instructions, looking for Instruction 4. For a moment, the room is silent except the sound of papers shuffling. Terry takes a pass. Might be wise if I give them time to find it and read it for themselves. I catch my breath.

"Personally, I think this instruction is the most important. It's the one that strikes fear in the hearts of prosecutors and gives a glimmer of hope to the defendant. While Theresa Crayon told us about Instruction 1, she never uttered a peep about Instruction 4. She didn't mention that we're supposed to presume the defendant to be innocent. She didn't mention that we're not supposed to consider the charges against him to be evidence against him. She was hoping we wouldn't actually read the instructions.

"By asking us to disbelieve Byron Case simply because he's the defendant, she's asking us to deprive him of the presumption of innocence. She's asking us to disbelieve him simply because he was the only one in the courtroom charged with a crime. She's asking us to relieve her of the burden of proof. I'm simply not going to do that.

"I'm not arguing we should automatically believe Byron Case. I'm arguing only that we should observe Instruction 4, that we assess his testimony in the same fashion as all other witnesses. Did he have the ability to observe and remember? Was his testimony reasonable? Did it comport with the other evidence?

"Each of you can weigh the evidence according to your interpretation of the instructions, but I'm immovable on this point. I won't deprive this defendant or any defendant of his basic Constitutional rights."

There's a knock on the door. The bailiff pops his head in and informs us that it's lunchtime. The jury room will be secure during lunch, so we can leave anything we want to leave, except ourselves. We won't be allowed to stay. Lunch break will last ninety minutes. Jury room will be open again in eighty minutes. Once we're all assembled, we need to ring the buzzer so that the court will know we've returned and are continuing our deliberations.

George bolts for the bathroom.

Lots of murmuring as people make their way out the door.

❖

As usual, I keep to myself during lunch. I take advantage of the hot dog cart and the park nearby. The weatherman was right: it's warm but overcast. I sit in the park, eat my dog, mustard and ketchup only, and wash it down with a diet Mountain Dew. I go for seconds. I watch the passersby, and think about the trial.

I conclude I'm satisfied with how we're doing. I managed to steer us clear of some of the mistakes I've seen during my previous deliberations.

I stroll around the park and the downtown area, then head back to the jury room.

I arrive five minutes early. Christina the bell-ringer is already there, as are Chad and George and a couple others. Everyone returns on time except for Tony. He's six minutes late. When he arrives, we give him the evil eye, but no one says anything. As soon as he enters, Christina walks over and rings the buzzer to let the court know we're back in business.

"Okay, looks like we're all here. Just a couple more minutes on the instructions, then we'll be discussing Deputy Epperson.

"Instruction 3 tells us we must follow all the instructions, not just some of them. It reinforces the point I've been trying to make. Instruction 4 tells us we must presume the defendant to be innocent. Instruction 1 says only that we may, not that we must, that we may consider motive when weighing testimony. I suggest that the only way we can follow both of these instructions is to presume Byron Case innocent and not use his desire to avoid prison as a reason to disbelieve him.

"Each of you will have to make your own choice. If anyone would like the floor to state their case, feel free."

No takers. Mostly they want to move on.

"Instructions 2 and 7 aren't particularly controversial, at least in my opinion. They tell us we must not consider questions, objections, opening statements, or closing statements as evidence. We must not speculate as to how a witness might have answered a question. We must disregard any answer, statement, remark, or exhibit the judge told us to disregard.

"This is, of course, easier said than done. We'll try to observe these instructions by explicitly summarizing the evidence of each witness, and just the evidence. We'll try to ignore all the rants, pleas, and obfuscation of the opening and closing statements. Even if we overheard or observed something during a sidebar, we'll not bring it up in here. We'll try to ignore the frothy eloquence and we'll make them show us.

"Finally --"

A soft cheer rises from the far side of the table.

"-- that brings us to Instruction 6, the last one to discuss. It tells us we must discuss this case fully with one another. We are to consider all the evidence and we are to listen to the views of our fellow jurors. After discussing all the evidence, and only after discussing all the evidence, each of us must decide our own vote. Our verdict must be unanimous, either Guilty or Not Guilty.

"And that's where we're headed now. We're going to begin considering the evidence by discussing the testimony of Deputy Epperson."

DELIBERATION: DEPUTY DAVID EPPERSON

"Here's how I'd like to proceed. Everyone, if you will, please scour your notes and your memories for any significant evidence testified to by David Epperson. Let's try not to consider quite yet what it might mean. Let's simply organize the facts as Epperson claimed them to be. I'll write on the board what we agree to be the significant facts, right here, just to the right of the elements for murder one. Once we have the summary up, then we'll discuss what it might mean.

"I'll begin. First off, Epperson testified he was a deputy with the Jackson County Sheriff's Office and that he discovered the body in Lincoln Cemetery."

I add those two pieces of evidence to the board.

"Now let's work around the room. We'll go clockwise. Sondra, just one piece of evidence."

Sondra looks at her notes and adds that Epperson found the body at 3:44 AM on October 23, 1997. Christina adds he was two-tenths of a mile from the entrance when he saw her lying there. Tony remembers that no one else was around. Chad says she was lying on her back, and her arms were above her head. Terry notes that her eyes were open. A number of people, including myself, found that creepy.

So around and around we go. When the unique evidence starts running low, people take a pass. Then I open it to anyone with anything left. When we're done, the list looks like this:

- Deputy for Jackson County Sheriff's Office
- Discovered body in Lincoln Cemetery, 0.2 miles from entry; routine patrol
- October 23, 1997, 3:44 AM; very dark, no lights, leaves on trees, pitch black
- No traffic, no one else around
- Lying on her back; arms above head; eyes open
- Gunshot wound to face, from bottom of nose into mouth
- Not breathing; no pulse; skin cold to touch; skin bluish gray
- Puddle of blood behind head
- Called for assistance; guarded gate after investigators arrived
- No ID; only item found was a key chain (so he was told)
- Body was that of Anastasia WitbolsFeugen (so he was told)

"Okay, there's his testimony, nice and concise. None of us alone could have remembered everything here, and none of us has all this in our notes. Okay, Jade came close. She seems to have a good set of notes. But for most of us, there's just too much to remember, too many witnesses."

"Okay, this next step is not pleasant. We're going to look at the picture of Anastasia's body."

I go to the evidence box which is sitting on the floor behind me. I pull out a manila folder. I open it and look inside. It's gruesome, but I try to control my reaction. As I study the photo, the room is absolutely silent. I give them my assessment.

"This photo is horrible. When you look at it, you feel like you just walked into someone's most private place at just the wrong time. But this photo is an important piece of evidence, and we're supposed to review the evidence before we decide our vote. So I'm going to pass it around. No one has to look at it. Anyone who does look, please be respectful."

The image is truly awful. She has that terrible gunshot wound in the middle of her face. I think Epperson is wrong in his description. It looks to me like the wound extends from her upper lip to the bridge of her nose, not the bottom of her nose.

She's lying on her back. Her arms are above her head and her eyes are partially open, just like Epperson said. One eye is more open than the other. One iris appears darker than the other.

Her shoulder length hair is fanned out above her head. From the photo, it looks to be light brown in color.

Her body is perpendicular to the roadway. Her heels are just touching the road. Her head and most of her body are on the grass.

The pool of blood beneath her head is not as large as I thought it might be. There's some blood running down her face from the wound. Not much though. It looks like most of the blood beneath her came from the back of her head.

She's wearing a tan coat with a beige or gray sweater underneath. The jeans are dark, maybe black. The shoes are black, low-cut, with thick soles. The clothing is intact, not torn.

She looks petite, sad, and lonely. I am suddenly jarred by the fact that my own daughter is very close to her in age. After all the testimony, objections, and admonitions, I realize I had become desensitized to the horrific violence suffered by this young woman. At this moment, looking at this photo, she is more human to me than she was during the trial. She is a beautiful young person, and the tragedy of her death chokes in my throat. I stand up, walk to the window and stare into the distance.

Behind me, the photo makes it way around the room. I hear two of the ladies gasp. I hear Vivian decline to look at all. When the photo has made its way around, I leave the comfort of the distant view, retrieve the photo, and return it to the evidence box. There is a duty to complete and an oath to fulfill.

"Did anyone see anything that looked strange?"

Chad makes a weak attempt at a joke, but it falls flat. Very flat.

"What about her hair?"

Liza lights up for the first time. She realizes what I'm asking about.

"It's all fanned out."

The guys give her the so-what look. Sondra and Christina nod, and Vivian looks up suddenly to give her a smile.

"Epperson didn't mention that, did he?"

He certainly did not. Liza explains what it might mean. When a woman wants her hair to lie nice and smooth and even, she starts by tilting her head forward and brushing her hair over her head, from back to front. Then she throws her head back. That causes her hair to fan out and fall evenly onto her back. Liza isn't sure Anastasia's hair would be fanned out like that just because she fell backwards.

Jade makes the point I was wondering about. Her hair might have been arranged for her after she was shot, by whoever shot her.

Chad chimes in with the thought that she might have been dragged. It would explain why her hair is fanned out like that and why her arms are above her head.

He gets up, walks to the evidence box, pulls out the folder and takes another look at the photo. He says he doesn't see anything that looks like drag marks. He hands the folder to me. I can't see any drag marks either. I pass the photo around again. This time everyone looks with more skeptical eyes.

It's Sondra's turn to notice something.

"There's no blood splatter on the ground."

As far as we know, there's no blood splatter anywhere. She thinks there should be some somewhere, but no one talked about it. We went through an entire murder trial, a gunshot wound straight through the head, and we heard nothing about blood splatter. Not on the ground. Not on Justin's clothes. Not on Byron's clothes. Not on the car. Nothing. She wishes we'd heard from a blood splatter expert. Several others agree.

The folder makes its way back to me and I return it to the evidence box. I ask for a five minute break. We won't have time to leave the jury room, but I need five minutes free from the intensity of the moment. Viewing that photo twice was more stressful than I anticipated. Some of the jurors lean back, sighing or stretching.

Vivian beats George to the bathroom. She's not as quick. Just closer.

❖

"Okay, everyone ready to go?"

A few grunts. I take that to mean yes.

"Because we've been disciplined in our deliberation, we have before us, on the board, Epperson's testimony sitting right beside the elements the State needs to prove murder one. Let's go through the elements and see which Epperson has helped prove.

"First one says that the murder had to take place on October 22, 1997. But as you can see, Epperson discovered the body on October 23, 1997. Since no one established time of death in this trial, not that I recall anyway, I suggest that his testimony does not contribute to proving this element."

Terry points out that Epperson said her skin was cold to the touch, so she had been out there a while, and it was only 3:44 in the morning when he found her. He thinks that means she probably was killed the previous day, else she still could have been a little bit warm. I try to disagree without offending.

"Seems to me that's a bit speculative. If we'd heard those words directly from Dr. Young, or Dr. Blanchard who testified in his place, or even the investigator from the ME's office who never testified, then I would more readily accept it as true. But none of that happened. Either the State didn't think they could prove time of death, or they didn't want to. I'm unwilling to accept the issue never occurred to them.

"So while I see your point, I don't believe Epperson's testimony comes anywhere close to proving Anastasia was murdered on the 22nd."

Well Terry sure as hell doesn't think there's any proof Anastasia was killed on the 23rd, either. I concede the point.

"The next element is that Anastasia was killed in Jackson County. What did Epperson contribute towards proving that element? Terry?"

Terry points out that Epperson worked for the Jackson County Sheriff's office and he was on routine patrol, ergo [he actually used the word "ergo"] that's where she was killed. Terry recalls, correctly I believe, that Epperson actually said that Lincoln Cemetery was in Jackson County.

Liza points out that she might have been killed elsewhere and dropped off at the cemetery. Terry counters with the pool of blood beneath her head. Sondra is still angry about the blood splatter issue and re-ignites.

"Where's the blood? They never talked about the blood splatter."

I try to keep it moving.

"I think they probably have this one covered, but I've got to say they were pretty lackadaisical here. I think they should have made this point painfully obvious to us. Let's move on.

"The third element was that Byron Case killed Anastasia. I believe the defense asked Epperson only one question on cross, and that was if he knew who killed Anastasia, or something like that."

Jade corrects me. As I said, she seems to have the best notes. Horton Lance asked him if he could tell whether Anastasia was killed by a stranger or an acquaintance. Epperson said "no."

"So that would be no. The fourth element is that --"

Chris, the quiet one, is apologetic but feels he simply must interrupt. If we're not going to take things for granted, then at this point, we're only assuming that the body was that of Anastasia. Epperson didn't know her personally. No friends or relatives came by and identified her while he was there. He didn't compare dental records. He only heard later that the body was that of Anastasia WitbolsFeugen.

Wish I had thought of that.

"Good thought, Chris. Not only that, he didn't even say who he heard that from. And now --"

Terry want's to know if we're kidding him. He thinks we must be, we gotta be. He thinks we're nit-picking, and he doesn't care for it.

"Fine. We don't really have to deliberate that since it's been established by other evidence. Moving on. The fourth element is that Anastasia died as the result of being shot. Epperson said he observed what appeared to be a gunshot wound, but I think that comes up short of proof."

Terry points out with some enthusiasm that the female ME who testified, Dr. Chase Blanchard, said that the cause of death was a gunshot wound to the head. I concede his point, and express my confidence we'll see that to be true when we consider Dr. Chase's testimony.

"The fifth element is that Byron Case deliberated before he shot Anastasia, even if he did so only for a microsecond. Epperson has nothing to add here. Nor does he have anything to add to the last point, that Byron Case shot Anastasia knowing it would probably kill her.

"So that covers Epperson's testimony. But there's something missing here that bothers me a lot. Epperson was the only one from the Jackson County Sheriff's office who testified. What about all the investigators who showed up? Why didn't any of them testify? What about the oft mentioned Sergeant Kilgore? Wasn't he the lead investigator? Why didn't he testify? Where was he?

"How about the investigator from the ME's office? He went to the scene. We don't even know his name. Why didn't he testify? Why is Epperson, who is not an investigator, who was asked to secure one of the entrances to the cemetery while others investigated, why was he the only one who provided testimony for the sheriff's office?

"It makes me suspicious, as if something is out there they don't want us to know about. Now, unless anyone has anything else on Epperson, we'll move on to the witness after Kelly. Kelly was next but we're going to hold discussion of her testimony until last. Next after Kelly is her mother, Debra."

DELIBERATION: DEBRA MOFFETT

Debra didn't claim to be a witness to Anastasia's death, so she can't provide any direct evidence. She does, however, provide times for some events, and I really like timeline data. A good timeline can be difficult to put together when restricted to only the bits and pieces we get to hear as jurors, but it can really pay off. People can fudge the truth, and people can just lie outright, but people can't be in two different places at the same time, and time can't run backwards.

"So let's do what we did with Epperson. Let's work around the room and summarize the evidence from Debra Moffett's testimony. Bonus points for anyone with specific times."

I erase what we had for Epperson, after adding his summary to my notebook. Then we start adding the evidence from Debra Moffett's testimony.

- Off work at 2:30 PM; picked Kelly up from school
- Home around 3 PM; Kelly went upstairs for "quite a while"
- Justin and Byron picked Kelly up; curfew was 8:30 PM
- Around 9:15 PM, Justin and Byron dropped Kelly off back home
- Debra upstairs; heard whispering and a phone call
- Kelly told her Anastasia got out of car
- Learned of Anastasia's death next day
- Byron and Kelly continued to see each other daily
- After holiday, Kelly started complaining about Byron
- Following spring, Byron upset by Kelly's drug use and infidelity
- Kelly deteriorated; in therapy; never mentioned homicide to therapist
- December 1999, Kelly broke up with Byron
- March 2000, Kelly told her Justin killed Anastasia
- June 2000, Debra told Kelly's rehab counselor what Kelly told her
- Kelly ran away from rehab; told her father that Byron killed Anastasia
- August 2000, Kelly told rehab counselor Justin killed Anastasia
- 20 minutes later, told mother and rehab counselor Byron killed Anastasia
- Rehab counselor recommended lawyer; met with lawyer next day
- Kelly called and recorded Byron at urging of Sheriff's department

"Something that jumps out at me is that Kelly changed her story frequently. Looking at the board, here's a list of who Kelly said killed Anastasia:

"Neither Justin nor Byron; as she told Debra that night.

"Neither, neither, neither, neither, neither; as she told Sergeant Kilgore five times.

"Justin; as she told Debra.

"Byron; as she told her father.

"Justin; as she told Maggie.

"And finally back to Byron, as she told both Maggie and Debra just minutes after telling Maggie it was Justin.

"For me, that's a problem."

Vivian speaks up. If her son ever came home and told her that he had witnessed a murder, she would be on the phone to the police like yesterday. She wants to know why Debra or Kelly's father didn't call the police. I don't have an answer for her.

Vivian flips through her notes, then answers her own question.

"It's because they knew she a lied about people like that. They knew she told Byron her father was an alcoholic who beat her. They figured she was lying again, especially since she changed her story back and forth."

Everyone lets Vivian's observation just lay there. No one comments on it, so I move on.

I rip four sheets of paper from my notebook. On each sheet, I add one time line item. Then I place the sheets of paper in the middle of the table, so the time line runs down the length of the table. So far, here's what we have.

3:00 PM	Kelly home from school
?:?? PM	Byron and Justin pick Kelly up
9:15 PM	Kelly returns home
3:44 AM	Epperson finds Anastasia's body

It's not much yet, but it's a start. We're only two witnesses into our deliberation. That's just two out of what, twenty?

"Unless anyone has anything more they want to say about Debra Moffett, we'll move on."

DELIBERATION: DIANE MARSHALL

Diane Marshall is, or was, Anastasia's step-mother. As most everyone else who testified, she has no direct knowledge of what happened among the four teens that night. Her testimony is of value to us because she added some important elements to our timeline.

Once again, we work around the room, but don't get too far before people start taking a pass. We come up with only the following:

- Picked Francesca up from school after work
- When they arrived home, Anastasia was waiting, wanting ride to Mount Washington Cemetery
- Dropped Anastasia at Mount Washington, just before 4:20 PM
- Anastasia scheduled to meet her friends at 5:00 PM
- Diane had second thoughts; dropped Francesca at hairdresser and then searched for Anastasia at 6:00 PM, unsuccessfully
- Bob, Anastasia's father, searched later that night, unsuccessfully

"I can't recall where I heard it in the testimony, but it seems like Anastasia lived three miles east of Mount Washington, up Truman Road, by the Truman House. I assume that Truman House is where Harry Truman lived. He was from Independence. The point is that we can assume it shouldn't take too long to drive from Mount Washington and Anastasia's house. In fact, people can walk three miles in an hour without too much effort. I do it every day. Well, most every day.

"So if Diane dropped Anastasia just before 4:20, they left the house some time after 4:00 PM, even accounting for the traffic that Diane talked about. We can add a few elements to the timeline."

I rip out four more sheets from my notebook. I record one timeline item per sheet, add the sheets to the timeline in the center of the table, rearranging them as appropriate. Now our timeline is beginning to take shape. The new items are shown in bold below.

3:00 PM Kelly home from school

?:?? PM Byron and Justin pick Kelly up

4:05 PM **Anastasia leaves home**

4:15 PM **Anastasia dropped at Truman entrance to Mount Washington**

5:00 PM **Anastasia expects to meet Justin at Mount Washington**

6:00 PM **Diane cannot find Anastasia at Mount Washington. Returns to her mother's house**

9:15 PM Kelly returns home

3:44 AM Epperson finds Anastasia's body

"Not bad after only three witnesses. I'm guessing there will be a couple of surprises if we keep with it. Let's take a ten-minute break."

George races unopposed for the bathroom.

DELIBERATION: FRANCESCA WITBOLSFEUGEN

Francesca is Anastasia's sister. Her testimony is similar to Diane Marshall's in that she contributes primarily to the timeline of events.

Around we go, this time working clockwise beginning with Jade. I mix up the order and starting point so we don't get into a rut. Francesca had more content in her testimony than did her step-mother.

- Diane picked her up at school at 3:30 PM; went straight home
- Anastasia was waiting; eager to go to Mount Washington
- Diane gave Anastasia a ride to Mount Washington
- Justin called 15 minutes later; said he was in Lenexa; surprised Anastasia left
- She became concerned; talked to her father about Anastasia being alone in the cemetery
- Went for haircut then to prayer meeting; left 6:45 PM; returned 8:30 to 9 PM
- Took another call from Justin at 9:30; Justin told her of a fight
- Remembers saying "You mean she's been out there an hour?"
- Father (Bob) and step-mother (Diane) arrive home between 10 and 10:20 PM
- She did not tell either of them about the second call from Justin
- Bob received a call from Justin; she then tells him about earlier call
- Bob left to hunt for Anastasia; had not returned by time she went to bed
- No call from Byron or Kelly that day. Just Justin.

Chris speaks first. He doesn't speak frequently, but he seems insightful, so I'm pleased to hear from him.

Chris wants to know where Anastasia's father was during the trial. Why didn't he testify? Why did the sister have to tell us about the phone call between Justin and the father? Why did the step-mother have to tell us about the father's search efforts?

We just keep coming up with evidence we think we should have, but don't. It's frustrating, but we have to work with what we've got.

As it turns out, Francesca gave us a lot. The new timeline items are in bold.

3:00 PM Kelly home from school

 ?:?? PM Byron and Justin pick Kelly up

3:30 PM **Diane picks Francesca up at school; drives straight home**

4:05 PM Diane and Anastasia leave home

4:15 PM Anastasia dropped at Truman entrance to Mount Washington

4:20 PM **Francesca takes 1st call from Justin**

5:00 PM Anastasia expects to meet Justin at Mount Washington

6:00 PM Diane cannot find Anastasia at Mount Washington; returns to her mother's house

6:45 PM **Francesca leaves for haircut / prayer meeting**

8:30 PM **Anastasia gets out of car 1 hr prior to Justin's 2nd call**

8:45 PM **Francesca returns home; 8:30 - 9 PM**

9:15 PM Kelly returns home

9:30 PM **Francesca receives second call from Justin**

10:10 PM **Bob (father) and Diane arrive at home; 10 to 10:20 PM**

??:?? PM **Justin calls third time; talks to Bob**

??:?? PM **Francesca tells of 2nd Justin phone call; Bob searches for Anastasia**

3:44 AM Epperson finds Anastasia's body

Chad notes there's a two-hour window when no one was at Anastasia's house. Between 6:45 and 8:45, Francesca is at a prayer meeting, Diane is at her mother's house, and Bob is at work.

Terry points out that Francesca returned home just about the time Justin told her Anastasia got out of the car. They're both right. That's what the timeline says. I'm glad to see people constructing arguments based on the evidence.

Christina notes that Francesca's second phone call from Justin corroborates the whispering phone call Debra Moffett overheard after Kelly returned home.

Chris asks Christina why she described the phone call as whispering. Terry answers for Christina, to Christina's noticeable chagrin.

"Because that's how Kelly's mother described it."

Chris counters with two interesting observations. First, if Justin and Byron were whispering downstairs, how did Debra Moffett hear them upstairs? Second, Francesca never mentioned that Justin was whispering or hard to hear when she talked to him.

I remain quiet and let them each make the best case they can. I think Chris made the better case this time. I hadn't thought of it that way. Now it seems to me as if Kelly's mother was exaggerating.

There's a timely knock at the door. It's the bailiff. He informs us we're done for the day. He's going to collect the evidence box and secure it elsewhere overnight, then return it to us tomorrow morning. We can and should leave our notes. The room will be locked overnight.

The first day of deliberation is over. It's now obvious that we won't be finished by the weekend.

DELIBERATION: GLEN COLLIVER

It's Friday morning. They opened the jury room to us at 8:30 AM. We're supposed to be deliberating as of right now. It's 9:00, and we're one person short. George is late. The door opens, but it's the bailiff, not George. The bailiff greets us good morning and drops off the evidence box. He reminds us to ring the buzzer when we're all assembled.

George arrives two minutes later, apologizing profusely. Christina rises and rings the buzzer. We're off and running. Day two.

"We just finished with Francesca. Next up is Glen Colliver. Let's put together the summary points of his testimony."

Glen Colliver is, or was, the manager at Mount Washington cemetery. He was potentially an interesting witness because he was the last to see the four teens just before the disputed events took place. Unfortunately, he doesn't really have all that much to offer. Here's all that we could extract:

- Saw young woman, possibly Anastasia, sitting alone at central memorial
- Saw young woman and young man standing outside a car
- Pulled up behind them to encourage them to leave cemetery; they did
- Recorded the license number; turned out to be Justin's car

Chad campaigned to have events from the following morning included. More specifically, he doesn't understand why I won't put in Glen's meeting with Anastasia's father the next morning. I don't believe that such evidence should impact our deliberation. It clutters our summarized evidence while adding nothing to help us decide whether or not Byron Case committed this crime. Chad drops the issue without conceding the point.

I continue the discussion.

"There was confusion over the time Glen saw Justin and Anastasia outside the car. He swears it was 9 PM. He remembers it was after dinner, and before a television show he always watched with his wife. He remembers his wife telling him to hurry or he'll miss the show.

"The police, on the other hand, recorded the time as 1900 hours, which is military time for 7 PM."

I'm probably one of the few people here or anywhere with a 24-hour clock hanging on the wall in my living room. It's from my Dad, when he was in the

Army Air Corps. Décor-wise, it goes with nothing else in the room, but it's staying right where it is.

"So how are we going to decide whether it happened closer to seven or closer to nine?"

Several pairs of eyes lean over the table and study the timeline we've assembled so far. Terry says it can't be 9 PM. Debra Moffett and Francesca both recall that the second phone call from Justin to Anastasia's house occurred a little after 9 PM. There wasn't time for everything to occur as either of them described if Glen saw them at 9 PM.

Jade makes an even better point. She points to the stipulation about the time of sunset. She's found that in her notes, which as I've mentioned previously are superior. The stipulation put the time of sunset at 6:30 PM, and Glen Colliver said he locks the gates at dusk.

"So it looks like it was more likely at 7:00 PM. It's an object lesson for us on memories. Even though a witness may be absolutely certain in his recollection, he might just be wrong. Memories can be awfully tricky things."

Because of Jade's insight, we have three new items to add to the timeline, rather than just two. As usual, the three new items are displayed in bold below. I'm going to display just those events surrounding the new additions.

> 5:00 PM Anastasia expects to meet Justin at Mount Washington
>
> ?:?? PM **Glen sees Anastasia at memorial in Mount Washington**
>
> 6:00 PM Diane cannot find Anastasia at Mount Washington
>
> 6:30 PM **Sunset**
>
> 6:45 PM Francesca leaves for haircut / prayer meeting
>
> 7:00 PM **Glen sees Anastasia and Justin outside car in Mount Washington**
>
> 8:30 PM Anastasia gets out of car (Justin's 2nd call to Francesca minus 1 hour)
>
> 8:45 PM Francesca returns home; 8:30 to 9 PM
>
> 9:15 PM Kelly returns home
>
> 9:30 PM Francesca receives second call from Justin

"That means the disputed events may have happened shortly after 7 PM, say 7:30 PM. This is an hour earlier than the 8:30 PM time Francesca sort-of, kind-of remembers."

Chad points out this means Anastasia's house might have been empty for more than an hour after the disputed events.

Deliberations are getting interesting.

DELIBERATION: JOHN BRUTON

John Bruton is Justin's father. He was in Tulsa the day the critical events took place.

- Paid Justin's condo, car, and living expenses only if Justin stayed in school
- Threatened to cut off funds when Justin planned to marry Anastasia
- Heard from Justin weekly. Visits from Justin occasionally, once with Anastasia
- Justin interested in guns; visited gun shows; unaware of Justin owning a gun
- Justin visited the weekend before murder / suicide; went to a gun show; did not apparently buy gun
- Learned from Byron of Anastasia's death and Justin's disappearance
- Drove to Kansas City; stayed in Justin's apartment; met Byron and Kelly there
- Byron told him that Anastasia got out of car at a stop light

"I don't see too much here. Somebody tell me what I'm missing."

Chris is on the "where's Anastasia's father" theme. He points out that Justin's father, who was in Tulsa at the time, testified, but Anastasia's father, who searched for her that night, and took calls from Justin, did not testify. When he has a point, he doesn't let go.

Christina has a brilliant thought. We might be looking at Justin's trip to the Tulsa gun show in the wrong light. Maybe he didn't go there to buy a gun. Maybe he went there to sell a gun. Maybe that's where the shotgun he bought from Wal-Mart went.

"That's a very interesting idea. Very interesting. Crayon and Fry want us to believe Justin had to buy a new shotgun to kill himself because Byron threw the other one away after he shot Anastasia. But maybe he bought the first shotgun because he was going to commit suicide. He had talked about it, but no one took him seriously. He didn't go through with it and sold the gun in Tulsa. Then the very next week, he gets in an argument with his girlfriend, she storms out of the car, ends up dead, and that does it for him. The suicide is back on. He gets the same type of gun he decided on earlier and finishes what he had started."

Sondra points to inconsistent arguments by the prosecution. They want us to think that Byron used the shotgun Justin bought from Wal-Mart, but they left no stone unturned in their defense of Kelly's claim that Byron used his father's shotgun. Nobody else ever saw any evidence of Dale Case having a shotgun, but the prosecution extracted from each such witness that Dale Case could have had the shotgun hanging on his wall when they weren't looking.

Christina puts the exclamation mark on the discussion she started. They not only wanted us to believe it was Justin's shotgun, they wanted us to believe it was Dale Case's shotgun, and they wanted us to believe it might not have been a shotgun at all, but a high powered rifle.

"I guess there was more in John Bruton's testimony that I realized."

DELIBERATION: JIM DODD

Jim Dodd was the employee at the Bullet Hole gun shop who sold Justin the shotgun he used to kill himself. There isn't a lot in his testimony. Tony passes. Christina notes the time Justin entered and Sondra remembers that Dodd said Justin didn't act strangely. We leave it up to Jade to remind us the specific type of gun Justin purchased.

- Justin entered store at 10 or 10:30 AM, October 23, 1997
- Purchased a Remington H70 shotgun and 5 rifled deer slugs
- Filled out all appropriate forms
- Did not act strangely in any fashion

"The prosecution's point with Jim Dodd seems to be that since Justin bought the shotgun at 10 or 10:30 AM, and that was before the radio broadcast news of her death, it proves Justin was acting out of guilt. Ergo, Byron did it."

Terry catches that I used his word, and gives me a nod. I ask him if he sees any flaw in the prosecution's argument. He sees the trap, the ergo trap. He's been leaning towards a Guilty vote, and pointing out any flaw in the prosecution's case goes against his nature. He knows, however, that if he doesn't say it, the next person will.

He concedes that maybe the evidence of Justin's guilty conscience indicates that Justin did it. It doesn't necessarily mean that Byron did it. On the other hand, though, Jim Dodd's testimony is certainly not inconsistent with Kelly's testimony.

Chris, who is now on the lookout for missing evidence, notes that nobody established when the radio first broadcast news of Anastasia's death. Several people said they heard it on the radio or saw it on television around five in the afternoon, but no one ever established when it was first broadcast.

Sondra takes the point a step further. They didn't actually have to broadcast Anastasia's name. All the press had to do is listen to the police scanners, which they do. They would have picked up on the activity at Lincoln Cemetery. They could have scooted on over and learned that the police had found the body of a young female. They could have that over the morning news, easy.

Jade completes the thought. Justin knew Anastasia wasn't home by midnight. He calls Byron at 9:00 AM. Byron finds it strange only in that Justin is usually sleeping at that time, so it is out of character for Justin to have called so early in the morning. Maybe Justin is fretting over Anastasia's safety, since she didn't come home. Byron tells Justin he's sleeping, he doesn't want to talk, and that doesn't help Justin's state of mind. Then Justin hears on the radio that the police have discovered the body of a young woman in Lincoln cemetery. He presumes the worst, and that shoves him over the edge. He decides to complete what he started earlier. He goes to the Bullet Hole gun shop, and calmly buys the same type of shotgun he purchased previously, a Remington H70 shotgun. He heads for a quiet place, and does himself in.

Terry thinks people are concocting complicated, convoluted stories and dismissing the most obvious explanations.

"I don't think anyone is dismissing the obvious explanation, Terry. I think we all see the obvious explanation as possible. The other jurors are simply exploring alternatives. If there are no other explanations, that would add weight to the prosecution's argument. The existence of alternative explanations, however diminishes the weight of their argument, that's all. It doesn't prove to me the prosecution isn't correct."

Terry suggests that no one can be expected to cover every single possibility, no matter how ludicrous. Terry wants to add Justin's trip to the gun shop to the timeline. I add it. Then he wants to add that the radio didn't broadcast news of Anastasia's death until 5 PM. I ask him where that's supported in Jim Dodd's evidence. He says he'll wait until we talk about Abraham Kneisley. I put it in the timeline anyway, as a reminder.

The timeline of events, limited to Thursday morning, now reflects the additions in bold.

> 3:44 AM Epperson finds Anastasia's body
>
> 10:15 AM **Justin buys shotgun from Bullet Hole (10 - 10:30)**
>
> 5:00 PM **[First radio broadcast of Anastasia's death, per Terry, see Kneisley's testimony]**

Just as I'm ready to move to the next witness, Chad comes alive.

"Remember when you wouldn't put Glen Colliver's meeting with Anastasia's father in the timeline?"

It's directed at me and my authoritarian decision on that subject.

"Yes."

"Well, you screwed up. If you had let us talk about what went on with Glen that morning, we would have the answer to this question about when it was on the radio."

My mind's racing back to Glen's testimony. I'm scanning my neurons for some combination of Glen and radio. I'm getting nothing.

Jade sees it before I do.

"Oh, he's right."

Then George sees it, and Sondra, and Tony. Pretty soon, I'll be alone. Chad gives me a hint.

"What prompted Glen to go over to Lincoln Cemetery that morning, and give the police his information about Anastasia's father?"

They're all looking at me. Even the ones who still haven't figured it out are acting as if they have. And it's still not coming to me. Crap!

He gives me another hint.

"His assistant told him, right? And how did his assistant learn of it?"

Only then do I see it.

"He heard it on the radio. You're right. And if I hadn't been so stubborn about discussing Glen's activities the following morning, we might have remembered this back then."

Okay, I really messed up. Nothing to do now but correct the error and try not to make the same mistake in the future.

We add a few elements to the timeline of events for the next morning. The new ones are in bold.

    3:44 AM Epperson finds Anastasia's body

    8:00 AM **Colliver opens gates to Mount Washington**

    8:00 AM **Colliver encounters father hunting for daughter. Sees picture of girl from previous night; takes father's info**

    8:00 AM **Mentions to assistant the events of previous evening**

    9:00 AM **Hears from assistant of a radio news report that may be related to the events of previous evening**

    9:00 AM **Travels to Lincoln Cemetery to share his knowledge with police**

  10:15 AM Justin buys shotgun from Bullet Hole (10 - 10:30)

    5:00 PM [First radio broadcast of Anastasia's death, per Terry, see Kneisley's testimony]

I'm pretty angry with myself. After lecturing everyone on the crucial role of evidence, I allowed my stubbornness to get in the way of considering critical evidence in a murder trial.

Another screw-up like that and I'll bench myself.

DELIBERATION: DETECTIVE ALBERT DEVALKENAERE

I have a real problem with DeValkenaere's testimony. I need to play it straight, though, and solicit unbiased input from the other jurors. I keep a straight face as I say:

"Okay, what do we have on Albert DeValkenaere? Chad, let's start with you and we'll work to your left."

Chad notes that DeValkenaere led the team that arrested Byron Case. Terry adds, as I expected, that DeValkenaere testified that Byron Case tried to escape.

"Escape or avoid arrest?"

"Okay avoid arrest. Nonetheless, it's evidence of guilt. Put it down."

"I don't believe DeValkenaere ever said that Byron Case tried to avoid arrest. Anybody have a specific note in that regard?"

"He ran back into his room when he saw the police. He tried to lock the door. I call that resisting arrest."

"Resist or avoid?"

"Resist. I say that's resisting arrest and evidence of guilt. Put it down."

"Anyone else think Byron resisted arrest?"

Chad, George, Vivian, Sondra, and Tony raise their hands. Terry counts for me and tells me that's six.

"Put it down."

I don't respond quickly enough for him. He gets up and walks around the table, determined. As he approaches I hand him the magic marker. He takes the marker and uses it to write, in large capital letters: BYRON CASE RESISTED ARREST. He hands me the marker and returns to his seat.

I'm hoping Chris will come to my rescue and state what seems to me to be obvious. I don't want to always be the lone voice challenging the prosecution case. But Chris doesn't save me.

Jade does.

"I have some questions about Officer DeValkenaere's testimony. I'm looking at my notes here, and I can't see how many officers were on the arrest team."

Manna from Heaven. Now I can just watch it unfold. Chad and Terry say "ten" in unison.

"Well according to my notes, he said the fugitive arrest team has up to ten members. Up to ten. I don't see anything in my notes where he said how many were actually on the team that night."

No response. She lets the silence grow heavy.

"Okay. I'll just add a note that it was somewhere between two and ten."

She writes in her notebook.

"Then I'll add a note that Officer Albert DeValkenaere is feeding us a bunch of crap."

She writes a little more. Suddenly she gets up and walks around the table. As she approaches, I hand her the marker and step back, way back. She's on a mission.

She writes in large capital letters: "BETWEEN TWO AND TEN PEOPLE ON THE ARREST TEAM!" She underlines it. She then completes the entire evidence list from her notes. I take a seat and watch, impressed. When she's done, it looks like this:

- Led team that arrested Byron Case
- BYRON CASE RESISTED ARREST
- BETWEEN TWO AND TEN PEOPLE ON THE ARREST TEAM!
- June 11, 2001, 1 PM
- KC Missouri PD, KC Kansas PD, and / or FBI; JCSD included in this arrest
- Unmarked cars; sirens off; tactical gear, 4" logos / text on vests
- Surrounded building; front door open; screen door ajar
- "Police. Anybody inside come to the door"; top of lungs 4 or 5 times
- Cover position near bedroom door as house is cleared
- "Police. Anybody inside come out"; continued yelling
- Case appears at bedroom door; sees police; attempts to close and lock door
- Door forced open; Case arrested
- Albert DeValkenaere is feeding us a bunch of crap!!

When finished, she places the marker on end in the middle of the table, challenging any one of us to pick it up. She calmly returns to her seat. Despite the stillness in the room, the marker topples over, rolls to the side of the table, and drops to the floor. Neither she nor anyone else has said a word since she stood up. I walk over, pick up the marker, add one more exclamation mark to her last item on the board.

- Albert DeValkenaere is feeding us a bunch of crap!!!

"How do we know that DeValkenaere is feeding us a bunch of crap? Let's start with Terry and work to his right."

Terry passes, as does Chad. Tony makes the now obvious point that maybe he said up to ten people on the arrest team to exaggerate how dangerous they thought Byron Case was. Christina adds that the information about all the departments and tactical gear tended to do the same thing, to make Byron Case seem dangerous.

Sondra now thinks it convenient that the front door was open and the screen door was ajar. Maybe that's the way that it was but it now seems kind of convenient.

Chris now rises to the occasion.

"If the front door was open and he was yelling at the top of his lungs, why didn't Byron hear him?"

Liza's turn.

"That's right. And he said he was right outside Byron's door, still yelling, and yet Byron seemed surprised to see the police were in his house. Doesn't make sense. Why wouldn't Byron hear all the yelling? Can't both be true. Can't be yelling at the top of his lungs right outside his door and have Byron surprised to see him."

George passes.

Vivian says:

"I walk out of my bedroom and see someone pointing a gun in my face, you can bet your ass I'd be shuttin' the door."

Now it's back to Jade. She's looking at her notes. She doesn't look up. She just smiles and says "Pass."

It was a tour de force. I almost add that it's all irrelevant, that it has nothing to do with whether or not Byron killed Anastasia. I think better of it. I pass.

"It's 10:45. Let's take a break. Please be back in 15."

George has established his claim on the restroom. He strolls in this time and we all just watch. Speculation, if any, is silent.

DELIBERATION: DR. CHASE BLANCHARD

Dr. Blanchard was a fill-in for Dr. Thomas Young, who, we were told, was out of town. Dr. Blanchard reviewed the autopsy report, autopsy photos, ME investigator report, and the toxicology report. Her testimony was, we were told, going to be based on that review. She went well beyond that, however, and that bothers me.

It seems I'm easily bothered by such things. I guess it's the price of being skeptical.

In a previous career, before I entered the glamorous world of custom database design, I was an aerospace engineer. I describe myself as a recovering engineer. My wife tells me "no way." She informs me that I'll always be an engineer. I'm starting to see her point.

We work around the room and summarize the testimonial evidence Dr. Blanchard had to offer. She actually provided quite a bit of detail.

- Autopsy: October 23, 1997 at 9:30 AM
- Height: five feet two inches; weight: 120 pounds
- Cause of death: gunshot; entry, tip of the nose; exit, back of head
- Muzzle was within six inches of nose; probably a contact wound
- Defect = entry wound; diameter = $\frac{3}{8}$-inch
- Trajectory of bullet slightly up if head in anatomical position
- Skull fragment found four feet away from body.
- Black Doc Martens shoes; dark gray socks; black denim jeans
- Light brown corduroy jacket; dark gray pullover shirt
- Black bra, black panties, sanitary napkin
- Clothes in place and undamaged; no apparent defensive wounds
- Small bills and change in back pocket; no purse or billfold
- Distorted lead bullet fragment recovered from hair at back of head
- Wound consistent with shotgun firing deer slug
- Wound inconsistent with shotgun firing pellet round
- Wound consistent with high-power rifle
- Wound consistent with high-power pistol, but not likely
- Toxicology negative for alcohol and drugs of abuse

"Let's discuss the non-ballistics issues first, please. Who wants to start?"

Christina suggests the lack of defensive wounds and the condition of Anastasia's clothing indicate she was shot by someone she knew.

"That's a reasonable conclusion. Not proof, but it seems reasonable."

Terry points out that Dr. Blanchard's testimony pretty much proves that Anastasia was murdered by gunshot. The elements for the murder in the first-degree charge are still on the board. One of them is that Byron Case killed Anastasia by shooting her.

"I think it's safe to say Dr. Blanchard has given us good reason to believe that Anastasia died as a result of being shot. Is there any other --"

Terry interrupts.

"Anastasia was a *homicide* victim."

He emphasizes the word "homicide" and stares at me. I'm silent. He clarifies:

"Anastasia didn't die because she just happened to be in a cross-fire. She was intentionally shot. Murdered. *Homicide.*"

Now I get it. I misspoke.

"Right. Dr. Blanchard said it was a homicide. Now, is there any other element up there she addressed or should have addressed?"

I look at Jade. She knows but she's not going to carry the water on this one. I look at Chris. He's quiet, as usual. I decide to wait everyone out. I take the last sip of a Diet Mountain Dew. It's warm and flat.

Liza breaks the silence.

"Why didn't she say anything about when Anastasia died? They can tell, can't they?"

I was hoping someone would bring that up.

"I'm not an ME, that's for sure, so I can't say how precisely they can establish a time of death. What strikes me is that Dr. Blanchard didn't even mention it, Theresa Crayon didn't even ask about it. Given that the prosecution must prove to us beyond a reasonable doubt that Anastasia was killed on the 22nd even though she was found on the 23rd, it seems they would be eager have the ME say something like:"

At this point, I assume my deep, radio announcer voice.

"Based on the body temperature and the state of rigor mortis, it's clear to me that the victim was killed sometime before midnight. I can't be any more precise than that, but she was definitely killed prior to midnight."

"Maybe they only do that in the movies or on TV, not in real life, but it annoys me. Every time we should be getting solid physical evidence or testimony from an individual directly involved in the case, we come up with zip. Sergeant Kilgore is MIA, Anastasia's father is too, and now the ME who actually conducted the autopsy is a no-show. His fill-in makes no effort to establish a time-of-death, which as you know is a critical element in this case, but she's on a soapbox about ballistics. It looks like they intend to hinge their entire case on Kelly and her veracity, without any corroborating physical evidence."

Terry calls me on it. He points out that now I'm the one jumping ahead of the witness we're discussing. He's correct, and I acknowledge it.

"Good call. Okay, what else, still excluding the ballistics please? George, you have any thoughts on her testimony?"

He looks up, surprised. I lead him.

"What about the toxicology report?"

"It was negative?"

"Not quite negative."

He looks at the board. He has more confidence in his answer this time.

"Negative for alcohol and drugs of abuse."

"What about sleeping pills?"

"Umm, umm --"

"We don't know, do we? She didn't tell us. Her answer was quite precise and quite limited. Negative for alcohol and drugs of abuse."

I resist the urge to do finger quotes around "of abuse."

"How about prescription drugs, or sleeping pills, pain killers, caffeine? How about poisons? Are we supposed to assume they're all absent? We weren't supposed to assume any alcohol or drugs of abuse, obviously, because she took the trouble to mention those. So why would we be expected to make assumptions about other possible toxicology findings? Her precise but narrow summary of the toxicology report triggers my suspicions."

Chad points out the defense attorney never asked about the toxicology report. If there was anything in the report that would help Byron, his attorney would surely have pointed it out to us.

"I'm not going to make any such assumption, and I caution others against doing so. You'd be throwing the presumption of innocence out the window. Remember, the defense has no burden to prove anything. It's the prosecution that has the burden of proof, and I expect them to provide me with the evidence that will prove their case. If they don't --"

I decide to let it hang. Probably went too far as it was.

Terry says I'm doing it again, making a big deal out of nothing. So what if there was something else in the tox report, even though there probably wasn't? Big deal. He informs me he would like me to get on with it, meaning the deliberations, and that I should do so for God's sake.

"I don't know what difference it might make, but I want the evidence. Once we get the evidence, we can then try to figure out if it makes a difference. She didn't give us the evidence, but I can speculate what difference it might make, if you'd like."

He passes and thereby avoids another of my harangues. If Anastasia was full of sleeping pills, for example, it would suggest Kelly's version of events is not accurate. Her version of events leaves no time for Anastasia to self-medicate. I have my thoughts on why Anastasia might have wanted to sedate herself somehow, but they're not fully formed and too speculative to delay us here.

"Okay, on to the ballistics. Here's my concern. She told us she was just going to fill in for Dr. Young by relaying the results of the autopsy and toxicology report. It seems to me, however, that she spent most of her time talking about ballistics. Why didn't they have a ballistics expert come and talk to us about the bullet fragment and about what kind of weapon it might have been fired from?

"I've fired various types of weapons on firing ranges, but I'm hardly a ballistics expert. However, I get the impression that Dr. Blanchard isn't well versed in ballistics either. First, she changes her story from her deposition to her trial testimony about the possibility of the weapon being a .22 handgun. During her deposition, she said it was possible. That's her word, 'possible.' I wrote it down. Jade can tell me if I got it wrong."

Jade gives me a little nod. That's what she has.

She says that it's funny we're even comparing Dr. Blanchard's deposition testimony to her trial testimony. We were given the impression that Blanchard testified at trial only because Dr. Young was out of town.

She punctuates her observations with:

"Duped again."

I withhold my thoughts on the subject.

"During her testimony, she said the wound was inconsistent. That was the word she used in court, 'inconsistent.' I wrote it down. Jade?"

Jade give me another nod. That's what she has.

"And then she tells us in court, when a person's freedom is at stake, when the prosecution's integrity is at stake, that there is no change in her position, that 'possible' and 'consistent' are not the same. When I heard her say that, I made sure I wrote that down, because I thought it was baloney. I underlined it, because I figured she's changing her story to go along with what the State, her employer, wants her to say. And then I put a large exclamation point beside it, because I conclude she'd rather shill for the State than give me a straight answer. So now I'm going to look at what she says very, very carefully."

I pause. I'm irritated again, or still, and they can tell. They figure best to let it be. It doesn't work.

"Unfortunately, it brings to mind Bill Clinton's 'I did not have sex with that woman' speech. After he got caught, he covered by saying it depends on what the meaning of 'is' is. Now I'm getting 'possible is not the same as consistent.' So I would like to look hard at the ballistics and see if we can find what they don't want us to find."

Silence.

"Okay, I'll start. The bullet hole, what they call the bullet defect, was three-eighths of an inch in diameter."

I turn to the board, do a little long division in front of them, dividing 3 by 8, and arrive at 0.325.

"The diameter of the defect is 0.325 inches. That's the diameter of a .32 caliber bullet. That's what caliber is, the inner diameter of the barrel expressed as a decimal fraction. I just know that. I also know that that a yard and a meter are close to the same length, with a meter being a bit longer, 39 inches I think."

I turn to the board again, and do a little more math. I come up with 8.33 millimeters.

"That's the size of a 8 or 9 mm bullet."

Chris speaks up, finally. Isn't a shotgun shell much larger in diameter than that? He doesn't know the exact size of a shotgun shell, but it seems to him that it might be twice the diameter of a bullet. So he would like to know, God bless him, how a shotgun slug left a hole that small.

Terry's all over it. Blanchard said it could have been a shotgun slug or a high powered rifle. Kelly said it was dark, that it could have been a high powered rifle. So it wasn't a shotgun. So what?

"That's my point, Terry. It doesn't seem like she's really much of a ballistics expert. Why should the jury have to figure this out? Why didn't she rule out a shotgun or at least explain how a shotgun slug could leave a hole that small? Again, it seems to me like she's shilling for the prosecution. Why didn't we get to hear from a real ballistics expert?"

George raises his hand without looking up. That's strange. No one's required to raise their hand. It works though. Everyone looks at him. It seems as if he has something to say, but is reluctant to say it. Whether he's trying to or not, he's turning it into a dramatic moment.

"I don't think Anastasia was shot with either a shotgun or a high-powered rifle."

He's captured out attention.

"First off, she's not much of an expert if she can't tell the difference between a wound caused by a shotgun shell and wound cause by a .22 handgun. You stick a shotgun in someone's face and pull the trigger, it's going to look a hell of a lot worse than that. A shotgun blast will be the worst but even a high-powered rifle will do more damage than that."

He raises his arm backward and, without looking, points to the evidence box where Anastasia's crime scene photo rests.

Terry asks sarcastically how he would know. Has he ever seen someone shot in the face?

George stuns everyone in the room.

"Yes."

He lets it hang there for a bit.

"Not in the face, maybe, but in the head for sure. We all have, haven't we? We saw Kennedy shot in the head with a high powered rifle, and we all saw what that did. It didn't just cause a little skull fragment to be thrown four feet away, and it didn't leave a little round hole. It caused a big chunk of Kennedy's skull to be thrown way up, and blood and brain sprayed out like a fountain, and it messed him up a whole lot more than that picture shows."

Again he swings his arm back and points at the evidence box without looking at it.

"And wherever the shot that killed Kennedy came from, it came from a long way away, not right in his face. So I don't think she was shot in the face with a high powered rifle. And I damned sure don't think she was shot in the face with a shotgun."

Seems like the deliberation process is causing George to reconsider some of his earlier notions. I call for a lunch break. He gets up and walks to the bathroom. The room is silent again as he exits. My thoughts are about matters more pressing than George's excretory functions.

DELIBERATION: DETECTIVE SCOTT ATWELL

No surprise what I had for lunch. Two hot dogs from the cart, two diet Mountain Dews. A quick stroll, some people-watching, a little contemplation and I'm ready to go.

Our exchange just before lunch, the deliberation of Dr. Blanchard's testimony, showed the beauty of having a jury of twelve selected at random. The cumulative knowledge and experience of any twelve American citizens is something to behold. The challenge is to take advantage of the cumulative mind before it locks itself into any position and becomes uncurious.

Things pick up as we deliberate Detective Scott Atwell's testimony. We're getting serious about wanting to figure out what really happened out there on that terrible night. That desire is a trap of a different sort, but I'll not dwell on that here. For now, I'm pleased with the way we're working together.

Here's what we come up with regarding Scott Atwell's testimony:

- Called to scene of Justin's death; Saturday, October 25, 1997
- Body found beside abandoned warehouse; 1:15 PM
- Body lying on back, perpendicular to building, head nearest the building
- Severe gunshot wound to head
- Remington H70 shotgun w/ 18" barrel parallel to body
- Muzzle against left armpit
- Justin's car nearby; nothing of interest in front or back seat of car
- In trunk: shotgun receipt, box with make, model and serial number of shotgun; box of 12-gauge slugs; three in box, two at scene
- Raining or drizzling for twelve hours; dry beneath body and car
- Detective Atwell informed Sergeant Kilgore of the shooting
- Gunshot wound determined to be self-inflicted; shooting recorded as suicide
- Toxicology report negative; no alcohol, no drugs

"Okay. Here we go. Did anyone ever figure out whether Detective Atwell and Judge Atwell were related?"

Apparently not.

"It would have been nice if they had clarified it, just mentioned it."

Apparently so.

"I assume not. Seems like that would be a serious conflict of interest. Anyway, how did Scott Atwell's testimony help the prosecution case, if at all? He was, after all, their final witness."

Terry starts.

"The fact that Justin killed himself indicates a guilty mind, and that's consistent with Kelly's testimony. He felt guilty because of his role in Anastasia's death, and he killed himself."

Christina points out it might also indicate Justin killed Anastasia himself, and felt guilty about that. Terry counters with:

"No evidence to that effect. None."

Sondra throws in that Justin might have felt guilty for causing Anastasia to get out of the car, for not going back for her, for leaving her alone that night.

Terry counters that Justin couldn't have known of Anastasia's death when he killed himself.

Chad reminds Terry about Glen Colliver going to Lincoln Cemetery at 9 AM because of a report that was on the radio sometime after 8 AM.

Chris comments quietly, almost to himself.

"Arguing over the time of the news reports doesn't mean anything if Justin killed her. That's the whole point isn't it? He killed himself because he killed her."

Terry tells Chris he's crazy.

All that discussion, and all I did was ask a simple question. I ask another.

"How did Atwell's testimony hurt the prosecution case, if at all?"

Chris is leafing through his notes, slowly. Without looking up he says:

"No blood on the car."

Chad asks Chris how he knows that, since there wasn't any testimony.

"If there was blood, we would have heard about it."

Chad says the rain might have washed it off. Chris points out there was no blood in the trunk.

"Should have been some blood in the trunk if Byron shot her point blank then threw the shotgun in the trunk. Should have been some blood. Rain didn't wash it away."

Chad points out that none of us are blood splatter experts and we're just guessing. Chris is unimpressed.

"Should have had an expert testify then."

Sondra lights up.

"This was my point that no one wanted to listen to before."

She glares at me. Now I'm wondering if I cut her off too quickly earlier when she wanted to discuss blood splatter in more detail. She's not going to let me cut her off again.

"Obviously we're not going to figure out where Anastasia's blood splattered, but we know this:"

She ticks off her list on her fingers.

"One: blood splattered. Somewhere. But not in Lincoln Cemetery and not on Justin's car. Two: lack of blood splatter is significant. I mean it. Please listen to me. This is a big deal. Three: I don't think Anastasia was killed where she was found. That one small skull fragment could have come loose finally when whoever shot her dumped her body there."

Chris says:

"Fair enough."

He makes a checkmark in his notebook. I have no idea what he's doing. Again without looking up, he adds:

"Should have found Byron's fingerprints on the trunk of the car, but they didn't."

No one asks Chris how he knows they didn't find any fingerprints.

"If Byron slammed the trunk lid, should have been some fingerprints. Rain won't wash them away. Oil and water."

He makes another check in his notebook. Then he puts down his pen and resumes a quiet posture.

That was way too easy. I just asked two simple questions.

DELIBERATION: DAWN WRIGHT

Dawn Wright was the first of the defense witnesses. We're working well together now, and it takes little time to summarize her testimony.

- Worked at Dairy Queen near Mount Washington
- Anastasia waited there for friends
- Anastasia said she had an argument w/ her boyfriend; had plans but no ride
- Anastasia said she called him and asked him to pick her up
- Anastasia said her boyfriend had made plans with his best friend; she was upset by that
- Anastasia made four or five calls from pay phone
- Anastasia wore baggy, light-colored jeans with flared legs that dragged the floor; sandals and socks; heavy coat or jacket, closed
- Dawn gave Anastasia a tampon; told police it was a Maxipad
- Dawn later saw tampon wrapper in bathroom
- Three people arrived in car to pick up Anastasia; two guys, one girl
- Long 4-door with back end like a Chevy Impala; maybe 2-door compact
- Guy in trench coat got out and argued with Anastasia; got in car and drove away
- Time was within the hour before closing, between 9 and 9:45 PM

"Dawn is a frustrating witness. She was one of the last people to see Anastasia alive and has valuable information, but she clearly has difficulty recalling details. I don't have any trouble believing that Anastasia was at the Dairy Queen that night, but beyond that I'm not sure which portion of Dawn's testimony is trustworthy, if any. For example, does anyone believe she is correct about the time Anastasia left the Dairy Queen? She said two guys and a girl dropped by and picked her up some time between 9 and 9:45.

"It's like a do-over of Glen Colliver's testimony. He said he was positive that he closed the Mount Washington gates near 9 PM, because it threatened to interfere with a television show he always watches. Now Dawn Wright says she is positive that Anastasia left for Mount Washington Cemetery some time after 9 PM, because it was during the final closing hour."

Terry and Jade make the same points they made previously. Debra Moffett and Francesca both recall that the second phone call from Justin to Anastasia's house occurred a little after 9 PM. That makes no sense if Anastasia didn't leave the Dairy Queen until after 9 PM. Sunset was at 6:30 PM, Glen closed the gates at dusk, and if Anastasia left the Dairy Queen after 9, the gates to the cemetery would have been locked.

It's confusing to be sure, but we elect to leave the timeline as it is. I ask everyone to keep in mind that both Glen Colliver and Dawn Wright provided testimony contrary to our timeline.

"Again this demonstrates how bad eyewitness testimony can be. Someone is way off here regarding times. We just need to do the best we can with what we have. I suspect we can add at least one item to the timeline though. Some time after being dropped off at the cemetery, probably some time after 5 PM when she was expecting to meet her friend or friends, but some time before 6 PM when Diane Marshall drove through Mount Washington searching for her, Anastasia seems to have walked to the Dairy Queen."

With that addition, the surrounding timeline segment looks like:

5:00 PM Anastasia expects to meet Justin at Mount Washington

?:?? PM Glen sees Anastasia at memorial in Mount Washington

?:?? PM **Anastasia walks from Mount Washington to Dairy Queen**

6:00 PM Diane cannot find Anastasia at Mount Washington

"There are more problems with Dawn's testimony. She can't be sure now if it was a large four door sedan or a two door compact. Justin drove neither, as I recall. He drove a --"

I flip through my notes.

"-- 1993 Honda Accord, two-door. That's a mid-size car, not a compact, really. It does have a back end somewhat like an Impala, depending on the model year of the Impala.

"And then there was the issue with the tampon. Dawn says she is positive she gave Anastasia a tampon, though she told the police it was a Maxipad. She told us she was embarrassed to say tampon to the police, so she said Maxipad. It doesn't seem to me that either is embarrassing, but what do I know?

"I'll tell you what I thought to be the most unusual aspect of her testimony, though. The prosecution wanted her to say it was a tampon. They brought it up on cross and re-cross. The defense didn't want her to say it was a tampon. They didn't bring it up on direct, and during re-direct they extracted an admission from her that her memory was probably better several years ago when she told the police it was a Maxipad.

"I can't imagine why the prosecution and defense would argue the way they did. They were each arguing against their own interest."

Blank looks.

"Because --"

I say slowly, waiting for the realization to strike.

"-- if it was a Tampon --"

Puzzled looks.

"-- then Byron is innocent."

Amazement, shock, silence, and finally:

"Ohhhhh, I get it."

It's Vivian. We haven't heard from her in a while.

"If it was a tampon when she left and a Maxipad when they found her, she sure as hell didn't change in the car."

Now most of them see it. Two of the guys still have wrinkled foreheads.

"Exactly. When and where did she change? If she got out of the car and walked away, she could have walked home or to a friend's house, or a store maybe, got hold of a sanitary napkin, and changed without anyone who testified knowing about it. If she never left the company of the other three, when and where did she change?"

Now everyone sees it.

"And it's not just the tampon --"

Says Christina.

"-- If she went home, she could have changed her clothes. That would explain why Dawn described Anastasia's clothes differently than what she was wearing when she was killed."

"Good thought," I say. "Hadn't occurred to me, seriously. Good thought."

"But there's no evidence she went home," says Terry.

"Maybe there is now."

That was Chris. Short and sweet.

DELIBERATION: JAMIE LYNN SMITH

"The next witness is Jamie Lynn Smith. She's the girl who shared an apartment with Byron when he moved temporarily to St. Louis. I'm not particularly impressed with her value as a witness. She knows less about this case than almost anyone so far, with the possible exception of Albert DeValkenaere, the cop who led the arrest team. Smith didn't know any of the players until well after the murder.

"Nonetheless, let's see what we can assemble from her testimony."

- Met Byron in Kansas City in May or June of 2000
- Moved to St. Louis on August 1, 2000
- Byron moved to St. Louis on September 13, 2000
- Byron withheld St. Louis address and phone number from Kelly
- Visited Byron in Kansas City sometimes between August 1 and September 13
- Kelly called Byron once when she was visiting
- Kelly claimed she had a room, but no food, no shower
- Kelly came by about an hour later; stayed for 2 or 3 hours
- Kelly upset about Byron moving and withholding contact information
- Kelly managed to obtain phone number and called frequently asking for Byron
- Jamie always told Kelly she had the wrong number

"Her testimony has to do with how people behaved almost three years after the murder. I'm not particularly fond of such testimony. I prefer the physical evidence, or testimonial evidence from people who knew the people involved, or witnesses to the events. This testimony is just too remote. But I want to give it a fair shake, so anybody have any observations?"

No one wants to say what everyone is thinking.

"Why do you think the defense brought her in to testify?"

Silence. I pick out Tony, since he's been the most quiet.

"Tony, any thoughts?"

"I guess they want us to think that maybe Kelly is doing this because, uh, out of spite, like she's pissed off because Byron left her and wouldn't tell her where he went."

"I'm guessing you're correct, and there may be something to that, or maybe not. As I said early on, I'm not as interested in people's motives, or what attorneys want to present as people's motives. If we can't envision any motive for Kelly to lie, would that mean we're obliged to vote Guilty? And if they can make it look like Kelly had a motive to lie, does that mean Byron didn't do it? That's why I really want to focus on the hard evidence. Each of you can decide for yourself what to make of the timing."

"Clock says 3:15. I have no reason to distrust it, so let's take a fifteen minute break."

Everyone sees it now. No way will we be done today. We'll be back here bright and early Monday morning. It's not even clear we will be able to finish Monday.

DELIBERATION: EVELYN CASE

Evelyn is Byron's mother. Christina notes that she did not bother to appear in court until it was time to testify. She wonders if that means anything. I point out that the prosecution and the defense can move to have potential witnesses excluded from the courtroom prior to their testimony. After they testify, they can stay. It's intended to prevent witnesses from adjusting their testimony based on what those before them say.

Jurors begin thinking back over the witness list so far. No one can recall any of the witnesses being in the courtroom prior to their testimony.

I remind everyone that it's dangerous to infer truth from witness behavior. We need to stick with the testimony and the physical evidence. We try to do just that with Evelyn Case's testimony.

- Byron came home between 10 and 11 PM that night
- Talked briefly; said Anastasia got out of car and walked away
- Divorced from Byron's father, Dale Case, after ten years of marriage
- Stayed in contact with Dale after divorce; shared custody of Byron
- Visited Dale's residence on occasion; never saw a hunting gun there
- Dale did not own firearm, did not hunt; both were anti-gun
- Byron had strep throat and fever when Kelly called in June of 2001

We don't spend much time discussing her testimony. It's pretty straightforward and pretty limited. She does add an element to the timeline, however. Here's what the end of that fateful day now looks like:

8:30 PM Anastasia gets out of car (Justin's 2nd call to Francesca minus one hour)

8:45 PM Francesca returns home; 8:30 - 9 PM

9:15 PM Kelly returns home

9:30 PM Francesca receives second call from Justin

10:30 PM **Byron arrives home (mother's apt) between 10 & 11**

DELIBERATION: NANCY NOLKER

"I think we can also make pretty quick work of Nancy Nolker's testimony."

And we would have too, had I not screwed up. Here's a brief summary of her brief testimony.

- Byron's aunt; Dale's sister
- Visited Dale's residence 4 or 5 times a year; never saw a gun there
- Cleared out Dale's house after he died; no evidence of a gun
- Never knew Dale and Byron to go shooting

"Between Evelyn Case and Nancy Nolker, the defense is pretty thoroughly rebutting Kelly's claim that Byron used his father's shotgun to shoot Anastasia."

Terry corrects me. Kelly's testimony was that Byron told her that he used his father's gun. She did not say that she knew it was Dale's shotgun, only that Byron told her it was. Neither of the last two witnesses refute that.

"I guess only Byron can refute what he told Kelly about this. For those of you who feel you can't believe his testimony because he doesn't want to go to prison, I guess that means whatever Kelly says, goes."

Now it sounds like I'm whining. This is my fault. I shouldn't have brought Kelly's testimony in yet. I should have just allowed Nancy's testimony to stand as it is. There will be time to tie things all together later.

Jade is working furiously through her notes, way up in the front of her notebook. She's hunting through Kelly's testimony. I consider just moving on to the next witness, rather than have Jade compound my error. But I'm too slow.

"Kelly also said that she saw a gun on the wall at Byron's father's house."

Others start turning back through their notes to Kelly's testimony. I try to put an end to it.

"Why don't we wait until we get to Kelly's testimony to discuss this."

Jade:

"You brought it up."

Me:

"Yes I did. My error. Now we can see why we shouldn't --"

Terry:

"Kelly also said that it might not have been the same gun."

Me:

"Now we can see why --"

Christina:

"But that's not the point. She said she saw a gun on the wall at Byron's father's house. These last two witnesses refute that. They make Kelly look bad."

Me:

"-- we should wait until we're discussing Kelly's tes --"

Terry:

"Just because neither of these last two saw the gun doesn't mean it wasn't there. They conceded they weren't there all the time. His father could have bought it shortly before Anastasia was shot, then Byron used it and threw it away. We don't know."

Me:

"-- timony before we begin weighing Nancy's evidence against Kelly's claims."

Christina:

"But we can't just be guessing that some strange coincidence happened just so we can accept Kelly's testimony. The prosecution has to prove its case beyond a reasonable doubt, and they rely exclusively on Kelly and now Kelly looks like she's --"

Me:

"Okay. I apologize. This is my fault. We're comparing Nancy's evidence against testimony we've yet to consider and we're on the verge of trying to decide if the State has met its burden. I started this and so once again, I apologize. We need to move on."

The jury is agitated now. I'm not sure that's a bad thing. I don't want us to be complacent and just go through the motions. I want people to take it seriously, and have some passion.

Either that, or I'm looking to put a happy face on the situation I created.

Time to move on.

DELIBERATION: ABRAHAM KNEISLEY

I'm glad to have Nancy Nolker behind me. Next up is Abraham Kneisley. He was, and I guess still is, Byron's friend. Let's see what everyone recalls or recorded about his testimony.

- Close friend of Byron; passing friend of Justin, Kelly, Anastasia
- House-sitting for friend; recently broke up with girlfriend
- Wanted Byron to take items to girlfriend's house; pick up some items
- Paged Byron; Byron called back 10 - 15 minutes after page
- Byron, Kelly, Justin went to see Abraham; arrived around 8:30 PM; 30 to 45 minutes after page
- They told of Anastasia getting out of car at 7:30 and walking away
- Talked less than fifteen minutes; departed on errand for Abraham
- No one acted strangely or drunk, or smelled of alcohol; no evidence of crying
- Learned of Anastasia's death next day, 5 PM news; informed Byron
- Justin asked him to help find a gun 6 to 8 weeks earlier; refused

"Any comments regarding Abraham's testimony? Just a reminder, to myself as well as everyone else, let's try not to get too far ahead of ourselves talking about other witnesses we have yet to deliberate."

Well, that put a damper on things.

"Crayon spent a good portion of her cross-examination making sure we knew that Abraham had seen the case file, read newspapers, listened to the radio, talked to a friend at a radio station. She pointed out that he was a friend of Byron's, that he had talked to Byron recently. What do you make of all that? Do you think that's fair ground for questioning Abraham's truthfulness?"

Terry thinks so, as does Tony, Chad, and a few others. The remainder are non-committal. Terry says he's not sure he can trust Abraham to tell the unbiased truth because he was and still is close friends with Byron.

"Are you suspicious of Debra Moffett because she is Kelly's mother, or Francesca because she's Anastasia's sister? Are you ready to dismiss their testimony?"

Shrug.

"Are you suspicious of Evelyn Case because she is Byron's mother?"

Terry ducks the question.

"She didn't really say anything that would help him."

I press the point.

"How about Nancy Nolker? She's Byron's aunt."

Shrug.

"Do you think Crayon prepared her witnesses before their testimony?"

Shrug.

"Of course she did. You think Crayon didn't know almost every single thing Kelly was going to say? You think Crayon didn't coach her on what would be important and what should be avoided? That's why I encourage you to look at the evidence, focus on the evidence. The attorneys, all of them, are trying to mess with our minds. They prep their own witnesses at the same time they tell us not to believe opposing witnesses who have been prepped. Don't let them do it. Focus on the facts and make up your own mind."

I tend to pound too hard on a point sometimes.

Okay, frequently.

Time to move on.

"To the extent we trust Abraham's testimony, he gave us some new items for the timeline."

7:00 PM	Glen sees Anastasia and Justin outside car in Mount Washington
7:30 PM	**Anastasia gets out of car (as per Abraham's testimony)**
7:45 PM	**Abraham pages Byron (30 to 45 minutes before their arrival)**
8:00 PM	**Abraham receives return call from Byron (10-15 minutes after page)**
8:15 PM	**Byron, Justin, Kelly arrive at Abraham's (temporary) residence**
8:30 PM	Anastasia gets out of car (Justin's 2nd call to Francesca: one hour)
8:30 PM	**Byron, Justin, Kelly depart Abraham's (temporary residence)**
9:15 PM	Kelly returns home
9:30 PM	Francesca receives second call from Justin

"It's starting to get interesting, and confusing. The time that Abraham gave for their departure fits reasonably well with the time Kelly's mother said they arrived at her place. They never really told us how long it took to get from Abraham's to Kelly's.

"Abraham, though, testified they told him Anastasia got out of the car at 7:30. Francesca's testimony puts it at 8:30. That seems like a significant difference.

"Abraham places their arrival time somewhere between 8 and 8:15 during his police interview, and 8:30 here during this trial. I put 8:15 in the timeline, but I can be wrong, obviously. If they arrived at 8:15, fifteen minutes after they responded to his page, and if they took the page while they were in transit back to Byron's condo, his time line fits in pretty nicely. That's a lot of ifs, though."

Terry nods in agreement. It's good that we're getting along so well.

They can see the clock. It's darn near 5. They know the bailiff will be knocking any minute now. They're packing up already. What a week!

DELIBERATION: DON RAND

It's Monday morning, 10:43, thirteen minutes past our delayed start time. The bailiff has been in and out delivering the evidence box. Christina's buzzer finger is armed and ready to go. George is here. He was six minutes early. We're waiting on Vivian. She enters and says only "Sorry I'm late." The room fills with "No problem" and "We understand." We're considerably more understanding than when George was late by just two minutes last Friday.

"We're down to just two witnesses before the big match-up between Kelly and Byron. Just two. So let's keep at it. Pull out your notes for Don Rand, and let's summarize what he had to say."

- Worked at Amoco station near Lincoln Cemetery
- Saw lady get out of eastbound car at stoplight near I-435 and Truman
- After dark; told police time was 8:30 PM
- 100 feet away
- She seemed upset; did not mention being upset to police
- She walked eastbound along Truman Road and disappeared
- Young, attractive, 5 foot 6 inches, 130 pounds, brown hair, looked like photo
- Police contacted him the next day, or the day after
- He did not talk later to young lady asking about Anastasia
- Can see road leading to cemetery; cannot see someone walking up there

"Who wants to start?"

No one, really. As usual. Just a gentle nudge to get them started.

"Tony?"

"He seems kinda confused."

"How so?"

"She wasn't upset, then she was. She was tall, but she wasn't, but it was her in the picture. You can see the road going up to the cemetery but you can't see if someone is walking on the road. That sort of thing."

"Terry?"

"I think he saw someone else. That simple."

"He did identify her photo."

"Said it looked like her, didn't say it was absolutely her. He's way off on the height. Five foot six or seven when she was only five foot two? Nobody can miss by that much."

"Most guys can."

It's Sondra.

"You'd be surprised."

The other ladies nod.

"Anybody have anything else to add to this mess?"

Nope.

"Okay. Let's just add the one item to the timeline, and get on with the next witness. Don Rand estimated this happened around 8:30 PM."

> 7:30 PM   Anastasia gets out of car (as per Abraham's testimony)
>
> 8:30 PM   Anastasia gets out of car (Justin's 2nd call to Francesca less one hour)
>
> 8:30 PM   **Don Rand sees Anastasia get out of car and walk east, same direction as he said the car had been driving.**

"Clearly, Don Rand's time coincides nicely with that inferred from Francesca's testimony. It conflicts by an hour with the testimony of Abraham Kneisley. I'm not sure we can expect any better agreement given the vagaries of eyewitness testimony and people's recollections."

"On to Dr. Edward Friedlander."

DELIBERATION: DR. EDWARD FRIEDLANDER

We quickly summarize the testimony of Dr. Edward Friedlander, the expert witness for the defense.

- Contact wound to nose
- Weapon could not be a shotgun firing pellets
- Weapon could be a pistol, rifle, or shotgun firing slug; somewhat surprised if shotgun.

"That was quick. He agrees that it was a contact wound to the nose. No one disputes that it was a contact wound to the nose. Unless someone wants to speak up, let's close the book on that issue.

"He says he'd be somewhat surprised if the murder weapon was a shotgun. He'd expect the entry wound to be larger. I guess he's talking about what we talked about before. The defect, the hole that is left when they put everything back in place was three-eighths of an inch. That's like a .32 caliber round, or an 8 or 9 mm round. As Chris pointed out, shotgun shells are twice that. So I guess I would have expected a larger defect as well.

"So now we have a second so-called expert witness and neither of them really educates us, or explains matters to us well enough that we can do our job.

"But that's it for the supporting cast, everyone. We've done a hell of a job so far. Now it's going to pay off. We have all that knowledge organized and at our fingertips, and we're ready to compare Kelly's and Byron's testimony."

DELIBERATION: MOFFETT V. CASE

"All right, this is it. I think we've put ourselves in the best possible position for comparing the testimony of Kelly and Byron.

"It doesn't always work out that a case hinges on the testimony of a single witness, but that's what we have here. The prosecution has provided no evidence whatsoever that Byron killed Anastasia other than the testimony of Kelly Moffett. Their case stands or falls on her credibility. Does anyone see it differently?"

Terry wants to know if I'm including the recorded phone call as part of Kelly's testimony.

"Yes, I include that. We'll be deliberating that as well. Absolutely.

"So here's what we're going to do. Using our timeline as a guide, we're going to walk through the events of that day, as best as we can, based on the information we've been given. We have two versions of events, Kelly's and Byron's. We're going to compare them. We're going to weigh them one against the other.

"In weighing them, each of us will use our own scale. For me, the scale will be heavily biased towards Byron. He's the defendant. He carries with him the presumption of innocence. Conversely, the scale will be heavily biased against Kelly. She represents the State's case. Without her, they have nothing to meet their burden of proof. But regardless of whether Byron's story is true or false, the prosecution still must prove to me beyond a reasonable doubt that Kelly's story is true.

"For me, it's not a matter of which is more likely true. It's whether Kelly's is true, beyond a reasonable doubt. That said, if there is some reasonable chance that Byron's version of events might be true, that means I have a reasonable doubt that Kelly's is true.

"Each of you will have to balance or bias your own scale. I can't do that for you, nor should you let me. I ask only that you think about the burden of proof and be conscious of it as you compare the evidence.

"Anyone have anything they wish to add before we proceed?"

Silence. And reflection.

"I'm going to put our timeline on the board, one segment at a time. I'm going to start with the segment leading up to where Justin and Byron pick Kelly up at her house. Then we're going to examine our notes of Kelly's testimony and Byron's testimony and add their timeline elements. Then we're going to try to make sense of it.

"And we'll do that over and over, one timeline segment at a time. When we're done, we'll take our first vote. If it's unanimous, we're done. If not, we'll deliberate a bit longer, but not too much longer. We're not going to badger anyone into changing their vote.

"We will not attempt obtain a unanimous verdict by volume of voice if we fail to obtain one by reason of argument. We will declare ourselves a hung jury and go home.

"So this is it."

❖

I ask the jury to begin with the portion of the time line leading up to Justin and Byron picking Kelly up from her house. I figure this shouldn't be too controversial, and I'm right. What I underestimate, however, is how difficult it is to fill in the timeline with Kelly's and Byron's testimony. They testified far longer than the others, so there is much more to remember and many more notes to pour through. Everyone is flipping furiously through their notebook, jumping from Kelly to Byron, from direct examination to cross-examination, making secondary notes on scraps of paper, volunteering tidbits as they discover them. It's frenetic, bordering on chaos, but it works. Over the course of forty minutes, we arrive at our first complete and consensus timeline segment.

It turns out Byron was substantially more specific about times than Kelly. When we couple Byron's times with the times provided by other witnesses, they seem to fit reasonably well. Furthermore, the sequence of events as told by Byron and Kelly match reasonably well, the exceptions being crucial.

The timeline segment follows. Consider all times approximate. Some are provided by the witness explicitly. Others are estimated by the jury. The initials of the witness contributing to each timeline element are included in parenthesis. Since there were two DMs, Diane Marshall and Debra Moffett, they are noted as DiM and DeM.

- 2:00 PM Justin talks to Anastasia by phone, early afternoon, time approx (BC); Justin and Anastasia had plans to meet; she cannot get ride; he cancels plans; Event must have occurred prior to Justin and Byron departing Justin's condo
- 3:00 PM Kelly home from school (DeM)
- 3:00 PM Justin and Byron depart Justin's condo (BC)
- 3:15 PM Kelly takes a nap, time approx (DeM, KM)
- 3:30 PM Diane picks Francesca up from school; drives straight home (DiM)
- 3:30 PM Justin and Byron arrive at Funcoland, in Lenexa (BC); Approximately 30 minute drive from condo; trade in games Justin brought back from Tulsa previous weekend; stay for approximately one hour; decide to pick up Kelly on way back; within 5 miles of her house

4:30 PM Justin and Byron depart Funcoland (BC)

4:40 PM Justin and Byron arrive at Kelly's house (KM, BC); Funcoland is within 5 miles of Kelly's house; Justin driving his blue-green Honda 2-door sedan

4:45 PM Justin, Byron, Kelly depart Kelly's house (DeM, KM, BC); Justin drives; Byron front seat; Kelly back seat

"Looks good, and we agree nothing there is particularly controversial. But this was the easy one."

Groans.

"From here, their stories diverge for a while."

❖

A knock at the door, and we're ejected from the room for lunch. I remind everyone that we have just an hour today. Be back by one.

I have a two and two, perhaps my final of the trial. Not much time for strolling, or people watching. I make my way back to the jury room with three minutes to spare. I almost cut it too close.

❖

"It was at this point that their stories diverge for a while. Kelly said that, after picking her up, Justin and Byron began telling her of their intent to kill Anastasia. Obviously, Byron denies that. Let's work on the timeline from that point to where Justin, Byron, and Kelly depart Kelly's house."

Notebooks flip, pencils scribble, tidbits arise from the commotion. Working at the marker board, I add, erase, move, and edit the tidbits as they float in. In just ten minutes, we have our next timeline segment. We actually have two. One as told by Byron and Kelly, the other as told by Diane Marshall and Francesca. Both lead up to the phone call made from the Phillips 66 gas station. They differ in the timing of the phone call by about thirty minutes. All things considered, that's not bad.

4:47 PM Byron & Justin tell Kelly they plan to kill Anastasia (KM only); Justin can't do it, so Byron will, using his father's shotgun; Kelly had earlier seen shotgun on wall at home of Byron's father; They plan to shoot Anastasia at secluded spot in Mount Washington; they want Kelly to call Anastasia to lure her in

4:50 PM Justin, Byron, Kelly arrive at Phillips 66 near Kelly's house (KM, BC);

4:52 PM Kelly calls Anastasia (KM only); Didn't know the phone number; they gave her a number or Justin may have dialed; Anastasia answered; said they were late and they should meet her at Dairy Queen

4:52 PM Justin calls Anastasia (BC only); Byron waits in car while Justin calls; cannot hear conversation

4:55 PM Justin, Byron, Kelly depart Phillips 66 (KM, BC); Kelly begins drinking; doesn't get drunk (KM only); Byron not drinking or acting drunk (KM direct testimony); Byron drunk; smelling of alcohol (KM interviews and deposition)

❖

4:05 PM Diane and Anastasia leave home (DiM)

4:15 PM Anastasia dropped at Truman entrance to Mt. Washington (DiM)

4:20 PM Francesca takes call from Justin (FW); 15 minutes after Anastasia leaves; did not talk to Kelly or Byron that day

5:00 PM Anastasia expects to meet Justin at Mt Washington (DiM)

5:05 PM Glen sees Anastasia at memorial in Mt Washington (GC)

5:15 PM Anastasia walks from Mt Washington to DQ (presumed)

"Here's where it gets interesting. Kelly says she placed a phone call to Anastasia from the Phillips 66 gas station near her house. Kelly says she actually talked to Anastasia. Byron, on the other hand, says that Justin made the call from the gas station, in an effort to get hold of Anastasia. Seems like one of them was lying to us. Any thoughts?"

Christina states that which is now obvious from the timeline. Francesca's testimony is consistent with Byron's testimony, and contradicts Kelly's.

"Yes. And that's doubly troublesome for the prosecution since Francesca is their witness, and no friend of Byron's.

Terry springs to Kelly's defense:

"Kelly said Justin called earlier."

Christina:

"How would she know that?"

Terry:

"Even Byron said Justin called earlier."

Christina:

"He said Justin called Anastasia earlier, not Francesca."

Terry:

"Maybe he's wrong."

Christina:

"But how did Justin talk to Francesca earlier? Look at the timeline. Francesca got off school at 3:30. When she got home, Anastasia was waiting. The first phone call she got that day from Justin was after Anastasia left, around 4:20 according to her testimony. Look at the timeline."

Terry:

"Justin could have called from Funcoland. Look at the timeline. Justin calls Francesca from Funcoland, and then Kelly calls Anastasia from the Phillips 66, just as she said. Kelly didn't say Anastasia was at home. She said they gave her a number to call. Look at the timeline."

I detect a hint of sarcasm in Terry's voice. Christina is not intimidated.

"Where was Anastasia when Kelly called her?"

Terry:

"She said she didn't know. Justin gave her the phone number, or Justin dialed, something like that."

Christina:

"Where do you think Anastasia was when Kelly called her? She couldn't have been at home. Francesca talked to Justin after Anastasia had already left for Mount Washington."

Terry:

"She could have been at the Dairy Queen."

Christina:

"The Dairy Queen employee --"

Me, being helpful:

"Dawn Wright."

Christina:

"-- yes, Dawn never reported Anastasia taking any calls, just going out to the pay phone and making calls. It's not clear you could hear the pay phone from inside and if you can, Dawn never heard anything, or never said anything about it if she did. There's no evidence Anastasia took a call from Kelly while she was at the Dairy Queen."

Sondra piles on.

"I don't think Anastasia would have even been at the Dairy Queen by the time they called from the gas station, whoever that was. Anastasia's stepmother said she expected to meet Justin at 5:00. She would have waited until sometime after that to walk to the Dairy Queen. That's why we agreed to add that item about Anastasia walking to the Dairy Queen around 5:15. Look at the timeline."

Perhaps a little sarcasm in her voice too.

Terry:

"You look at the timeline. It says Kelly called Anastasia at 4:52, like we can get that close. We all agree the times are approximate. They could have been at the Phillips after 5, easy."

Christina:

"But if Anastasia got a call from Kelly soon after she arrived at the Dairy Queen, why did she keep calling someone on the phone?"

Terry:

"Who knows? But that doesn't matter. The fact is that Kelly's testimony is consistent with the timeline."

Sondra:

"To you, maybe, but you sure have to fill in a lot of the blanks for her --"

Me, again being helpful:

"For the prosecution."

Sondra:

"-- yes, for the prosecution to try and make it all fit, and then it just barely fits if it fits at all."

I interject.

"Why would they call Anastasia at the Dairy Queen to lure her to the Dairy Queen?"

Terry gives me a puzzled look.

"What?"

Me:

"If they needed Kelly to lure Anastasia to the Dairy Queen, why would they expect Anastasia to be already at the Dairy Queen. No need to lure here to where she already is."

Vivian interjects.

"Don't make any sense to me. No sense at all."

I think she's talking about my last convoluted statement. She's not.

"If I'm going to kill someone, I don't go out of my way to take no witness along with me, and I sure as hell don't trick her into going someplace she's already at. It makes no sense."

Classic Vivian.

"No sir. No sense at all."

Terry looks like he just swallowed a bee.

❖

"Let's work the next segment. That will be from when they depart the gas station to when they arrive at Dairy Queen."

Twenty minutes later, we have it.

5:20 PM Justin, Byron, Kelly arrive at Justin's condo (BC); Justin's condo is 25 to 30 minutes from Kelly's house; message on answering machine from Anastasia; Anastasia has arranged a ride; wants to meet Justin

5:35 PM Justin, Byron, Kelly arrive at Dairy Queen (KM); went straight from Phillips 66; approximately 40 minute drive; Anastasia upset Justin is late but treats Kelly nicely.

5:40 PM Justin receives phone call from Anastasia (BC); she is at Dairy Queen; wants Justin to meet her at Dairy Queen; phone call comes in after 5 PM, closer to 6 PM

6:00 PM Diane cannot find Anastasia at Mount Washington (DiM)

6:05 PM Justin completes phone call with Anastasia (BC); phone call lasts 20 to 30 minutes

6:10 PM Justin, Byron, Kelly depart Justin's condo (BC)

6:30 PM Sunset (Stipulation)

6:40 PM Justin, Byron, Kelly arrive at Dairy Queen (BC); Anastasia upset Justin was late and that Byron and Kelly came along

"The obvious conflict here is that Kelly testified they traveled straight from the Phillips 66 to Dairy Queen. Byron testified they returned first to Justin's condo to play video games, received a phone call from Anastasia, and only then proceeded to the Dairy Queen.

"If Kelly's version is true, if she indeed lured Anastasia into a fatal trap, it would make no sense to stop at Byron's condo and play video games along the way. If, on the other hand, Byron's version is true, something equivalent to a stop at Justin's condo is necessary to provide an opportunity for Anastasia to contact them and inform them of her expectations and whereabouts. Each is telling a story segment consistent with their overall claim. Can we discern through other testimony presented to us which story segment is more likely true? Anyone?"

Terry gives it a try.

"Kelly has no reason to lie. Byron does. I'd go with Kelly's."

Groans. I hear someone mutter "Jesus Christ." I'm surprised and pleased. It seems like someone understands.

"Well, you'd be wrong."

It's Chris. It's the first time I recall him directing a response at another juror. Always before, he'd make an insightful observation to no one in particular, then return to his quiet place. This time, his comment is clearly a shot across Terry's bow. The broadside follows.

"If they went straight from the gas station to the Dairy Queen, they would have arrived well before sunset. They left the gas station no later than 4:55. It takes no more than 40 minutes to get from there to the Dairy Queen. They would have arrived no later than 5:35. They would have picked Anastasia up, driven around for fifteen minutes, and arrived at the mausoleum no later than 5:50. Sunset was 6:30. Even Kelly described the groundskeeper by his headlights. They couldn't see him, just his headlights. They only assumed it was the groundskeeper. If they drove straight there, they would have arrived too early for the events as they were described by Glen Colliver, Byron Case, and Kelly herself."

Jade:

"Not only that, if Anastasia received a call from Kelly soon after arriving at Dairy Queen, she wouldn't have kept making calls, unless she was calling someone other than Justin. We have no evidence she was trying to call anyone other than Justin."

Terry:

"You guys keep putting so much faith in the timeline. We don't know if we got all the times right. You guys were guessing at most of them. You tell me, who got up there on the witness stand and said they left the gas station no later than 4:55? Who? No one. Talk about not having any evidence."

❖

"This next timeline segment is going to be the most controversial. This is the one where Byron either shoots Anastasia in the face, or Anastasia gets out of the car and walks away. I suggest we do this segment one at a time, Kelly then Byron. So let's put together our sequence of events from the time they leave Dairy Queen to the time they return to Justin's condo. Just Kelly, for now."

Because we don't have to flip back and forth between the two testimonies, this one goes a little faster than I had come to expect. We're done in about twenty minutes.

> 5:45 PM Justin, Byron, Kelly, Anastasia depart Dairy Queen (KM); Justin drives; Anastasia front right; Byron left rear; Kelly right rear
>
> 6:00 PM Justin, Byron, Kelly, Anastasia arrive at mausoleum (KM); After leaving Diary Queen, drive around for 15 minutes; Justin and Anastasia get out of car to talk; Headlights appear behind them; they figure it's the grounds-keeper
>
> 6:10 PM Justin, Byron, Kelly, Anastasia depart Mount Washington (KM); get lost inside Mt. Washington; exit where they entered; Drive south on Brookside Avenue; west on Truman Road
>
> 6:15 PM Justin, Byron, Kelly, Anastasia enter Lincoln Cemetery (KM); down Truman Road past Erotic City; little dirt road; past stone building

6:20 PM Justin, Byron, Kelly, Anastasia stop in Lincoln Cemetery (KM); Near circle drive; Justin and Anastasia get out; talk on driver's side of car; Justin by driver's door; Anastasia by rear driver's side window; Byron gets out; opens trunk; steps toward Anastasia, raises gun; cannot see type of gun (as per testimony); old double-barrel shotgun (as per interview); Justin waves arms; says something in German; Anastasia staring at Justin; Byron steps towards Anastasia; shoots her from 5 feet away; Anastasia blown backwards; Kelly screams, turns away, then turns back; Kelly can see Anastasia's feet; knows Anastasia must be on her back

6:30 PM Justin, Byron, Kelly depart Lincoln Cemetery (KM); Justin drives; Byron in front seat; Kelly in back seat; No blood on Justin or Byron; Justin pale, crying, shaking; Kelly crying; Byron calm; they stop near industrial park, near RR tracks, near Lincoln cemetery; Byron throws gun away; Byron switches places with Justin; drives away

7:00 PM Justin, Byron, Kelly return to Justin's condo (KM); devise story; 30 minute drive from Lincoln to Justin's condo

7:00 PM Glen sees Anastasia and Justin outside car in Mount Washington (GC)

"Obviously, this is important. This timeline segment encapsulates the only evidence that Byron killed Anastasia in Jackson County on 22 October by shooting her with premeditation. There is no other evidence for most of the elements that the State absolutely must prove to us beyond a reasonable doubt. Not even the phone transcript provides any evidence as to location, date, means or premeditation. This is it. This is the ball game.

"Picking up on Chris's point, it seems to me as if it starts off badly for Kelly. Without the stop at Justin's condo, they arrive way too early to make sense. Kelly's story has Anastasia shot and the three survivors back at Justin's condo at just about the same time Glen Colliver is chasing the four of them from Mount Washington.

"I commented up front about the value of timelines. They're hard to put together, but they frequently help clarify matters. I acknowledge Terry's concern that our timeline isn't perfect, but we can only do our best with the evidence we have. As I see it, if we can't reconstruct the sequence of events, the prosecution cannot have proved it's case. The fact that we're trying so hard to make sense of such shoddy evidence means that we're giving the prosecution an incredibly generous benefit of the doubt.

"Timelines can point out holes in witness testimony. Time can't run backwards. People can't be in two different places at the same time. And now, people can't be both dead and alive at the same time. It seems to me as if we're having difficulty fitting Kelly's story into a reasonable timeline.

"Terry, any of this make sense to you?"

Shrug.

"Something about it bother you?"

Shrug. He's bothered by something.

"Anybody else? Yes, Christina."

"I don't see how Anastasia gets shot in the face, falls backwards, and ends up with her feet on the road and her head on the grass if she was facing Justin when she was shot. Seems to me like Anastasia would have to be facing the car with her back to the grass. And it seems like Byron would then have to be standing between her and the car, facing Anastasia with his back to the car."

Sondra:

"Not only that, Kelly said Anastasia was standing near the rear window, so Byron would have to be between her and the window. That means he would have been blocking Kelly's view."

Jade:

"And Kelly said Anastasia was just standing there, looking at Justin. It doesn't make sense."

Christina:

"That's right. It doesn't make sense."

Me:

"Sounds to me like Kelly is describing a rear-quarter shot, not a face-to-face shooting."

Terry offers an alternative.

"Maybe Anastasia saw Justin waving his arms at Byron, and turned to see what was going on just as Byron fired."

Christina:

"That's not what Kelly said. Kelly said that Anastasia was looking at Justin as Byron approached from the rear. Anyway, if it happened that way, how did Anastasia fall perpendicular to the road?"

Sondra:

"And why was the piece of her skull found north of her head, not up the road a ways? And why wasn't Justin covered with blood from the exit wound, or maybe even hit himself after the bullet passed through Anastasia?"

Terry:

"Look, she conceded it was dark. I think it's understandable she can't recreate it all exactly."

Sondra:

"It wouldn't be all that dark at 6:30 when Kelly's timeline places the shooting. And that's another thing. Why isn't there any blood and stuff on the ground? I think she was shot somewhere else and moved there."

Terry:

"Did they also move the little piece of skull? Seriously."

Sondra:

"When you get shot in the face with a shotgun, is it no muss, no fuss? Is there nothing to clean up except one little piece of skull? Seriously yourself."

Time to intervene.

"Good discussion. Let's see if --"

Terry:

"She said it might have been a rifle."

Christina:

"And she said he was five feet away. That's what she told Kilgore, before she knew it was a contact wound I'll bet. Maybe the rifle had a five foot barrel. Seriously, maybe he shot her with a rifle that had a five foot barrel. Not."

Terry:

"Christ almighty. She said it was a guesstimate. It happened four years ago, five years ago. When Crayon walked up to her and said 'This far?', Kelly kept saying no until Crayon was really close. She didn't have to guess how far in numbers, she could just remember how far by looking."

Me, trying to get a word in.

"Let's see if --"

Sondra:

"Just like when she looked at the wall. Kilgore asked her if five feet is like from here to the wall, and Kelly said maybe farther. Not closer, farther. And I'm not happy with all the swearing, either."

Still trying to get a word in.

"-- if maybe we can --"

Chris silences us all by speaking, quietly.

"Kelly said she could see Anastasia's feet. She couldn't, though."

A new subject and a new puzzle. Couple that with having something worthwhile to say each time you speak up, and Chris can command attention. And he just threw it out there and left us all hanging.

"Why is that Chris? Why couldn't Kelly see Anastasia's feet?"

I guess it's up to me to be Chris' straight man.

"Because she was sitting in the rear passenger seat."

He's right. I see it. I'm going to share it with the others when --

Christina:

"That's right! Gosh, I should have thought of that."

She actually said "Gosh." Now she has the floor.

"Look, if you're sitting in the back seat, behind the driver's seat, you could stick your head out the window, look down, and see her feet. But if you're in the seat on the passenger side of the car, and you look out the driver's side window, all you can see is stuff in the distance. You can't see down. The side of the car is in the way."

Sondra:

"Not only that, her feet would be the last thing you would see. Anastasia's head was farther from the car than her feet. If you lean over from where you're sitting and start to look out, the first thing you'll see is Anastasia's head. The last thing you'll see are her feet."

Silence. People are thinking. That's good. I think.

I allow some time to pass, then I dare suggest we move on.

"Let's see what we can do with how Byron tells this portion of the story. Let's look at his timeline segment from when they leave Dairy Queen to when they arrive back at Justin's condo."

Nothing. I wait a bit. Still nothing.

"But first let's take a break. Let's make it twenty."

George heads for the bathroom. The others push back and walk out slowly. I think the prosecution's goose is cooked.

❖

It happens. In theory, you're not supposed to make up your mind until the jury has discussed all the evidence, but you can't control thoughts that just pop into your head. Even if you have premature thoughts of guilt or innocence, you must control them. You control them by keeping an open mind. Easier said than done, though.

I don't think the prosecution will get a unanimous Guilty vote from this jury. I don't know that the defense will get a unanimous Not Guilty vote, either. I need to just press ahead and keep trying to do this job properly.

The mood isn't quite so heavy when we're all back in place. I think we're all ready to move on.

"Now let's see what we can do with Byron's version of events. Let's look at his timeline from when they leave Dairy Queen to when they arrive back at Justin's condo."

It goes pretty quickly. About ten minutes.

6:45 PM   Justin, Byron, Kelly, Anastasia depart Dairy Queen (BC); Justin drives; Anastasia in front; Byron behind her; Kelly behind Justin

7:00 PM   Justin, Byron, Kelly, Anastasia arrive at mausoleum (BC); After DQ, drive around 15 minutes; stop at mausoleum; Justin and Anastasia get out of car to talk; headlights appear behind them; figure it's the groundskeeper

7:00 PM   Glen sees Anastasia and Justin outside car in Mount Washington (GC)

7:10 PM   Justin, Byron, Kelly, Anastasia depart Mt Washington (BC); get lost inside Mt Washington; exit where they entered; drive south on Brookside Avenue; west on Truman Road

7:15 PM   Justin, Byron, Kelly, Anastasia arrive stop at stoplight (BC); Anastasia jumps out; Byron estimates time as 7:30 PM; Abraham Kneisley says Byron told him 7:30 (AK); Francesca places time as 8:30, one hour before 1st phone call (FW); Don Rand sees woman he identified as Anastasia walk by at 8:30 (DR)

7:45 PM   Justin, Byron, Kelly return to Justin's condo (BC); Byron estimates ride back takes 30 minutes; As they walk in, Byron receives page from Abraham (BC & AK); Byron calls Abraham; AK wants items ferried to ex-girlfriend

7:55 PM   Abraham receives return call from Byron (AK); 10 to 15 minutes after page

8:00 PM   Justin, Byron, Kelly depart Justin's condo (BC); They were there just a few minutes

8:15 PM   Justin, Byron, Kelly arrive at Abraham's (temporary) residence (BC); 35 to 40 minutes after Abraham paged Byron (AK); Abraham house-sitting for friend; pick up sack, perhaps having pants inside, and a letter, maybe

8:35 PM   Byron, Justin, Kelly depart Abraham's (temporary) residence (BC, AK)

8:55 PM   Justin, Byron, Kelly arrive at Kelly's house (BC); 20-minute drive from where Abraham was staying; Byron mentions that Anastasia got out of car; Justin calls Anastasia's house; talks to Francesca; Francesca places time of Justin phone call at 9:30 (FW)

"Byron's lying."

It's Terry.

"He's telling everyone that Anastasia got out of the car and walked away around 7:15 or 7:30 or whatever. He said 7:30 to his pal Abraham, at least that's what Abraham tells us. And now Byron tells us indirectly from all his little it's about twenty minutes from here to here, and I'm pretty sure this happened about this time. But Francesca and Don Rand put the lie to his story, didn't they? Francesca says Justin told her that Anastasia got out of the car at 8:30, and Don Rand says it was 8:30. That's too close to be a coincidence. You look at the timeline. It's your timeline. It's your turn to look at it.

"Justin and Byron and Abraham couldn't keep their story straight, and that's why the times are off, and that's why Byron's story is falling apart as we talk about it."

"So you believe --"

I ask,

"-- that Anastasia did in fact get out of the car, just as Byron said, just as Kelly said for three years, but she got out an hour later than Byron claimed?"

Terry:

"That's not what I'm saying at all. I'm saying Justin lied to Francesca, and Don Rand is full of beans. He didn't see Anastasia. He saw someone else entirely."

Back to me:

"So it was just a coincidence?"

Terry:

"What?"

Me:

"You said that it couldn't be a coincidence that Francesca and Don Rand both timed it at 8:30. But if Francesca timed it at 8:30 because that's what Justin told her, and if Don Rand timed it at 8:30 because he saw some other woman walking by at that time, then it was just a coincidence they gave the same time."

Terry:

"Who cares? You're dodging the point. Byron and Justin made up a story to cover their ass, they got confused about the times, and it's coming back to haunt them right here and now."

Me:

"It seems like Glen Colliver was off by two hours, telling the police he closed the gates at 7 PM, and telling us he closed the gates at 9 PM. It seems like Dawn Wright was off by more than two hours. She said Anastasia left during closing hour, between 9 and 10 PM, though we know Kelly was home right around 9. People are bad about times, dates, figures, memories. To me it's amazing we've put together a timeline that holds together as well as it does four years after the fact, based just upon the testimony of people having a hard time remembering. I guess I'm just not as bothered by the time discrepancy as you are."

"I think he has a point about Don Rand, though."

It's Jade.

"We talked about this before, and I've reviewed my notes. He said she got out of an eastbound car. Byron says they were heading west, back towards Justin's apartment. Don described the woman he saw as five feet, six or seven inches tall. Anastasia was only five feet two inches tall, according to the autopsy report. Don also told the police that the woman was not upset. He told us she was, that he knew so because she walked rapidly. He said he doesn't know if he saw her get out of the car or not. Well if he doesn't know, who should we check with? It's his testimony."

A little sarcasm there. She's not done yet.

"And finally, it doesn't sound to me as if he was very certain that it was Anastasia. They showed him only two pictures, one of a guy and one of a girl. He said the girl looked like her. He didn't say that's her, he said it looked like her."

Pretty impressive take down of Don Rand's testimony.

"Well there goes Byron's alibi, eastbound up Truman Road."

That's a little parting shot from Terry.

"We're a little late on the break everyone. Let's come back in fifteen. We'll go over the phone call and we'll vote."

DELIBERATION: PHONE CALL OF JUNE 5, 2001

The jury is just about used up. I check with them to see if they want to cover events later than the arrival back at Byron's condo. They do not. They are not particularly interested in what happened later that day, or that month, that year, or years following. They know Justin committed suicide and Kelly's life went south. At this point, they don't find it relevant. I guess I agree.

They are, however, exceptionally interested in discussing the recorded phone call from Kelly to Byron. I understand that. We agree we'll discuss the phone call, then we'll vote.

It's been a long time coming. Three days of disciplined deliberation has taken its toll. I don't share with my fellow jurors that my previous deliberation lasted eight days. Three days, eight days, it's a pittance either way compared to the lifetime of injustice and anguish we'll inflict with a bad verdict.

The jury sucks it up and, relying heavily on Jade's note taking prowess, we compile our final summary.

- Recording is of poor quality; particularly hard to hear Byron
- Kelly asks Byron twice why he had to kill Anastasia; Byron does not respond
- Byron advises Kelly to tell police that she cannot remember what happened
- Byron tells Kelly they shouldn't be talking about the case
- Byron tells Kelly he has been granted immunity in the case
- Byron tells Kelly he told the police everything

"I'll begin discussion, if I may. I have no intention of being coy. The tape is damning. It makes Byron look guilty. That bothers me because I can't see how anything else in this trial implicates him. Each of you will weigh Kelly's testimony best you can, but for me she's not credible. I don't know why she's lying, but I'm sure she is. Her story simply doesn't hold water. She was caught too many times in too many lies: the phone call, the shotgun, the drinking, the position of the players, the distance of the shot, the direction of the shot, her ability to see Anastasia's feet.

"I'm particularly bothered by her ever-changing story. For three years it wasn't Byron or Justin, then it was Justin, then Byron, then Justin, then Byron. Even Fry begins his closing argument talking about what a liar she is. That's simply stunning. How anyone can believe this woman beyond a reasonable doubt is absolutely beyond me.

"But then there's that darn tape staring me in the face. I say that metaphorically, of course, because we don't have the tape. We haven't been allowed to bring that tape in here along with the other evidence. We haven't been allowed to listen to it over and over and over again, to see if we might be able to hear what it says.

"So maybe if we can't have the tape itself, we'll get the transcript. But we don't get that either. We're told the transcript is not evidence. To compound the problem, we're told that the tape is not evidence. The only evidence, we're instructed, is our recollection of what was on the tape.

"The transcript itself raises huge questions. We never learned who transcribed the tape, and we never learned how they could hear it if we couldn't.

"And who do they have to substantiate the transcript as being valid? Kelly, that's who. Not an acoustics expert or even an independent Joe Q. Citizen off the street, but the very person the State is relying upon to put Byron Case away.

"So how could Kelly hear that tape clearly if we couldn't? I have an answer to that one as well. I don't think she could. It seems at one point Crayon even asked Kelly something along the line of 'And with the aid of the transcript you were able to hear what was on the tape.'

"It's amateur time, everyone. We have a police department who can't make a decent recording and a DA who has the chief witness corroborate the evidence which corroborates her own testimony which corroborates the evidence. And around we go."

I look to Jade for help on this point. She gives me a nod. I hope others saw that.

"So we're supposed to rely on our collective memories and our notes. You guys know that's ridiculous. Hard as it is to take notes fast enough when someone is testifying, that's nothing compared to how impossible it is to take good notes while listening to a crappy recording while reading an unsubstantiated transcript that we're not to consider as evidence. It irritated me then, and it's angering me now, so I'll just yield to anyone who wants the floor."

This is Terry's big chance, and he doesn't disappoint.

"He's guilty. It's as simple as that. You guys can draw on the board all you want, but when push gets to shove, he's guilty. Kelly twice asks him why he felt the need to kill Anastasia. Not just once, but twice. And he said nothing. Nothing!

"If Kelly asked me why I killed Anastasia, I'd tell her she's crazy. If she asked a second time, I'd tell her she's fuckin' crazy. And that's it. That's the case right there, and that's why I'm voting Guilty. You guys can keep drawing and making your little timelines, but he did it and you know he did it, and I'm damned sure not going to let him walk out of here free and clear to kill someone else."

The room is stone quiet. Terry just put to words what everyone has been thinking about all along.

"You think the tape proves Byron killed Anastasia?"

"You got that right."

"Because he didn't say anything when Kelly accused him?"

"That's what I'm saying."

"Even if he had strep throat and a fever?"

"Sounded lucid to me. Agreed to meet her at the park the next day. I'm not buying the death's doorstep excuse."

"Did Byron say he shot her?"

"Didn't have to. Kelly told us."

"Did Byron say he shot her in Jackson County?"

"Nope. Didn't have to."

"Did Byron say he shot her in on the 22nd of October?"

"Nope."

"Did Byron say he killed her in any fashion?"

"He sure did, when he just sat there and took it while Kelly twice accused him of murder. I know where you're going with this, but I'm not buying. Byron didn't have to tell us how, where, when, and why. We didn't have to hear it from his mouth. We heard it from Kelly. What Byron told us during the phone call is that we should believe Kelly. You can play private detective and hot shot lawyer all you want with your gotta show this and gotta show that and he was here but she was there. What you can't get around is that when push came to shove, he didn't say squat when Kelly flat out accused him of murder, TWICE. He just told her they shouldn't talk about it."

"You're focusing on what Byron didn't say. You're using absence of evidence as proof of guilt. How about when Byron said he told the police everything? To me that sounds like he's got nothing to hide."

I'm dying here.

"If he's got nothing to hide, why is he telling Kelly to just say she can't remember? Why is he telling her they shouldn't talk about it? It only gets worse for him when he finally does open his mouth."

I'm getting pummeled. When Terry was getting beat up earlier by the other jurors, I felt a bit smug. It's not so easy being on the receiving end, though. The other jurors looked to me to come up with something about the tape, and I didn't. Now when I scan the room, they're not looking to me at all. They're taking meaningless notes, or scribbling, or twirling their pencils, all while gravely considering the weighty issues before us. I've become the gruesome traffic accident you're not supposed to stare at.

"Sorry to get off subject here, but I had a pretty nice ball point pen when this whole thing started."

It's Chris. He's come to my rescue. At least I hope.

"And, uh, now it's gone. So, uh, Terry, why did you feel the need to steal my pen?"

Terry's caught off guard, as we all are. But he sees the trap and knows he has to respond quickly. He remembers his line perfectly.

"You're crazy."

"I'm not kidding. My pen's gone. Why'd you steal my pen?"

Terry smiles as he recalls his second line.

"You're not just crazy, you're fuckin' crazy."

"Maybe so, but I would still like an answer. Why did you steal my pen?"

"Look. I can play this silly little game as long as you want. You can ask me as many times as you want, and every time you ask me, I'm going to give you the same answer. You're crazy."

"That's good. Because the first time you don't answer, that'll be all the proof I need you really stole my pen."

THE VOTE

"Does anyone have anything more they want to discuss prior to our vote?"

"No one?"

The tension is palpable. I have a knot in my stomach.

"Okay. Here's how we're going to do this. Everyone please tear a blank sheet of paper from your notebook. In the middle of it, write Guilty or Not Guilty, as your conscience dictates. Fold the paper twice, top-to-bottom first, then side-to-side. Then pass your votes this way. I'll mix them up, then I'll read them one by one."

My hand trembles, just barely, as I write my vote. I assume no one else will notice. They'll be wrestling with their own demons.

I fold my ballot and wait patiently as pieces of paper are scribbled upon, folded, and passed from person to person. I'm careful not to look at any of the others as they vote. Instead, I just look at my folded piece of paper sitting on table before me. If I'm so confident that I fulfilled my oath, why do I feel so nervous? Why do I feel as if I might throw up?

When all other eleven ballots arrive, I lift them and drop them several times to scramble them. I allow myself to sit for a moment.

"Lots of juries simply use a show of hands. I prefer a secret ballot."

I realize that I'm looking at the pile of ballots rather than at the jurors. It's just the way I feel right now. I'm voting as part of a group, but it feels as if it's one of the most personal things I'll ever do.

"I want each vote to reflect a conclusion of a single juror based on that juror's deliberation and conscience. I don't want peer pressure and group dynamics to influence anyone's vote."

I was specific about the manner in folding the paper because previously, without such instruction, I was able to associate some votes with some jurors due to the way they folded the paper. I didn't say anything to anyone, but I felt then like I had violated someone's privacy. I'm trying to avoid that here.

"Most people here suspect they can guess the votes of many of their fellow jurors. Maybe that's so, but a blind vote still gives everyone the best opportunity for voting their conscience. That's why I asked for ballots.

"I'll announce the votes and lay them out as I count them. Guilty votes, if any, I'll place to my left. Not Guilty votes, if any, I'll place to my right. When I'm done, anyone who wants to check my count will be free to do so.

I take a deep breath, unfold the first ballot, and begin the count.

"Guilty."

I'm crushed, but I try not to let it show. I place the ballot to my left, unfolded, the word "Guilty" visible to all.

I unfold the next ballot, and read it out loud.

"Not Guilty."

All of us now realize that the vote will not be unanimous, that we won't have a verdict this round. It seems as if the jury itself exhales. It seems disappointed and relieved at the same time. I place the ballot to my right.

I unfold the next.

"Not Guilty."

Ballot goes to the right. I unfold the next.

"Not Guilty."

Another on the pile to the right. I wonder if I did that sub-consciously, placing the repository for my preferred vote to the right.

"Not Guilty."

That was my vote. I recognize my own handwriting.

"Guilty."

I place that one on the pile to the left.

"Guilty."

This is tough. I can't imagine anyone is happy with how the vote is playing out.

"Guilty."

Wow. I'm shocked at the divide. I'm thinking about where we'll go from here.

"Not Guilty."

Everyone's dismayed, though I'm not sure anyone expected a unanimous vote. Not really.

"Guilty."

Still it's hard to accept when the realization sets in.

"Not Guilty."

I can feel my tension ease. It's hard to accept the vote, but I guess it was the uncertainty that was most responsible for the knots.

"Not Guilty."

That's it. I pick up the pile to the left and count through them, placing them back on the table one at a time.

"One, two, three, four, five, Guilty."

I do the same for the right hand pile.

"One, two, three, four, five, six, seven, Not Guilty."

I lean back in my chair, and say nothing. No one else says anything either. We just sit there.

❖

Chad breaks the ice.

"What do we do now?"

It's time to provide reassurance, even though I am far from sure we'll ever reach unanimous consent.

"It's not unusual for the first ballot to be split. My understanding is that's the norm, not the exception. Yet most juries end up with a unanimous vote.

"Of the three previous juries I was on, one was a unanimous Not Guilty after the first ballot. Another was split 10 to 2 Guilty until the fifth ballot, when it changed to a unanimous Guilty vote. The third one started out 11 to 1 Guilty on the first ballot, and ended up hung as 10 to 2 Not Guilty. Nine people changed their votes.

"While getting a unanimous verdict is a reasonable goal, it's far from the most important goal of a jury deliberation. I'm sure the judge and the prosecution won't agree with me, but I believe the most important goal is that the jury fulfills its oath.

"That means deliberating all the evidence, together, as a jury, in accordance with the instructions we have been provided. We each get to decide if we've done that.

"It means presuming the defendant to be innocent. We each get to decide if we've done that.

"And finally it means demanding the prosecution prove each and every element of the crime beyond a reasonable doubt before we find the defendant Guilty. That's where we're at right now. If we each vote Not Guilty unless we believe in good conscience the prosecution has proved its case beyond a reasonable doubt, then we can all go home and take comfort that we did our duty, and did it well.

"I propose one more round of voting. Before we vote, however, I would like to go around the table and have each of us tell the others two things. First, I would like each of us, in turn, to identify the single piece of evidence that is most incriminating. What most seems to make Byron guilty.

"Also, I would like each of us to identify which piece of evidence most seems to make Byron innocent.

"And finally, this time around, I suggest that we not attempt to convince any other juror. I ask that instead that this be a final moment of self-reflection. If

I vote Not Guilty, what is going to bother me the most about my vote later? If I vote Guilty, what question will always nag at me?

"If you don't want to share your thoughts with the rest of us, that's fine.

"If we look critically at our own reasons for our vote, we will have fulfilled our oath regardless of the outcome."

I let that settle.

"Everybody in?"

Lot's of "yeah's" and a "let's do it."

"It's been a pleasure, everyone. I'm proud to be a member of this jury."

"If no one objects, I'll get it rolling. Then we'll go counterclockwise. Sondra will get the last word."

They're ready.

"Okay, I tell you the one thing that makes me most suspicious of the State's case. It's the ballistics. More specifically, I don't see how a shotgun slug fits through that hole. She said it was a shotgun and she changed to a rifle, possibly, late in the game when the shotgun story started falling apart.

"Now here's what's bothers me most about the defense case. It's the tape. Why didn't he tell her she was crazy? Why didn't he ask her what the hell she was talking about? Why did he try to get her not to talk about it? That really bothers me. But then I ask myself, if Kelly really saw Byron kill Anastasia, why is she lying about how it really happened? I don't get it.

"It's not very satisfying, I know. But those are the two ends of the spectrum from my perspective. Thank you for listening.

"Chris, you're up."

Chris is most bothered by the tape as well. He doesn't understand any better than I do. In terms of problems for the State, he is most bothered that they didn't offer any evidence of blood on the car. If they had found Anastasia's blood on the side of the car, or in the trunk, or on the floorboard, or anywhere, it would be a slam dunk vote.

Liza is bothered that there was no blood splatter to be found. That's evidence to her that Anastasia had been moved there after she was shot. If Anastasia had been moved there, then Kelly's story is a lie. Like Terry and me, she is bothered as well by the June 5 phone call.

George has really been quiet since he made his argument the weapon could not have been a shotgun or a high-powered rifle. It's therefore not surprising that, for him, the weakest point of the State's case was that Byron allegedly shot Anastasia with a shotgun or a high-powered rifle. He believes the wound would have been far more serious. He's not happy about the phone call, but doesn't expand on that thought.

Vivian doesn't trust Kelly, period.

"She lied and lied and lied. I won't be believing her now. But Byron knows something about what happened. That's why he doesn't want to talk about it on the phone or anywhere."

Jade is bothered by Kelly's description of the shooting. She doesn't understand how Byron could have inflicted a contact wound to Anastasia's nose from five feet behind. Like everyone else, she finds the tape suspicious.

Terry thinks the tape is the strongest piece of evidence proving Byron to be Guilty. He agrees with Jade though, that Kelly's positioning of the people that night is troublesome.

Chad volunteers that he voted Guilty previously because of the tape. The thing that bothers him most is Kelly claiming she saw Anastasia's feet. He knows that might seem strange, but that's what bothers him. On the other hand, if she was just going to lie about it, why didn't she just say she was in the back seat on the driver's side? That's what Byron said. If she had just gone along with that, she would have been able to see everything. It doesn't make sense.

Tony asks to pass. He says he's thought about it, and thanks everyone.

Christina agrees with Jade and Terry about Byron being five feet behind Anastasia, though Blanchard said it was a contact wound. She surprises everyone by not mentioning the tape. She is completely put off by the defense theory that Anastasia was killed by a complete stranger. There's no evidence of attempted rape or attempted robbery, and there's no reason for Anastasia to cut through Lincoln, and there's no evidence she tried to resist, but the defense is arguing that she was killed by a stranger.

Sondra is with Liza. The lack of blood splatter on the ground, on the car, on any of their clothes makes no sense. Others have talked about the lack of blood on the car or on the ground, but she wants to add that no blood was noticed on the clothes. Kelly never said that Byron or Justin changed clothes, but Kelly's mother never said anything about seeing blood on them.

Sondra on the other hand is now torn on what most makes Byron look guilty. She was thinking the phone call until just a minute ago when Christina talked about the defense theory of an unknown, deranged shooter. Now she can't decide which of the two she thinks is more damaging.

I'm tempted to explain that a crazy defense theory is not evidence of guilt, but it was my rule that no one could argue or correct anyone this time around. I let it go.

"Okay. This is it. It's going to be another paper ballot, so we all know what to do. It won't take long at all, one way or another. Christina, please ring the buzzer one last time. We'll be done before they ask us back to the courtroom.

"Almost time to go home."

INTERLUDE

Harry Truman is famous for the small, rectangular sign he kept on his desk. "The Buck Stops Here." Many others since have invoked those words. Few have acted true to them.

Harry lived just up the road from Lincoln Cemetery. Travel east three miles along Truman Road, turn right on Delaware, and there you are. Harry moved there in 1919 when he married Bess. They returned there after his presidency. He died there in 1972. Bess died there in 1982.

Fifteen years and four days later, Don Rand thought he saw Anastasia walking east along Truman Road. Anastasia lived just a stone's throw from Harry's house. Home was so close, but something went terribly wrong.

Jurors are routinely pressed by the State into making decisions that will alter the lives of others. In our legal system, the buck stops in the jury deliberation room. As a juror, you own your verdict. It becomes part of you. You think of it often.

If you are lucky, your thoughts will comfort you that the system works, that as a juror you helped bring an evil person to justice or, more importantly, you helped save an innocent person from the excesses of an authoritarian government. It's a romantic thought.

The reality is far from romantic, however. Juries convict twenty-five percent of the factually innocent brought before them. Juries also acquit fifteen percent of defendants who are factually guilty. As a juror, you should be aware of the harsh possibilities.

Though you do not ask to sit in judgment, the buck will stop with you. If you free a guilty person to do evil again, no one will stop you. If you condemn an innocent to ruination, you will be unable to take back your vote. The buck will stop with you.

To ease your burden, I offer a decision making strategy that gives you the best chance of living with your verdict, regardless of what you might learn after trial, regardless of what events may unfold. As with Harry Truman's short and pithy motto, my strategy is easy to express but difficult to follow.

Do your duty. Stand fast to your oath.

That's it. Follow the jury instructions. Presume innocence. Don't just say the words, act on them. Convict if and only if the State proves beyond a reasonable doubt each and every element of its case. Acquit otherwise. Be skeptical of everyone. Be unmoved by pleas for justice and cries from beyond the grave. Ignore the machinations and theatrics of the courtroom actors. Above all, do not relinquish your decision to others. Listen to their arguments, but not their emotion or prejudices. Rely on the evidence, only on the evidence, and be skeptical of that.

Do your duty. Stand fast to your oath. Go home and wait for the other shoe to drop.

ACT III
AFTERMATH

VERDICT

The case was submitted to the jury at 10:25 AM on May 2, 2002.

At 11:06, the actual jury, not our literary jury, communicated to the court that they wanted the audiotape and associated transcript delivered to the jury room. They also wanted to see the receipts for the shotguns that Justin purchased, the pictures of Justin and Byron's cars, all other photographs, the transcript of Kelly's testimony, and the transcript of Francesca's testimony.

Judge Atwell cleared the courtroom of everyone other than courtroom personnel, the attorneys, and the defendant. He ordered the door locked to prevent entry of anyone other than the jurors. He called the jurors back to the courtroom and responded directly to their requests.

"Ladies and gentlemen, what I'm going to do, in situations such as this, where there is audio or visual evidence, I generally bring the jury back down and play for their benefit in my presence, and that's the practice I intend to do today. So what we'll do, we will play the tape, the tape that was admitted. The transcript will be provided to you, so you can listen to it with the transcript again.

"As I told you before and would apply equally strongly now, the transcript itself is not evidence. It's only meant to assist you into listening to the tape itself. The evidence is your collective memory of what the tape says.

"So I brought you down for that purpose. While you're here, I'm going to go ahead, normally I would answer in writing to these other requests, but I'll go ahead and tell you the answers if that's all right.

"First of all, we have gathered together all of the evidence that has been admitted, and with the exception, there is a videotape of Mr. Bruton buying the firearm which we don't have a videotape machine readily available, so we didn't include that. Everything else that's in evidence will be provided to you when you return to the jury room; photographs, documents, all those things.

"Regarding the transcript of Francesca and Kelly, Ms. Moffett and the victim's sister, Francesca WitbolsFeugen, I am not allowed to provide you transcripts of any witness' testimony, so you must be guided by your collective memory of the testimony as you recall it.

"With that being said, let's pass out the transcript for the tape. Also, ladies and gentlemen, I have locked the courtroom door so we can preserve the dignity of your deliberations. So no one else can be in the room while you listen to the tape."

The Court played the tape for the jury one more time. The bailiff then gathered the transcript, and Judge Atwell instructed the jury to return to the jury room.

At 2:20 PM, four hours after the jury began deliberating, the actual jury, not our literary jury, informed the court it had reached a decision. The jurors were brought back to the courtroom, which was once again open to the public.

"Everyone, please be seated. My understanding is the jury has reached verdicts; is that correct?"

The foreperson said "Yes."

"Would you please pass the jury instructions and verdict forms to Mr. Cotton?"

The bailiff took the documents from the foreperson and delivered them to Judge Atwell. He reviewed them, briefly.

"The verdicts appear in proper order. The Court will now publish the verdict.

"As to Count One, we, the jury, find the defendant Byron Case, Guilty of Murder in the First Degree as submitted in instruction number five.

The defense asked that the jurors be polled. Each juror was asked in turn "Is this your verdict?" Each juror said "Yes." Judge Atwell spoke to them as a group for the last time in the courtroom.

"Ladies and gentlemen, first of all, I want to thank you as sincerely as I can for your service in this case. This was an extremely well-tried case. It was a case that needed to be resolved, and I think you all were very attentive, and I appreciate your service.

"What I'm going to do, I'm going to ask you to briefly return to the jury room. I'll be up there. If you got any questions of me, you're welcome to ask questions of me at that time if you would like to. Then you'll be released.

"I will also tell you at this point in time, the admonition regarding talking or not talking about the case no longer applies. There are occasions which, when the lawyers who try the cases sometimes like to talk to the jury about what things were persuasive, what things were meaningful. You certainly can talk to them if you wish. You need not. It's your right not to also.

I would suggest, if you do talk to any of the lawyers about the case, I think it's important not to discuss the particular votes of any juror or to discuss what any particular juror said, but just what you did as a group.

"Again, I really appreciate the work that you have done in a very difficult case, and I really, really appreciate it. I'm going to ask that you go briefly to the jury room. I'll be there in a few moments.

And for the last time in the case of Missouri v. Byron Case, the jurors heard "All rise, please. Jury is free to go to the jury room."

❖

Judge Atwell thanked the jury for being "attentive" in this "very difficult" case. The actual jury, however, didn't seem to find the case so difficult.

They were out for a grand total of 3 hours and 45 minutes. Their deliberations spanned a 90 lunch break and included 20 minutes in the courtroom listening to the tape a second time. Assuming they broke for lunch, they spent no more 2 hours and 5 minutes deliberating the fate of Byron Case. From the perspective of a skeptical juror, that is troubling. Such a monumental decision deserves more thought and more time.

Judge Atwell bears much of the responsibility for the brief deliberations. He made two rulings which seriously inhibited the jurors from engaging in comprehensive deliberations. The first was to forbid jurors from taking notes.

I'm not suggesting that Judge Atwell's ruling on this matter was improper in a legal sense, or even that it was unusual. I understand that many Judges consider note-taking to be a distraction, and that some judges fear notes might be granted undue significance. Imagine, however, our own literary deliberations without ready access to our twelve sets of notes. While no single juror had complete notes, collectively we did a pretty good job of covering the significant testimony as presented during the trial. Our notes allowed us to summarize the testimony of each witness and to build the timeline. In the absence of those notes, we would have had difficulty remembering just the witness names with precision.

I wasn't surprised then to learn that the jurors asked the judge for copies of transcripts of Kelly's testimony, Francesca's testimony, the tape, and other items of evidence. Nor was I surprised when the judge would not allow the jurors to take the transcripts into the jury room. Witness transcripts are never allowed in the jury room, as far as I know. Lawyers can sometimes get daily transcripts, but jurors ... never.

What did surprise me was that Judge Atwell did not have the testimony read back to the jury, though he allowed the tape to be played for them one additional time. Clearly the actual jury had questions about Kelly and Francesca's testimony. Just as clearly, those questions remained unanswered. Byron Case was convicted of first degree murder by a jury that was self-confessedly uncertain regarding the evidence of the State's primary witnesses.

Atwell's prohibition of notes combined with his refusal to re-read witness testimony deprived the jurors of any realistic opportunity to capture the nuance and subtlety of the testimonial evidence. Instead the jurors were left most likely to recall the performance elements of the trial, the drama rather than the facts. They were likely to recall most vividly that which they had heard most recently. No wonder the State insists on closing both first and last.

I have yet to be on a jury in which I was forbidden to take notes. If I find myself in such circumstance, I will ask frequently and repeatedly to have large portions of testimony re-read to me in open court. If the State refuses me this reasonable request, I will likely revert to my default verdict of Not Guilty.

JUDICIAL RESOLUTION

For the crime of murder in the first degree, Byron Case was sentenced to life in prison without possibility of parole.

Byron appealed his conviction based on two contentions. First, Byron argued that there was insufficient evidence to convict him since the testimony of the State's key witness was marred by contradictions and was uncorroborated. Second, Byron argued that the trial court violated rules of evidence by allowing the State to admit the phone recording.

With respect to the insufficiency contention, Byron's attorney argued that the prosecution's case relied almost exclusively on Kelly's testimony. Since Kelly's testimony was both contradictory and uncorroborated, Judge Atwell should have, as a matter of law, declared the defendant Not Guilty rather than submitting the case to the jury.

With respect to the recorded phone call, Byron argued that the conversation did not constitute a tacit admission and therefore should have been excluded as hearsay.

Take note that Byron did not argue that the jury's verdict was incorrect, that he was actually innocent. Actual innocence is not a valid basis for appeal, with rare exception. Courts up to and including the U.S. Supreme Court operate under the assumption that if the trial was conducted fairly and the jury unanimously voted Guilty, the defendant is in fact Guilty. Appeals, therefore, almost always attempt to find fault with the trial procedure rather than with the jury's decision.

Byron, in his appeal, did not fault the jury. He faulted the court for allowing the case to go the jury at all, and also for allowing the jury to hear the phone recordings. The appeals court made short work of his appeal. It ruled that Kelly's testimony was neither uncorroborated nor contradictory. Kelly's testimony was corroborated by the phone recordings. Furthermore, Kelly's testimony was not contradictory in a technical sense, since contradictions with pre-trial testimony and contradictions with other witness were legally excluded from Byron's legal argument. The court declared further that Kelly's testimony wasn't contradictory even with other testimony in the case. To complete the hat trick, the court declared that even if Kelly's testimony was contradictory, it was inconsequential to the verdict.

Before the trial, Byron was legally presumed innocent. Since the Guilty verdict, Byron has been legally presumed Guilty. By law, the appeals court weighed the evidence in a light most favorable to the prosecution. To understand how powerful the presumption of guilt can be, consider the following excerpt from the appellate court's ruling.

Case's claim that Kelly's testimony about the shooting flatly contradicted the medical evidence is false. According to the medical evidence, the muzzle of the gun used to kill Anastasia was less than six inches away from her when she was shot . . . Kelly did testify that Case was five feet away from Anastasia when he shot her, but she characterized her testimony about this matter as a 'guesstimate.' If the gun was three feet long and Kelly's guesstimate was off by two feet, then her testimony is consistent with the medical evidence that the muzzle was less than six inches from Anastasia when she was shot. Kelly's testimony about the shooting was not inconsistent with the medical evidence.

The court failed to address the issue of whether an entry wound on the nose could have been caused by a shot from the rear. It didn't have to. If it had elected to it would merely have pointed out that Anastasia could have turned her head just before she was shot. The appellate court, which works from a presumption of guilt, has no difficulty reconciling a contact wound to the nose with a rear quarter shot from five feet away. The jury, which supposedly worked from a presumption of innocence, should have had considerable problem with that contradiction.

With respect to the tape, the appeals court agreed with the prosecution that the conversation constituted a tacit admission. The tape was therefore not excluded by hearsay rules.

> A defendant makes a tacit admission of guilt when the defendant fails to respond to or significantly acquiesces in the import of an inculpatory statement by making an equivocal, ambivalent, or evasive response when the inculpatory statement was made in the presence and hearing of the accused, and was sufficiently direct, as would naturally call for a reply.

If someone asked you why you felt the need to kill John Kennedy, and you simply stared at them, that would clearly fit within Missouri's definition of a tacit admission. You failed to respond.

If instead of remaining silent you told the person to "Shut the fuck up," that too would be a tacit admission. That exact response has already been judged as a tacit admission by the State of Missouri. "We shouldn't talk about this" would also be a tacit admission, since that's what Byron allegedly said. "Maybe I did, maybe I didn't" would certainly be a tacit admission, since it's equivocal.

It's difficult to determine how eloquent one might have to be to avoid tacitly admitting to the assassination. I'm guessing "Have a nice day" might be insufficient, since it's ambivalent. "Bite me" is not much different than "Shut the fuck up." "I don't know what you're talking about" might be ruled evasive, as could "I've got to be getting home."

I suggest something along the line of: "I did not kill John Kennedy, nor did I have any agent act in my stead, nor did I have any role whatsoever in his assassination, either before or afterwards, nor do I know of anyone who actually participated in or contemplated his assassination." Think quickly though. If you try something such as "I'll need to check with my attorney before responding to your statement," that will almost certainly qualify as tacit admission in Missouri.

The appeals court cited the following portion of the Byron / Kelly conversation as the tacit admission:

> Kelly told Case, who was at his residence: [The police have] called a bunch again. They called while I was in rehab, they showed up out there. Yeah. I don't understand, like seriously, what all went on or whatever, and I seriously, I hate to say this, but why, seriously, why did you have to kill her? What was the whole fucking big deal? Could you explain that to me? Because I don't get it. Seriously. Justin's dead for no reason, she's dead for no reason. It's just all fucked up. And for some reason they're talking to me, because you won't talk. So I'm fucked. And it makes me look horrible because everybody already knows that I'm a fucking crack-head, that I'm a coke-head, that I'm an alcoholic and don't remember shit. And if I tried to talk to them, nothing's going to add up. So, I mean if you could seriously explain to me as to why you actually felt the need to kill her, then that would really help me feel better about the whole fucking thing. I mean, was there seriously any reason to all this?

> Case responded by saying, 'We shouldn't talk about this.' Kelly said, 'Why?' Case then repeated, 'Probably because we shouldn't talk about this.'

Byron didn't stand a chance. The vote to affirm the verdict was three to zero.

❖

Byron filed a second appeal, this time claiming ineffective assistance of counsel. Byron claimed his public defender, Horton Lance, made a major error when Kelly blurted out in court that she had taken a lie detector test. Before the trial, Judge Atwell had ruled that lie detector and stress test results were not to be mentioned in court. Lie detector and stress tests are deemed unproven and are almost always inadmissible.

Kelly's outburst left the impression that she took and passed a lie detector test to prove that she saw Byron shoot Anastasia. Kelly did in fact take a test, a stress test rather than a lie detector test. Significantly, Kelly took that stress test while she was still claiming Anastasia got out of the car and walked away. She took neither a stress test nor a lie detector test after she changed her story to claim Byron shot Anastasia.

Horton Lance objected, as he should have. Judge Atwell quickly realized the magnitude of the error. He called a sidebar and offered the defense a mistrial. Against Byron's initial wishes, Horton Lance declined the offer. Lance explained he was concerned Abraham Kneisley and Tara McDowell might be unable or unwilling to fly back for a second trial. Lance didn't ask them if they would be available, he simply declined the mistrial. Lance asked Judge Atwell instead to issue a strong cautionary statement to the jury. Judge Atwell told the jury to ignore what Kelly had blurted out, thereby bringing further attention to the lie detector test she seemingly took and passed.

Byron also argued that Lance was injudicious in his questioning, should have called additional witnesses, and should have argued more effectively to exclude the phone conversations. Once again, Byron had little reason for hope. The standard for effective counsel is so low that it excludes almost no one.

In California v. Garrison, for example, it was uncontested that Garrison's attorney was an alcoholic at the time of the trial. The attorney consumed alcohol before, during, and after trial. The bailiff confirmed the attorney always smelled of alcohol. On the second day of jury selection, the attorney was arrested for driving drunk to the courthouse. His blood alcohol level was 0.27. The attorney died of alcoholism after the trial. Nonetheless, Garrison lost his ineffective-counsel appeal. Garrison failed to show that the attorney's alcoholism had any impact on the outcome.

In United States v. Muyet, the appellate court acknowledged that Muyet's attorney slept through portions of the trial. The court denied the ineffective-assistance claim because the attorney was not "in a state of unconsciousness (actually snoring in the courtroom) throughout the trial." Since Muyet failed to convince the court that the verdict would have been different had the attorney been awake throughout the trial, the attorney's conduct was deemed to meet "prevailing professional norms."

In California v. Smith, Smith alleged and the appellate court agreed that the defense attorney suffered mental illness during the trial. The attorney feared for his own safety because he believed he and his client were targets of a murder conspiracy involving the victim's relatives and friends. The attorney shared his conspiracy theory with the jury during his opening statement. When discussing the case, he alternated between stupor and laughter. He told his secretary that he was crazy, that he wanted to go to an asylum. His associate, his secretary, and his private investigator supported the claim that their boss and colleague was mentally ill. The appellate court ruled that "although there is merit to the argument that a mentally unstable attorney may make errors of judgment," the mental illness by itself was insufficient evidence that the attorney was ineffective.

In Virginia v. Honaker, the defendant was charged with rape, though he was a hundred miles away at the time of the crime. The state serologist testified to the presence of sperm in the rapist's semen. The defense attorney failed to introduce into evidence the rather significant fact that Honaker had a vasectomy. Honaker was convicted and sentenced to three life sentences plus 34 years. He lost his appeals. He served ten years before DNA testing cleared him.

The surfeit of bad defense attorneys should come as no surprise. In Mississippi, the State will pay private counsel no more than $1,000 for representing indigent defendants in a non-death-penalty case. In some rural sections of Texas, the limit is $800. The State of Virginia will pay no more than $305 for defending an indigent client against any felony charge punishable by less than twenty years. The extra $5 is a nice touch.

Public defenders, on the other hand, are frequently hamstrung by their caseload. The American Bar Association cites studies indicating that public defenders can competently handle 150 to 200 cases at a time. Some public defenders' offices are being sued because they exceed that number. Some offices are rejecting cases to stay below that number. From my perspective, even 150 cases at a time seems amazingly high. It can't leave much time for tending to each case.

The New Orleans Public Defender's office handles 50,000 criminal, municipal, traffic, and juvenile cases a year. It employs just 42 attorneys. Assuming 250 work days in a year, the office needs to clear nearly five cases per day per attorney. Assuming ten hour workdays, that's two hours per case per attorney.

These public defender statistics should reflect poorly on our legal system, not on the attorneys themselves. Unfortunately, such onerous workloads will, on occasion, cause public defenders to make decisions that are not in the best interest of their clients.

In the trial of Missouri v. Case, Horton Lance declined a judge's offer for a mistrial. The appellate court refused to second guess that decision. Compared to the drunken, sleep-deprived, mentally-unbalanced attorneys who pass competency muster, Horton Lance must have looked like Clarence Darrow.

AFTERMATH: GUNS

In the trial of Missouri v. Case, the State argued out of one side of its mouth that Anastasia WitbolsFeugen was killed by a shotgun blast to the nose, fired from point blank range. The defense attempted to refute that argument, in part, by persuading the prosecution's ballistic non-expert to concede the weapon might have been a .22 caliber handgun. The State, appalled that their non-expert conceded such a thing, responded by having the non expert assign a low probability to the possibility. When all was said and done, the jury learned that the weapon could have been anything from the largest of shotguns to the smallest of handguns. There was no way of narrowing it down further.

Quite simply, the ballistics portion of the trial was a circus. As the players in the ballistic circus streamed from their tiny clown car, they ran madcap about center ring tripping over huge ballistic clues. It was funny, I suppose, because the clues were obvious to anyone not having orange hair, a big red nose, and gigantic shoes.

Here's one of the clues none of the clowns could see. The bullet fragment found at the back of Anastasia's skull weighed 56 grains.

Perhaps you don't recall Dr. Young found a single bullet fragment while examining Anastasia's body. He wasn't there to tell you, of course, but Dr. Blanchard read from his autopsy report. He mentioned the fragment twice in that report; once to say he found it, once to say he sent it to the crime lab. No significance was made of the fragment by either the prosecution or defense.

Even if you do recall some mention of the fragment, you had no way to know that it weighed fifty-six grains. Dr. Blanchard didn't mention this during her trial testimony. She didn't even know of it prior to her deposition. I quote from her deposition.

> Lance: There is a lab report somewhere. You may not have seen it. It says the bullet fragment weighed 56.1 grains. Does that mean anything to you?
> Blanchard: No. That is beyond my area of expertise.
> Lance: Do you know how much a grain of a bullet is?
> Blanchard: No.

And that's it. I'm not holding anything back from her deposition. Honestly, that's it. Horton Lance asked Dr. Blanchard nothing more about the fragment. Theresa Crayon asked Dr. Blanchard nothing at all about the fragment. The only other testimony remotely regarding the fragment was a further admission from Dr. Blanchard that she is not a ballistics expert. "This is criminalistics. I'm a forensic pathologist. It's related, but it's not my area, just like ballistics is not my area."

Theresa Crayon was there in the same room at the same time, asking questions and presumably listening to answers. She knew Dr. Blanchard was not an expert. She knew Dr. Young had sent the fragment to the crime lab. She knew the crime lab had conducted an analysis of the fragment and wrote a ballistics report. She knew that actual ballistics experts worked in the crime lab, and that she could subpoena one of them to testify. She could even subpoena the very person who examined the bullet fragment, the one who wrote the ballistics report.

Instead, Theresa Crayon decided to have Dr. Blanchard present to the jury the scant ballistics evidence the State was willing to present. Though Dr. Blanchard had apparently not even read the ballistics report, Theresa Crayon had her testify in place of the person who conducted the ballistics analysis.

Lance did not object to Dr. Blanchard testifying as a ballistics expert. Nor did he subpoena the actual examiner from the crime lab. Instead, he called in an expert of his own, Dr. Friedlander. Like the others, Dr. Friedlander was unable to rule out a .22 caliber handgun as the murder weapon.

Hogwash!

In the face of both prosecution and defense experts telling me it is impossible to exclude a .22 caliber weapon, in the face of my boundless inexperience with respect to ballistics, even in the face of those seemingly insurmountable odds, I hereby boldly claim that Anastasia WitbolsFeugen was absolutely, positively not killed by a .22 caliber weapon.

I make that claim with confidence simply because I examined the evidence. It wasn't a particularly difficult thing to do. After just ten minutes on the Internet, I'm ready to pontificate on the significance of a bullet fragment weighing fifty-six grains.

A grain, when used in the context of ballistics, is an English measure of weight: seven thousand grains equals one pound. In other words, a fifty-six grain bullet fragment isn't all that large. If you put the bullet fragment on a good digital kitchen scale, the scale would read one-eighth ounce. If you instructed your scale to display weight in grams rather than ounces, the scale would read four grams. Most kitchen scales have a precision no better that two grams, because a gram is really small. A grain is smaller still.

Now, with the discussion of grains and kitchen scales behind us, we're ready for the big .22 caliber finale. The heaviest commonly used .22 caliber bullet weighs forty grains.

At this point, if you believe that a fifty-six grain bullet fragment can be left behind by a forty-grain bullet, read no further. Put down this book and turn on your television. If you happen to receive a summons for jury duty, fill out the attached form in purple crayon and tape it to your forehead.

If, on the other hand, you realize that a fifty-six grain bullet fragment did not and cannot come from a forty-grain bullet, you have more credibility as a ballistics expert than all the clowns who prosecuted, defended, and testified in the case of Missouri v. Case.

❖

In one sense, it makes no difference that the murder weapon was not a .22 caliber handgun or rifle. That fact neither proves nor disproves Kelly's claim that Byron shot Anastasia with a shotgun. It has no direct bearing of whether Byron Case is factually innocent or factually guilty of the crime for which he was convicted. It was pure silliness for the prosecution and defense to spar over that point. It was particularly silly for Horton Lance to do so. He won the inconsequential battle but lost the meaningful war. His client was hauled away in chains.

I detailed the .22 caliber issue for two reasons. First, as a skeptical juror, you now realize that experts are not always as expert as their résumés and expensive suits might suggest. Second, you will hopefully give careful consideration to the conclusions that follow, even though they may differ from those of experts who testified at trial. Hopefully, you will not automatically reject bold statements such as --

❖

Anastasia WitbolsFeugen was not killed with a shotgun.

This conclusion required only slightly more investigation than my ten minute in-depth .22 caliber analysis. I simply read Justin Bruton's autopsy report and looked at gruesome pictures in a book. Let's consider first the autopsy report.

The description of Justin's wound is gruesome, but unfortunately that's the point. From Justin's autopsy, we obtain a sense of how much damage is caused by a shotgun blast to the head, fired from point blank range. I won't be giving too much away if I tell you beforehand that the damage is far more severe than that suffered by Anastasia. Skip forward if you wish to accept this claim without reading the details.

Under the autopsy section labeled "EXTERNAL EXAMINATION" we find:

> The body is that of a tall, Caucasian, young adult male, estimated at 170 pounds, consistent with a height of approximately 6 feet when the head is partially reconstructed.

> The body lies on its back. The calvarium has been eviscerated with comminution and loss of structure of the vault. The scalp and residual bone of the vault has been turned down over the face.

Under the section labeled "EVIDENCE OF INJURY" we find:

> The palate has been destroyed and the calvarial vault eviscerated with extensive comminution of the base of the skull, as well as the lateral and rostral aspects of the calvarium. The scalp has been split

open with multiple tears approximately radiating from the central parietum and the flaps of tissue have been turned backwards onto the structures of the face. The jaw is fractured in multiple locations.

X-ray of the head demonstrates no retained projectile.

Forgive me for being blunt, but the top of Justin's head was literally blown off by the shotgun blast. Bits of skull attached to flaps of skin folded over Justin's face. The ME attempted to return these folds to their original position so that Justin's height could be measured. The effort was only partially successful. Justin's skull cap (calvarium vault) had been destroyed (eviscerated). The base, side (lateral), and front (rostral) portions of his skull had been splintered (comminuted). His jaw had been fractured in multiple locations.

Anastasia's wound was horrific and fatal, but considerably less severe than Justin's. Anastasia's skull was fractured but remained in place. Justin's skull lost its shape and structure. Anastasia's exit wound was large, but only one small fragment of skull was ejected. Justin's exit wound approximated the top of his head. Only fragments of his skull cap remained.

In addition to reading Justin's autopsy report, I examined a series of pictures showing shotgun wounds to the head. By "examined" I mean that I looked quickly then looked away. All of the images showed far more extensive damage than that suffered by Anastasia. To my untrained eye, it seems unlikely that Anastasia's wound was caused by a shotgun.

The book to which I've referred is *Gunshot Wounds: Practical Aspects of Firearms, Ballistics, and Forensic Techniques* by Dr. Vincent J.M. DiMaio, M.D.

Dr. DiMaio served in the U.S. Army, assigned to the Forensic Pathology Branch within the Armed Forces Institute of Pathology. He later served as consultant to the Assassination Records Review Board in Washington D.C., and later still as a consultant to the United Nations Office of the Prosecutor for the International Criminal Tribunal for the former Yugoslavia. Until 2007, he was the Chief Medical Examiner for Bexar County in Texas, the county that includes San Antonio.

More sensationally, Dr. DiMaio was one of four experts selected to perform the autopsy on the exhumed body of Lee Harvey Oswald. He testified for the defense during the first trial of Phil Spector, spending three days on the witness stand.

Dr. DiMaio seems to have some expertise with respect to gunshot wounds. I'm guessing that, as a minimum, he would have figured out that a .22 caliber bullet would not leave behind a 56 grain fragment.

I didn't just glance at the pictures in Dr. DiMaio's book, I took the trouble to read large portions of the text. With respect to shotgun contact wounds to the head, DiMaio writes: "The entrance is often bisected by large lacerations extending to the top of the head." That's interesting. Anastasia's wound extended only from the top of her lip to the bridge of her nose. It didn't extend to the top of her head.

Here's an even more interesting claim from his book. "The wound entrance from a shotgun slug is circular in shape, with a diameter approximately that of the slug."

Whoa!

If DiMaio is correct about that, it gives us a nice, clear cut way of determining whether Anastasia was killed by a shotgun blast.

Everyone agreed that if the weapon used to kill Anastasia was a shotgun, it must have fired a slug rather than a pellet round. That's because no pellets were found in the X ray of Anastasia's skull. So if Dr. DiMaio is correct, the diameter of the bullet hole would be approximately the same diameter as a shotgun slug.

Let's compare. Once Dr. Young moved Anastasia's skin back into place, the bullet defect, i.e. the bullet hole, was ⅜-inch in diameter. That's 0.375 inches.

Now let me quickly check the Internet for the size of a shotgun slug. Here we go. That was easy. It seems a 12-gauge shotgun slug has a diameter of 0.75 inches.

Holy cow! The bullet is twice the diameter of the bullet hole, just as Chris, our literary co-juror, suspected.

Excluding a shotgun as the murder weapon now seems almost as easy as eliminating a .22 caliber weapon. A ¾-inch shotgun slug couldn't have left just a ⅜-inch hole, at least not according to Dr. DiMaio's book.

To make sure I wasn't overlooking something, I checked DiMaio's slug size / bullet hole claim against statements made by other ballistics experts. Here's a sampling of what I found:

"Most wounds inflicted with a shotgun in contact with the body will result in a wound diameter approximately the same as the diameter of the shotgun's bore." This is from *Criminal Investigation: A Contemporary Perspective*, Second Edition, by Ronald F. Becker.

"The effects of a contact range shotgun discharge are devastating and frequently lethal. ... The diameter of the defect equates very closely with the internal diameter of the muzzle." This is from *Terminal Ballistics: A Text and Atlas of Gunshot Wounds* by Malcolm Dodd and Karen Byrne.

"The entrance wound from a shotgun will vary depending on how far the muzzle of the shotgun was from the victim. If the shot was fired from less than 12 inches away, the wound will be approximately ¾-inch in diameter." I found this quote in *Criminal Investigation: Law and Practice*, Second Edition, by Michael F. Brown.

"It would surprise me [if it was a shotgun], because I would expect the entry to be bigger, but I can't tell you that it wasn't [a shotgun]." That's testimony from Dr. Edward Friedlander, the defense expert from the trial of Byron Case. He's more timid in his conclusion than Dr. DiMaio, or Ronald F.

Becker, or Michael F. Brown, or Malcolm Dodd and Karen Byrne. At least it occurred to Friedlander that the bullet hole was small compared to a shotgun slug.

"The most likely [weapon used] is a rifle or a handgun. Shotgun is possible, but less likely in my opinion." That's from the deposition testimony from Dr. Chase Blanchard, the self described ballistics non expert used by Theresa Crayon to present the ballistics evidence to the jury. Once again, Dr. Blanchard is more timid than the authors I cited above. At least she suspected during her deposition, for whatever reason, that the murder weapon was not likely a shotgun.

"[The autopsy findings are] not consistent with a handgun. [Shotgun is] a good possibility ... about the same as a high powered rifle. I couldn't tell. Either of those two." That's from trial testimony by Dr. Blanchard, the self described ballistics non expert used by Theresa Crayon to present the ballistics evidence to the jury. Blanchard changed her testimony substantially sometime between deposition and trial, changed it in a fashion quite favorable to the prosecution.

While the in court argument regarding a .22 caliber weapon was inconsequential and distracting, the argument over the shotgun was monumentally important. When Kelly began changing her story, when she began claiming Byron shot Anastasia, she was explicit that Byron shot Anastasia with a shotgun.

Kelly first told that to Jackson County Prosecutor Bob Beaird, in the presence others. From the summary of that meeting, we find:

> Byron got out and told her [Kelly] to stay in car. She [Kelly] was watching out the back side driver's window and could see them [Justin and Anastasia] a few feet away. Byron popped the trunk (she is not sure if he got the keys from the ignition) and closed the trunk. She saw him with a shotgun and Justin was yelling at him in German. Byron went over to victim and shot her in head. He put the gun back in the trunk and they got in the car.

According to these notes, Kelly is unambiguous about seeing Byron with a shotgun. Two days later, Sergeant Kilgore interviewed Kelly. That meeting was recorded and transcribed. The relevant segment of that interview follows.

Kelly:	When he had gotten out of the car, the keys were in the ignition, so he like grabbed the keys. I could hear him, you know, like open the trunk. And got out the gun and shot her. And she was pretty close to the car. I like saw the whole thing that happened. The whole time Justin was yelling at her.
Kilgore:	Exactly what did you see?
Kelly:	I saw him get the gun out, just go do a little, I don't know what he did, just the whole --
Kilgore:	Tell me what you think he did. What did you hear?

Kelly:	Well I don't think I heard that little, 'cause I could, they were still talking so much. I don't think he did the little, the little chink chink thing, but I don't, I don't think he did that. I just saw him messing with it.
Kilgore:	What you're describing to me is like a pump shotgun?
Kelly:	No, I'm not sure if he did that. I saw him kinda fiddling with it for a couple seconds. But he just grabbed it out and walked around the side of the car. I think it was double barreled, though, 'cause it looked like an old gun.

Kelly repeated her claim that Byron shot Anastasia with a shotgun, adding that it was a double barrel shotgun. Double-barrel shotguns typically break open to allow the shooter to place the cartridge directly into the barrel. With double barrel-shotguns, you do not insert the cartridges into a slot on the side of the weapon then pump them into the barrel.

Sergeant Kilgore by this point was convinced that Kelly is claiming Byron shot Anastasia with a shotgun. He asks her "Did he hold the shotgun up with the end of it to his shoulder like you would hold a rifle?" After stammering a bit, she replied "yeah, it was probably up." She did not correct Sergeant Kilgore's characterization of the weapon as a shotgun.

As the trial approached, the prosecution had a problem. Kelly said that Byron shot Anastasia with a shotgun. Dr. Blanchard had testified during deposition, however, that the weapon used to kill Anastasia was probably not a shotgun. That could raise reasonable doubt in the minds of reasonable jurors. For that prosecution, that's a problem.

Fortunately for the prosecution, Kelly changed her story for the jury. Kelly told them that the weapon might have been a rifle. Whatever the weapon was, she told them, it was long and black. And it was dark out that night so it was hard to see the gun, but not so dark that she couldn't see what happened to Anastasia, and she's just trying to tell the truth the best she can.

That would have been sufficient for most jurors, but more fortunately still for the prosecution, Blanchard changed her story as well. No longer was the weapon most likely a rifle or a handgun. No longer was it unlikely to be a shotgun. When testifying before the jury, the autopsy report was suddenly not consistent with a handgun, and the weapon was most likely a shotgun or a high-powered rifle. "Not consistent" became different than "possible," and "unlikely" came to mean "likely." Or so the jurors were to presume.

All in all, it worked out pretty well for the prosecution.

However --

❖

Anastasia WitbolsFeugen was not killed by a high-powered rifle, either.

Rifles and handguns fire similar size bullets, much smaller in diameter than a shotgun slug, much closer in diameter to the circular defect of Anastasia's wound. A rifle is considerably more powerful than a handgun, however, because the long barrel allows more powder a longer time to expand as it accelerates the bullet down the barrel. Bullets fired from rifles fly in excess of 2400 feet per second. Few shotguns or handguns, by comparison, have muzzle velocities greater than 1600 feet per second.

There's one more thing you should know about bullets, particularly bullets fired from rifles. Bullets are either soft nosed or jacketed.

The primary material in any bullet is lead, because lead is heavy and lead is cheap. With lead, you literally get more bang for your buck. Lead is also soft. It will deform, expand, and fragment upon entry. It will tend to remain in the body. It will thereby transfer all its energy to the target. Lead bullets have what is commonly known as high stopping power. Soft-nose bullets are well designed for bringing down deer. They are classified as hunting ammunition.

The military and some other shooters use rounds that penetrate targets cleanly, without fragmentation, frequently without deformation. The reason for this is that human targets, unlike deer, tend to hide behind walls. The military needs ammunition that will penetrate. Military bullets therefore protect the soft lead nose with a jacket made from a metal substantially harder than lead. When the jacket covers the entire length of a bullet, the bullet is known as having a full metal jacket.

Now that you're sufficiently versed in bullet design, you're in a good position to understand why I'm confident as a non-expert that Anastasia was not shot with a rifle.

We'll first consider the possibility of a rifle firing a bullet with full metal jacketing. This won't take long. I'll simply quote from DiMaio's *Gunshot Wounds*.

> Military bullets, by virtue of their full metal jackets, tend to pass through the body intact, thus producing less extensive injuries than hunting ammunition. Military bullets usually do not fragment in the body or shed fragments of lead in their paths. Because of the high velocity of such military rounds as well as their tough construction, it is possible for such bullets to pass through more than one individual before coming to rest. These bullets may be almost virginal in appearance after recovery from the body. . . . Full metal-jacketed rifle bullets almost invariably exit if the deceased is the primary target and is within a few hundred yards of the muzzle of the weapon.

That leaves us only to consider a rifle firing a lead nose bullet. Once again, from Gunshot Wounds:

> X-rays of individuals shot with hunting ammunition usually show a characteristic radiologic picture that is seen almost exclusively with

this form of rifle ammunition: the so-called "lead snowstorm." As the expanding hunting bullet moves through the body, fragments of the lead break off the lead core and are hurled out into the surrounding tissues. An x-ray shows scores, if not hundreds, of small radiopaque bullet fragments scattered along the wound track (the lead snowstorm). ... This picture is not seen with handgun bullets, nor, with rare exception, with full metal-jacketed rifle bullets.

And there you go. Anastasia was not shot with a .22 caliber weapon, a shotgun firing a pellet round, a shotgun firing a slug, a rifle firing a fully jacketed bullet, or a rifle firing a lead-nose bullet. We now know this because a .22 caliber bullet would not have left behind a 56 grain fragment, because no pellets showed up in the X ray, because a jacketed bullet would have penetrated cleanly, and because a lead nose bullet fired from a rifle would have left a "lead snowstorm." That leaves --

❖

A handgun.

Not just any handgun, though. It couldn't be too large and powerful, like the Dirty Harry .44 Magnum, because it would have created damage more akin to Justin's wound than Anastasia's. DiMaio explains this, too.

Contact wounds of the head with handguns, while often producing secondary skull fractures, do not ordinarily produce the massive injuries seen in high-velocity rifles and shotguns. Massive injuries from contact handgun wounds of the head, when they do occur, are associated with Magnum calibers. ... These cartridges can inflict contact wounds that in their severity mimic wounds from rifles and shotguns.

On the other hand, the handgun couldn't have been too small or it would not have left behind a 56 grain fragment.

Handguns which fit the bill of being not too powerful and not too anemic include the standard .357 revolver, the standard .38 revolver, and the 9mm semi automatic pistol. All fire bullets having a diameter close to the ⅜-inch diameter of the defect in Anastasia's wound. All fire bullets which are sufficiently massive to leave behind a 56 grain fragment.

A real ballistics expert might have been able to further narrow the possibilities. In the play book of Missouri v. Case, however, neither side condescended to introduce even a ballistics report.

❖

During testimony, we learned from Justin's father that Justin traveled to Tulsa on the weekend prior to Anastasia's death. We learned also that Justin went to a gun show while he was down there.

What we didn't learn was that Justin talked to his father after the gun show about seeing a handgun he really liked. It cost $350, so Justin didn't buy it. At least, that's what Justin told his father. I guess Crayon figured that was just more information the jurors should not hear.

If Justin bought a handgun at the gun show in Tulsa, just days before Anastasia was killed, he didn't tell his father. We know, however, that Justin was not completely forthcoming with his father regarding his gun ownership. Justin, for example, did not tell his father that he bought a shotgun from Wal-Mart and later sold it, possibly at a Tulsa gun show. Neither apparently did Justin inform his father that he asked Abraham Kneisley to help him acquire a gun.

❖

During testimony, we learned that there were no defensive wounds on Anastasia's body. There were no bruises, no scratches, no wounds to her hands where she tried to shield her face from the bullet. She was not shot from behind as she tried to flee, nor was she shot in the side of the head as she turned away. She was looking right at the shooter, eye to eye. The two of them were separated only by a gun and a finger on a trigger.

It's almost as if Anastasia just stood there and allowed someone to shoot her, with a handgun, in the nose, just days after Justin was looking at pistols in Tulsa.

It makes me wonder about --

AFTERMATH : SUICIDE

From a Sergeant Kilgore interview of Betsy Owens, Anastasia's biological mother, I offer for your consideration the following quotes:

"I just spoke to her that Wednesday. I spoke to her Monday and Tuesday and Wednesday of that week. She called me at work. This was kind of unusual, and because my boss was out of town, I was able to take the opportunity to talk with her for about an hour each time. So we talked about a whole lot of subjects. Monday she was a little depressed. Not wanting to live, that sort of thing."

"[S]he felt like Justin had gone down to see his parents and when he came back he was colder to her than he had been . . . when she had seen him last on the Thursday before. And this was either Monday or Tuesday she said this, after she had seen him."

"[W]ell originally a month or so before she had called up and asked if my brothers would prescribe her sleeping pills. Two of my brothers are doctors, and they had prescribed antibiotics for her in the past, or things like that, you know. I said no, sleeping pills are restricted drugs, and . . . they're not going to lose their license over it."

"[S]he was wanting something where she could, you know, just, she didn't want to do an act of death where she did it."

"[S]he didn't want to live, but she really didn't want to die and go through painful things . . . not one that she would kinda be active at. And I could see her saying something, well if you're going to leave me, kill me, or something. I can see her saying something like that."

"[B]ack in September she called up and asked if she could come down and have supper, she and Franci, and could I make spaghetti. And it was just the way she was talking I felt like, this was just kind of a last supper."

"I took her over to see the new house we were building, and she said she won't see it completed. I was like, well sure you're going to see it, you'll be out here to, you know, on Christmas Eve to open Christmas gifts, you'll see it completed. Well the house was completed a day or two days after she died we closed on it. So she never did get to see it completed."

"I could see it being a suicide thing, and then the others seeing what damage occurred, and chickening out, you know. Wait a minute, I don't think I want this. I can see Stasi being the leader that she was, saying well I'll go first. . . . I don't know. It's possible. I don't know."

❖

From a Kilgore interview of Robert WitbolsFeugen, Anastasia's biological father, I offer the following exchange:

Q: Did she cut her wrists?

A: Oh, I, no, I think she, she probably tried that three, on three different occasions and she complained that the razors you know, the safety razors --

Q: When was the last time she tried it?

A: Umm, if she tried, I don't know about it. She talked about it as recently as two or three weeks ago.

Q: She talked to you about cutting her wrists?

A: Yeah. She said would I please go out and buy some better razor blades, she wanted to cut her wrists.

Q: When was the last time she actually cut herself?

A: It was, uh, would have been about that same time frame, two weeks ago.

❖

From a letter Anastasia left on Justin's computer.

"I wish I could kill myself. I wanted to do it before but I couldn't because I firmly believed that you would come back to me. I hate life. Life is a big joke to be played on the ones who don't want to feel it. I never wanted to feel life."

AFTERMATH: EYES

"Knowledge comes by eyes always open."

At least according to an essay entitled *Old Age*, written long ago by Ralph Waldo Emerson.

Perhaps you recall from the deliberations that I was bothered by Anastasia's eyes, that they remained open in death. It seemed strange, at least to me, since she was shot by a gun that was touching the tip her nose. I would have closed my eyes.

Perhaps my eyes would have opened afterwards, as I fell, or as I lay there. I simply didn't know. Recently, I Googled to find out.

What I found, I didn't expect.

I was trying to learn if eyes naturally open or close upon death, or if they can open or close after death. That's what I was hoping to learn. It wasn't that big of a deal, just a curiosity actually. It shouldn't have taken me very long, but I was side tracked and have yet to find the answer to my initial question. I did learn something unexpected, though. Something significant.

When a person dies, the body undergoes a series of time-dependent physiological changes. Some changes occur immediately, some occur over a period of minutes, hours, or days. The existence or absence of these changes provides insight into the time since the body ceased functioning. While the post mortem changes don't allow the time of death to be established precisely, they do provide insight.

It turns out that eyes exhibit some of the earliest postmortem changes. I discovered fairly early in my research that the corneas become cloudy within 12 hours of death. This seemed significant. It brought to mind something I read in Anastasia's autopsy report. Anastasia's corneas were still clear at the time of her autopsy. I repeat the entire paragraph from the autopsy report:

> Rigor mortis is well developed and generalized. Livor mortis is faint and posterior, mostly in the buttocks and legs. Livor mortis is mostly fixed but focally blanching. The corneas are clear.

Dr. Young started the autopsy at 9:30 AM on Thursday morning. He noted that Anastasia's corneas were clear. Not cloudy. Clear.

If it is strictly true that the eyes will cloud over within 12 hours of death, that meant Anastasia was killed no earlier than 9:30 PM on Wednesday night. That's two hours later than Kelly placed the shooting. That's after Byron and Justin dropped Kelly off at her house.

I realized that things are never that simple. Anastasia's body had been wrapped in a tarp for transport and had then been kept refrigerated before the autopsy. Perhaps such actions delay corneal cloudiness. Also, it's likely that 12 hours is not a hard upper limit. Anastasia's clear corneas were suggestive, but not compelling. I continued my research.

I found a site that limited the 12 hour rule-of-thumb to eyes that were closed. Then I found another with the same limitation. Then another, and another. These sites gave a different value for eyes that remained open after death. These sites claimed that if the eyes remained open, their corneas would cloud over within three hours.

Holy smokes!

Deputy Epperson said Anastasia's eyes were open at 3:44 AM when he found her. Crime scene photos confirm that. Dr. Young reported her corneas were clear as of 9:30 AM. Autopsy photos confirm that. Sometime in between, Anastasia's body was wrapped in a white tarp and refrigerated. While that confuses what happened after her transport to the morgue, it's obvious Anastasia's corneas must have been clear at 3:44 AM when she was found. They must also have been clear at 5:05 AM when the investigator from the Medical Examiner's office arrived, before she was transported.

Anastasia must have been killed in the wee hours of Thursday morning, some time after 2:05 AM. At least that's the way I interpret the evidence. I admit that I am even less of an expert on post-mortem ocular changes than I am on contact-wound ballistics, so I should reference my sources.

Many of the claims for the three-hour limit seem to stem from a presentation by Dr. Michael M. Baden. In his presentation (search: "time of death" "corneal cloudiness" "baden"), Dr. Baden provides a table that says that the eyes cloud over within twelve hours if closed and within three hours if open. I accept those numbers as approximately true, based on Dr. Baden's experience and stature within the forensic pathology community.

Dr. Baden has been a medical examiner for nearly five decades and has performed more than 20,000 autopsies. He was the Chief Medical Examiner for New York City. He was the chief forensic pathologist for the United States House of Representative Select Committee on Assassination. Certainly you remember that select committee. They're the ones who re-opened the investigation into the assassinations of John F. Kennedy and Martin Luther King, Jr. They used Dr. Baden as their chief pathologist.

Dr. Baden examined the remains of Tsar Nicholas. He participated in the re-autopsy of fallen civil rights activist Medgar Evers. He participated in the autopsies of victims from TWA Flight 800, may they forever rest in peace.

He has been an expert witness for both prosecution and defense in celebrity cases involving John Belushi, Christian Brando, Billy Martin, Robert Blake, Phil Spector, and O. J. Simpson. He has investigated deaths in Croatia, Serbia, Israel, the Gaza Strip, the West Bank, Monaco, Panama, England, Canada, and Zimbabwe. He has taught in most of these United States and in

China, Taiwan, Kuwait, Australia, France, Italy, Ecuador, Puerto Rico, and Columbia. He sits on the boards of professional organizations with lofty names.

Dr. Baden has been around the pathology block more than a few times. When he speaks on a subject such as corneal cloudiness, I listen. He is not the only one, however, to state that corneas will cloud within three hours if the eyes remain open. A couple of other citations follow.

"Another eye change is corneal clouding. It occurs 2 to 3 h after death, if the eyes are open, and by 24 h if they are shut." That's from *Forensic Pathology of Trauma: Common Problems for the Pathologist* by Michael J. Shkrum and David A. Ramsey.

"When the eyes remain open, a thin film may be observed within minutes on the corneal surface, and within two or three hours corneal cloudiness develops. If the eyes are closed, the appearance of the corneal film may be delayed by hours and that of corneal cloudiness by twenty-four hours or longer." That one is from *Spitz and Fisher's Medicolegal Investigation of Death: Guidelines for the Application of Pathology to Crime Investigation* by Werner U. Spitz.

"Within 3 or 4 h after death, the corneas begin to cloud. The effect is most useful in determining whether or not the death was very recent." This last one is from *The Handbook of Autopsy Practice*, Third Edition, by Jergen Ludwig. He makes no distinction between eyes open or eyes closed. He does make clear though, that lack of corneal cloudiness demonstrates that "the death was very recent."

❖

In 1862 Ralph Waldo Emerson wrote that knowledge comes by eyes always open.

A century later, Dr. Michael Baden performed his first autopsy. A half century later still, Dr. Baden performed autopsy number 20,000, or thereabouts. Dr. Baden's presentation teaches that those eyes which remain open and clear after death impart knowledge of a recent passing. Doctors Shkrum, Ramsey, Spitz, and Ludwig agree.

Because Anastasia died with her eyes open, and because Anastasia's corneas were clear when she was transported, it's likely that she was killed in the early morning hours of the day she was found. If that is true, Kelly fabricated her story that Byron Case killed Anastasia WitbolsFeugen. She was not killed on October 22, as alleged by Kelly Moffett. If that is true, Byron Case is serving a life sentence for a crime he did not commit.

AFTERMATH: RIGOR

As Anastasia lay there with her eyes open, staring upwards into infinite darkness, her eyelids began to stiffen. A bit thereafter, her other facial muscles and her jaw became rigid. The muscles did not noticeably move or contort her features. They merely stiffened against any external effort to move them.

The rigidity progressed to her neck and then to her arms. Her elbows may have flexed slightly. Then the muscles of her torso stiffened. Finally, after approximately five hours, the muscles in her legs stiffened. Her knees, as did her elbows, may have flexed slightly in the process.

Anastasia's bout with rigor mortis was a natural, temporary phenomenon. After thirty six hours or so, the rigor passed quietly and she relaxed once again, for the final time.

❖

Boyd Harlan arrived at the crime scene at 5:05 AM, assuming we can trust Sergeant Kilgore's notes of that morning. Boyd was the investigator for the medical examiner's office. He made a cursory examination of Anastasia's body. He then had the body wrapped in a white tarp and transported to the morgue. There it was refrigerated until the autopsy.

The tarp and refrigeration slowed down the normal pace of post mortem changes. A time of death estimate would therefore best be based on the postmortem changes observed, or missing, prior to her transport. Deputy Epperson told us about her eyes. Boyd Harlan tells us about her state of rigor. Below, I present the entire narrative from his report.

> UWF found on the road in Lincoln Cemetery by a JCSD deputy on patrol.
>
> The body is found lying supine on the ground on the road in the cemetery. A single GSW to the face is noted.
>
> The body is at 2+ rigor mortis.
>
> The body is fully dressed and post mortem lividity is not assessable.
>
> Coagulated blood is noted directly under the head and shoulders of the body and a small piece of skull is recovered from the grass about 18 inches to 2 feet from the head. There are no other body parts or blood splatter found near the body.

The report is nowhere as thorough or as impressive as I thought it would be, given how proud Dr. Blanchard seemed that their office had their own investigator. Nonetheless, the narrative provides a significant clue as to the time Anastasia was shot in the nose from point blank range.

Boyd Harlan described Anastasia's rigor as two plus. In my recent email exchange with Dr. Thomas Young, he explained that two plus meant Anastasia's rigor was "moderately formed and not fully developed." It is a subjective description despite being assigned a numerical value. Such is the nature of a time-of-death analysis.

By now, you probably suspect I spent a few hours at the keyboard trying to educate myself about rigor mortis. Indeed I did. I was particularly interested in the rate at which it progresses. As usual, I was in for a surprise.

The surprise this time was that the definitive study dates back to 1872.

Wow! 1872. The ink was barely dry on Emerson's *Old Age*.

During that study, Dr. P. F. Niderkorn made hourly observations of 114 bodies from the time of their death to the time when rigor mortis was fully developed. From his data, I prepared the table below. Assuming his results are accurate and broadly applicable, we know the following about how quickly rigor develops:

2 hours since death:	1% chance rigor is complete
3 hours	20% chance
4	40%
5	55%
6	68%
7	77%
8	87%
9	92%
10	96%
11	98%
12 hours	99% chance
13 hours since death:	100% chance rigor is complete

Niderkorn's data, summarized in the table above, allow us to compare two different scenarios. The first scenario is that told by Kelly, of witnessing Anastasia being murdered soon after sunset on Wednesday, around 7:30 PM. The second scenario is that told by Anastasia's eyes, of being shot in the early morning hours of the next day. Anastasia's rigor will tell us which of the two is more likely true.

Under Kelly's scenario, Anastasia had been dead for approximately nine hours before Boyd Harlan examined her body. According to Niderkorn's data, there's a 94% chance rigor mortis would have been fully complete by that time. In fact, the rigor was only two plus, in the words of Boyd Harlan, only moderate in the words of Dr. Thomas Young. Based on Anastasia's state of rigor and Dr. Niderkorn's data, it is statistically impossible that Kelly's story is correct.

I state this, not as fact, but as a skeptical juror weighing evidence previously withheld from me.

Under the second scenario, the one told by Anastasia's eyes, she would have been killed less than three hours before being wrapped in the white tarp, transported to the morgue, and refrigerated. Boyd Harlan arrived at the scene at 5:05 AM. Presume Anastasia was shot at 2:35 AM. That's within the three hour window for clear corneas. Assume further that rigor was 50% developed, causing Boyd Harlan to record it as two plus, which Dr. Young translates as moderate. Rigor would have then have been complete in five hours, assuming she had not been found, wrapped, and refrigerated.

According to Niderkorn's data, this timing is not only reasonable, but likely. In more than 50 percent of the cases he monitored, rigor mortis became complete within five hours.

Death in the early morning hours of Thursday, October 23, 1997 is consistent both with Anastasia's clear corneas and her state of rigor. I accept this as a reasonable and likely possibility from the perspective of a skeptical juror who bothered to question the State of Missouri regarding its prosecution and imprisonment of Byron Case.

AFTERMATH: TELEPHONE

Kelly Moffett played us for chumps. You, me, Terry, Jade, Chris, the other literary jurors, the actual jurors, the family members, the press, the appellate court, the entire public, the U.S. Constitution, and the Bill of Rights. She played us all for chumps.

She had considerable help, of course: Kilgore, Crayon, Judge Atwell, Horton Lance. They played their roles perfectly. Kilgore set up a crappy recording system, allowed Kelly to make the recording with zero oversight, then screwed up the transcript frequently and in crucial detail. Crayon decided to have an expert enhance the tape, but hired some guy who couldn't find his own back pocket if he had a third hand already there.

Judge Atwell took the trouble to actually compare the inaccurate transcript with the crappy tape, but declared the transcription to be "excellent." He concluded, based on the erroneous transcript, that the tape was a tacit confession.

Horton Lance made a brief cameo appearance to object here and there in Walter Mitty fashion.

Crayon re-entered from stage left and exacerbated the charade by having Kelly corroborate her own tape, a tape that not even Kelly could understand without reference to the transcription. That returns us right back where we started with Kelly just sitting there smiling at our foolishness.

Fry closed the in-court portion of this macabre comedy with the following, less than reassuring words. "Labeling Kelly Moffett a liar here today isn't a hard thing for you to do. It's when she lied. When she lied, not if she lied. Let me tell you, she lied."

But the show wasn't over. It went on the road. After the courtroom, it made its first stop in the jury room. Atwell decided it would be best if the jurors had access to neither the crappy, inaudible tape nor the Kelly corroborated, inaccurate transcript. He told us instead that the evidence would be our collective memory of what the tape said.

Really? Our collective memory was the evidence? Really?

That would be shocking even if we could have actually heard the tape, even if Kilgore's transcription was actually worth a spit and a half. Our collective memory was the evidence? Will we have to spend the rest of our collective lives together in the Jackson County evidence room? Will we play the role of the closing cast in Fahrenheit 451?

After the jury room, the Kelly and Crayon show moved on to the appellate court. There, the appellate judges all agreed with Atwell that the tape represented a tacit admission. Of that, there could be no doubt. As proof, they cited two portions of the transcript, both of which had been mangled by Sergeant Kilgore, both of which had been uncorrected by Crayon's nameless audio-restoration expert, both of which had been declared by Judge Atwell as excellently transcribed, and both of which had been corroborated by Kelly herself, who was then called a liar, not by the defense, but by the prosecution, while Horton Lance just sat there.

So it wasn't just Kelly playing us for chumps. It was all of them. It was the entire judicial system. Sure, Kelly was right there at the beginning, and Kelly was right there at the end, but she couldn't have done it without all the others. They can all take a bow.

And by others, I include us, the jurors.

Don't sit there looking innocent and naïve. I warned you they were going to try to manipulate us. I warned you to trust none of them. There were sufficient warning signs that something was amiss, but we were tired, and we had been deliberating a long time, and we wanted to go home, and we had grand plans for Tuesday, and Terry was really starting to get on our nerves. Besides, we had already made up our minds, we already knew the truth, so what was the point anyway?

The point is that as skeptical jurors, we should have figured out something was amiss. We shouldn't have rendered our verdict without a thorough and skeptical review of all the evidence. And if we weren't absolutely positive beyond a reasonable doubt, we should have voted Not Guilty. Each and every one of us should have voted Not Guilty. That's what we should have done.

❖

That tape has always bugged me. How could Kelly tell such a cockamamie story of what happened that night, a story that could not possibly be true, yet still record a phone call with Byron that makes him seem so guilty? Why was Kelly so confident that Byron wouldn't call her crazy, right there on the tape, right there within earshot of the police, when she twice asked him why he felt the need to kill Anastasia? How could she be so sure Byron would say "We shouldn't talk about this" not just once but twice, and thereby make the tape admissible in court?

Because that tape has always bugged me so, I finally decided to check it out. This is something an actual juror should never, ever do during the course of a trial or during deliberation. Never. Ever. But the verdict has long since been settled, and the jury has long since been released, and I am no longer under an admonition to remain selectively ignorant.

I secured a digital copy of the tape recording, obtained a copy of the transcript as signed by Sergeant Kilgore, and then took the trouble to listen to the tape (digital copy thereof) and compare it to the transcript.

Uh, oh.

I guess you already know what I discovered. I guess you know why I have such a sour attitude regarding the State's role in this fiasco. The transcript is not an accurate representation of what is on the tape. It varies from the tape in the most crucial of details.

I was duped, and it pisses me off.

❖

I'll begin this sorry tale by telling you what I learned about the tape's history. Along the way, I'll tell you what the tape really says. I'll tell you where you can listen to the entire tape, if you wish, and where you can read the entire transcript. I'll allow you compare the two. I'll grant you that which Judge Atwell denied us and denied the real jury. I'll give you the opportunity to listen to the recording as frequently as you want, to read the transcript as often as you wish, to compare them as carefully as you desire.

I'll begin at the beginning. The recording was the brain child of none other than Kelly Moffett herself. On September 19, 2000, almost three years after Anastasia's murder, Kelly's attorney contacted the Jackson County Prosecutor's Office and offered to implicate Byron Case in return for Kelly Moffett's immunity. Later that day, Kelly talked to the prosecutors and, in their words, "offered to tape-record a conversation with Byron Case and try to get him to admit to the shooting." The next day, Kelly was interviewed by Sergeant Kilgore at the Mainstream Women's Center.

Kilgore:	I understand that the times you and I have previously talked, that you were not entirely truthful with me.
Kelly:	Yeah.
Kilgore:	That is correct?
Kelly:	Yeah, that's correct.
Kilgore:	Okay, and you are now willing to be truthful with me?
Kelly:	Yes.

The Sheriff's office was not apparently all that excited about Kelly's offer to record a conversation with Byron. I'm basing my conclusion on the 11 week delay between Kelly's offer and the next step taken to implement her plan. It wasn't until December 5th that Kilgore checked with the Kansas sheriff's office and the Kansas prosecutor's office to determine whether it would be legal to allow Kelly to tape a phone conversation with Byron, without Byron's knowledge. Recall that Kelly lived in Kansas, not Missouri. Apparently it was deemed legal, because later that day Kilgore hooked a tape recorder to a phone he provided and installed in the living room at Kelly Moffett's house.

I don't know what sort of equipment Kilgore used, or how he connected it. The integrity of the recording equipment was never established for the jury. I suspect it was an induction coil, stuck to the handset by a suction cup, with a wire leading from the Kilgore-provided phone down to a Kilgore-provided cassette recorder. There weren't as many recording options in 2000 as there are today, and the induction coil / suction cup setup was pretty common. Whatever the recording arrangement, it was not up to the task.

While Kilgore was still at Kelly's house on that 5th of December, Kelly attempted to call Byron in St. Louis. Kelly had Byron's phone number because Kilgore had given it to her. Kilgore obtained the phone number from Byron's probation officer. Recall from Byron's testimony that he had been convicted of stealing and placed on probation.

In any case, when Kelly attempted to call Byron, she reached his answering machine. She left a message and asked Byron to call her back. He didn't.

For seven months, nothing. No contact with Byron, no arrest warrant, nothing. Then on the night of June 5, 2001, Kelly Moffett finally contacted Byron Case by phone. Kelly recorded the call and informed the prosecutor's office the next day. Kilgore wrote of that in his report, explaining how he learned of the call from Ms. McGowan of the Jackson County Prosecutor's Office:

> Ms. McGowan informed me that Byron Case has returned to the Kansas City area and that Kelly Moffett had made telephone contact with Case *"out of the blue"* the previous night.

"Out of the blue." Interesting choice of words. The italics are mine, by the way. The quotation marks are in the original.

I interpret the words to mean Ms. McGowan used them to express surprise that Kelly had made contact with Byron. I considered then the possibility that Kelly was behaving in a rogue fashion, placing calls to the surprise of the prosecutor's office. Perhaps Kelly had been instructed not to attempt calls without someone from the prosecutor's office being present. Perhaps the prosecutor's office felt that if Kelly made the calls in their absence, someone might later question the integrity of the phone call. As a juror, though, I wouldn't have known one way or the other. Ms. McGowan never testified. Nor did Sergeant Kilgore, though he was the lead investigator in the case.

Kilgore retrieved the tape and transcribed it. I presume he transcribed it since he signed his name at the bottom of the transcription. He did less than a stellar job, as you will see in the following chapters.

AFTERMATH: "HELLO"

Here are the first seven lines of the transcript Kilgore made of that call. Feel free to read them as frequently as you wish. Mark them up, cut them out, frame them. They're yours.

Kelly:	Case, Byron Case. Byron Brooke Case. Byron Brook Christopher Case, actually.
Unk:	Hello.
Kelly:	Is Byron there? (Waits while answering machine plays) My God he's there! Shhh. Shhh, be quiet. Hello? (Disconnect, re-dial)
Unk:	(Recorded message) (Disconnect, re-dial).
Unk:	Where's he at?
Kelly:	His mom's house.
Byron:	Hello.

In addition to the painful realization that we were once again manipulated, there's a whole lot to be learned from those seven lines.

Kelly's friend, Angie, is there. You remember from the trial when Kelly explained that the other voice was that of her friend. No? Okay. I'll refer to the actual transcript.

> That was my friend, Angie. She was staying the night at my house that night and since I hadn't been able to get in touch with him, I figured nobody would answer, but the second he actually picked up, I made her go down in the basement.

I'll allow you decide for yourself whether Kelly committed perjury. Sure looks like it to me. The way I see it, Kelly didn't tell Angie to go to the basement. She told her to "Shhh." She told her to "Shhh, be quiet." Kelly had an opportunity to send Angie to the basement before the phone call, and before each of the two re-dials. She had an opportunity to send Angie to the basement while the answering machine message was playing, twice. But Kelly didn't take advantage of any of those five opportunities. We never heard anything along the line of "Go to the basement, Angie."

We know also that just before Byron picks up the phone, Angie is still there saying "Where's he at?"

At least that's what the transcript says. That's not, however, what I hear on the phone recording.

If you want to have a chance to actually hear both sides of the digitally preserved phone conversation, particularly Byron's side, an iPod probably isn't going to do the trick. Neither will the Windows Media Player, a Blackberry, or an ear trumpet. You're going to need a little more acoustic muscle.

So that I could better hear the recording, I downloaded the latest version of Audacity, a free sound editor. Audacity provides features such as filtering, tempo control, waveform display, and spectral analysis. The waveform display actually allows the user to view the recording, plotted as decibels versus time.

When I play my digital copy of the crappy tape recording on Audacity, and listen through a pair of good headphones, I have a better shot of figuring out what was actually said. Coupling this poor man's sound studio with my vast inexperience as a sound engineer, here's what I think Angie said just before Byron picked up:

Unk: Where's he calling me {unintelligible}

Holy moley!

I think the unintelligible portion was "at" followed by another word or two which Kelly inconveniently (and rudely I might add) talked over. As usual, Kelly's voice is the dominant voice in the conversation. I realize the word "at" seems to make no sense, but that's my best guess as to what I hear. If I'm transcribing, it's incumbent upon me to record what I hear, not what I expect to hear. If I'm uncertain about what I hear, I should make that clear to the reader. In this case, I described my transcription as "what I think I hear" and I described the most uncertain portion as {unintelligible}.

While I'm not positive about what UNK said at that point, I'm confident it wasn't "Where's he at?" as Kilgore claimed. UNK spoke at least six syllables. Kilgore's translation has only three. I'm presuming that Kilgore was guessing, using Kelly's response as a cue.

What UNK said may be important. If I am correct, if UNK actually said "Where is he calling me {unintelligible}," it suggests that UNK was listening on a different telephone line. Perhaps UNK was listening on Kelly's living room phone while Kelly was using the Kilgore-provided phone. UNK's question also suggests that UNK perceived herself to be a significant participant in the phone call. It wasn't "Where is he calling you {inaudible}." It was "Where is he calling me {unintelligible}."

That sentence triggered something; maybe it was a neuron. Before I had ever listened to that portion of the tape, back when I first read Kilgore's transcription, I took pause at the first line in the transcript. Remember it? It said:

Kelly: Case, Byron Case. Byron Brook Case. Byron Brook Christopher Case, actually.

It seemed out of place that Angie was asking about Byron's full name just as they were trying to contact him late at night. Perhaps Kelly said: "Hey, I know what we can do. We can call Byron and get that recording for the police. If I get through, I'll send you to the basement, okay?" Angie then replied: "Okay. What's his full name?"

It didn't work for me, but I didn't know what to make of it. After hearing UNK say "Where is he calling me {inaudible}," it struck me that UNK may have been asking about Byron's full name because UNK was filling out some sort of form. Perhaps UNK was not Angie, as Kelly testified in court. I only have Kelly's word for it that the other person was Angie. No one from the Sheriff's office was there when Kelly placed the call. No one from the Prosecutor's office was there. We have only Kelly's testimony for what went on in her living room that night. Speaking for myself, I'll not accept as a fact the person was Angie. I'm pretty tired of being duped by Kelly Moffett.

Just this morning, just hours before I typed this, I remembered something David Fry said during his closing argument. It seemed a bit strange to me during the trial, but things were happening fast, and it got past me before it could register. Now after all this time, it suddenly came back to me. I repeat the portion of Fry's closing argument below.

> Another thing I want you to remember about that tape and ask to hear it, he's so sick, his mother or a woman, goes and gets him. You can hear it. It's not in the transcript, but you'll hear it. 'Byron, Byron, Byron, telephone.' Mom knows he's so sick. Goes and gets him. Comes to the phone. There is a lot of conversation before he says, "We shouldn't talk about this."

> He's a liar. You have to come back and say, "There is a liar." You have to do that.

Wow.

Let's consider the possibilities. The first possibility is that David Fry was correct and honest with us when he told this to us during his carefully-prepared closing argument. That would be a problem. Note that he said: "It's not in the transcript, but you'll hear it." That would be the problem. It means the transcription would not have been complete and accurate.

Why would they have given us an incomplete transcription? What else might have been missing? How did the transcription get admitted into evidence without being complete and accurate? What other evidence was not complete and accurate? How often does this happen that the Jackson County Prosecutor's Office presents evidence they know is not complete and accurate?

The second possibility is that David Fry was inaccurate, that he simply made an honest, albeit clumsy, mistake. Byron's mother never yelled: "Byron, Byron, telephone." It's not in the transcript, and it's not on the tape. Kelly said "Case, Byron Case. Byron Brooke Case. Byron Brook Christopher Case, actually." Fry unwittingly thought it was Evelyn Case saying "Byron, Byron, Byron, telephone." After all each phrasing includes three instances of Byron. So it wasn't dishonesty, it was misunderstanding and lack of follow-up. I think this is the best case scenario for Fry.

A third possibility is that Fry was intentionally deceiving us in an effort to misdirect us. He knew there was something fishy about Kelly's three-Byron line in the transcript. He may have even known exactly what went on in Kelly's living room that prompted it. In this third scenario, Kelly's three-Byron answer had far more significance for the prosecution than it did for us, the jurors. Fry dealt with it by falsely attributing the three-Byron sentence to Byron's mother rather than Kelly. Fry cleverly disguised the false attribution as a clumsy argument that Byron wasn't really sick that day, or his mother wouldn't have said "Byron, Byron, Byron, telephone." Or something like that. Fry then had the gall to tell us we had to come back and tell Byron he's a liar.

We had to do it. David Fry told us so.

❖

There's something else important to be gleaned from the first seven lines. Someone pushed the "record" button prior to Byron picking up the phone and saying "Hello." We know that because that portion of the transcript is recorded. It's so simple, really, but so important.

Pushing the "record" button before Byron picks up makes sense, of course. The recording would not otherwise include the initial exchange between the two callers, and that would be leaving the dueling parties to argue over what was said prior to the beginning of the recording. This simple observation, however, is a reminder that Kelly probably recorded over fragments of her other unsuccessful calls to Byron. I don't know if those fragments still exist at the beginning of the tape, or if Kelly rewound the tape and recorded over them with each new phone call. It makes no difference actually, other than the destruction of evidence issue. The important point, now that I finally get around to it, is that Kelly had the capability to record over whatever she wanted.

It took me a few days to realize it was important. Kelly's ability to tape over, to erase, a conversation with Byron gave her absolute confidence the police would never hear a denial from Byron. All Kelly had to do was erase any call that did not go her way. It would be easy as pie, but only if no one from the sheriff's office or prosecutor's office was around. It would also be better if her parents weren't home or were upstairs asleep. Late at night perhaps, say around 11:30 PM.

Take note that I'm not claiming Kelly ever recorded over, ever erased a conversation with Byron. I'm saying only that she knew she could. That knowledge gave her ultimate control over what the police would hear. That knowledge gave her confidence to ask outrageous questions, unsupervised by Sergeant Kilgore, without fear Byron's answers would give her away.

In just the first seven lines of the phone call, the following possibilities bubble to the surface.

Kelly may have perjured herself in court when she testified she sent Angie to the basement.

Kilgore's transcription is in error, reflecting what he expected someone to say rather than what was actually said.

Angie, or whoever was there with Kelly that night, may have been listening to the call on a separate line.

Angie, or whoever was there with Kelly that night, was asking about Byron's full name as the phone call was being placed to Byron.

No one from the prosecutor's office or the sheriff's office was with Kelly when she placed the call. That could be what caused Ms. McGowan to describe the call as coming from "out of the blue."

The call was placed late at night, presumably when Kelly's parents were asleep. There is no evidence Kelly's parents heard any portion of the phone call as it was occurring.

Assuming only Kelly was there, that leaves no one other than Kelly to attest to the integrity of the call. Well, Kelly and Angie, or whoever was there with Kelly that night.

That means that Kelly could, if she wished, erase or record over any phone call not to her liking.

❖

And that is from the first seven lines of the transcript. There's plenty more to come, but right now I need a break. I'm guessing you do too.

AFTERMATH: BEEPS

Beep beep.

Beep.

Beep beep beep.

Beep.

Riiiinnnngggg.

❖

While Kelly and Byron were talking on the telephone, someone was pushing the number buttons on a phone somewhere. It was happening close enough to Kilgore's microphone that the beeps were preserved on Kilgore's cassette recorder. The beeps are there today, audible to anyone who can hear Kelly. There is no need for special equipment. The sound waves from those beeps went in Kilgore's ears just as surely as did the sound waves from Kelly's voice. Kilgore, however, declined to note the beeps in his transcription.

An immediate thought might be that either Kelly or Byron inadvertently pressed some telephone buttons while speaking.

No. That's not what happened. Neither Kelly nor Byron commented on the beeping. Neither of them said "Oops" or "Sorry, that's me." Not only that, each beep was characteristic of a single button. None of the beeps were compound beeps, caused by pressing two or more buttons at a time. It was no accident.

Big deal, someone pushed a couple of buttons. So what?

Actually, there were seven beeps. Just the right number for a local call.

Okay. That probably means someone was pushing one of the buttons over and over, because of nervousness or something, and they just happened to do it seven times.

Nope. That's not what happened either. There were five different numbers among the seven button pushes.

That doesn't mean that someone wasn't pressing a variety of numbers nervously. They were impatient perhaps, and they just happened to press five different buttons a total of seven times.

No. That's not the explanation. Not even close. None of the scenarios mentioned are actually possible. Something else happened. Something nefarious.

After someone pushed five different buttons for a grand total of seven times, a ringback tone is heard on the tape. A ringback tone is what the caller hears to indicate the phone is ringing on the other end of the line. The ringback tone captured on the Kelly / Byron recording is not as loud as the beeps from the button pushes, but it's there. And there's no doubt what one is hearing.

The ringback tone means that the button pushes were not happening on Byron's phone or Kilgore's phone, or on any phone on which any other person was listening. If you already have a connection and are talking to someone, you can push all the buttons you want. It will never create another connection. It will never cause another ringback tone to be heard on your phone. Not until you hang up, break the old connection, and place an entirely new call.

Here's what possibly, probably, most likely happened.

Someone was in the room with Kelly. I'm not talking about someone down in the basement or upstairs sleeping. I'm talking someone right there beside Kelly, someone listening on the Moffett phone as Kelly spoke on the Kilgore phone. Same phone line, different phones. That person, Angie or UNK or whomever, for some reason placed a local call using another phone not connected to the Byron / Kelly call. Perhaps the other phone was a cell phone. When the button pushes on that other phone created a connection, the ringback tone sounded. Those beeps and that ringback tone made their way on the tape recording of the Kelly / Byron phone call.

It seems as if something improper was happening on Kelly's end of the phone call. Someone else was in the room. Someone who wanted to hear the call, and wanted to know from whence Byron was calling. Someone who was interested in Byron's full name. And that person attempted to place a phone call soon after Kelly made contact with Byron.

❖

Beep beep.

Beep.

Beep beep beep.

Beep.

Riiiinnnngggg.

AFTERMATH: "IF"

I'm going to skip forward in the phone transcription to the point where Byron twice told Kelly that they "shouldn't talk about this." From my perspective, these two phrases have no significance with respect to whether or not Byron Case is factually innocent or factually guilty. From the perspective of the State of Missouri, it had substantial significance. The Missouri appellate court cited those two phrases explicitly in their determination that the tape did in fact constitute a tacit admission, that the tape was properly presented to the jury.

Let's take a look back at the relevant portion of Kilgore's transcription:

Byron:	We shouldn't talk about this?
Kelly:	Why?
Byron:	Probably because we shouldn't talk about this?
Kelly:	Of course, we should.
Byron:	Except, at least, if I need to talk to you.
Kelly:	What do you mean? Yeah, I would love for you to talk to me about it --

The transcription seems pretty convincing that Byron refused to talk to Kelly about it, whatever "it" was. The problem is that this transcription segment of six lines contains four lines with egregious transcription errors. That's not bad considering Kilgore only screws up Byron's lines and Byron has only three lines. Let's see how Kilgore managed to pull that off by considering the segment line by line.

❖

First line, Byron speaking: "We shouldn't talk about this."

When I listen to that line, I hear Byron say "We should talk about this," without the negation of the word "should." I hear Byron say just the opposite of what Kilgore writes.

Now --

I'll concede that Byron paused ever so slightly after saying "should," perhaps for emphasis.

I'll concede that the negation would fit nicely in that pause.

I'll concede that someone not listening carefully, someone listening with a preconceived notion might hear "shouldn't."

I'll even concede that when I isolate just that word and listen to it over and over, I can perhaps, maybe, possibly hear "shouldn't."

I'll concede each of these points, but when I just listen to the tape, I still hear "should." As a transcriber, I would have written "should." If I was uncertain, I would have written "{unintelligible}." In no case would I have written the word "shouldn't." I would not put to paper that which I cannot hear with certainty.

❖

Second line, Kelly responding: "Why?"

Note that Kelly doesn't say "Why not?" She says "Why?" A small point, but a small point in favor of those arguing Byron said "should."

❖

Third line, Byron speaking: "Probably because we shouldn't talk about this."

I don't hear the word "probably." I just don't hear it. I don't believe it's there. It's a relatively small point, but it reflects poorly once again on the accuracy of Kilgore's transcription.

Also, I can't determine whether Byron said "cause" or "because." I would have transcribed it as {'Cause or Because}. Another small point, but another ding on Kilgore's credibility as a transcriber.

The most significant portion of the third line, of course, is where Byron repeats "should" or "shouldn't." Once again, I clearly hear the word "should" with no negation. Concessions are as before.

❖

Fourth line, Kelly speaking: "Of course, we should."

Kelly's response here is telling. She has a habit of beginning her response by repeating what Byron just said. Below, I provide examples from throughout the transcript. In each case, the italics are mine.

| Byron: | I'm sure really surprised that they called again. |
| Kelly: | *That they called again.* They've called a bunch again. |

| Byron: | You free all day? |
| Kelly: | *Yes, I'm free all day.* |

| Byron: | That works. |
| Kelly: | *That works?* |

| Byron: | What's good for you? |
| Kelly: | *When is good?* Any time. |

Kelly:	Okay, I'll be there. You'll be in all black, I assume.
Byron:	Probably not.
Kelly:	*Probably not.* Really? I'm impressed.

| Byron: | {unintelligible} *we should* talk about this. |
| Kelly: | Of course *we should.* |

All right, I sneaked that last one in with my transcription rather than Kilgore's. It allows you to see how Kelly's tendency to repeat what Byron just said tends to support the argument that Byron said "should."

From here, the transcription becomes even more disturbing.

❖

Fifth line, Byron speaking: "Except, at least, if I need to talk to you."

Holy Cow! Kilgore's not even close.

Here's what I hear: "Umm, {unintelligible}, at least I need to talk to you."

Now this may look similar to what Kilgore wrote, but it's not. Where Kilgore has "except," I have "{unintelligible}." I'm not sure what was there, but I'm sure it wasn't "except." I believe the words were actually "there's stuff" followed by a slight pause as Byron reformulated what he was going to say. I'm not sure, though, hence my transcription reads "{unintelligible}."

That's not the most troublesome portion of the line though. Not by a long shot.

Kilgore added a word. Kilgore added the word "if."

That word is absolutely, positively, no way on God's green Earth in there. That word, that little two-letter word dramatically transformed the meaning of what Byron said. By inserting it, Kilgore failed to create an accurate record reflecting Byron's expressed need to talk to Kelly, much less his willingness to talk to her. Kilgore created instead a false record in which Byron is unwilling to talk to Kelly now, but might talk to her later, but only if he felt the need to do so.

Kilgore's transcription is a stunning, and disturbing, distortion of what Byron said. On this point, there is no confusion. The word "if" is simply not there in the tape. No amount of filtering, tempo change, or spectrum analysis can make it seem as if it might kind-of possibly be there. Kilgore simply inserted the word in the transcript at a critical point. He thereby made a false record of what Byron Case actually said and actually meant.

Could it get any worse than that?

Unfortunately --

❖

Sixth line, Kelly speaking: "What do you mean? Yeah. I would love for you to talk to me about it --"

I added the ellipsis to indicate Kelly said more than I presented. That's an understatement. Kilgore has Kelly going on for nine typewritten lines without pause. By doing so, Kilgore once again distorts for the reader what was actually on the tape. In fact, Kelly pauses at several points within Kilgore's uninterrupted paragraph, as if she is waiting for a response from Byron.

More disturbingly, it seems Kelly is actually listening to Byron, actually hearing him speak even though the recorder cannot.

That's what I believe happened. That's what I intend to show you, literally. Once you understand it, you will understand the extent to which Kelly can and does manipulate this phone call.

Here's my, not Kilgore's, initial transcription of what Kilgore presents as just one line.

> Kelly: Whadda you mean?
> Byron: [No response.]
> Kelly: Yeah. I would love for you to talk to me about it --"

No big deal, right?

Wrong.

Something suspicious is going on. After Kelly said "Whadda you mean?" there was a 1.5 second pause. I recorded it as no response from Byron. I was wrong initially when making my own transcription, and I now admit it to one and all. Byron did respond, and Byron's response caused Kelly to say "Yeah." Kilgore excluded Byron's portion of the conversation from the transcript. He even erased the time during which Byron was speaking, leaving Kelly to respond "Yeah" to a statement Byron ostensibly never made.

I'm guessing, right?

Wrong.

To see if Byron actually said anything during that pause, I applied a sophisticated audio technique called "turning up the volume." Here's my amended transcription of what Kilgore presented as just one line:

> Kelly: Whadda you mean?
> Byron: {unintelligible} talk to {me} {unintelligible}
> Kelly: Yeah. I would love for you to talk to me about it --"

Holy Spumoni!

Byron says something which is clear to Kelly but barely audible on the tape. Byron says something about talking to Kelly, and Kelly responds with "Yeah. I would love for you to talk to me." Once again, for the fourth time, I believe it's fair to say that Kelly's response indicates Byron is saying he wants to talk to her. That's a big deal, certainly, but not the biggest of deals in that segment.

Not by a long shot.

❖

Somehow, some way, the recording device is not consistently hearing what Byron is saying. Moments before, Byron was easily heard by the recording system when he said "We should talk about this," twice, and when he said "At least, I need to talk to you." There may be an argument about how intelligible Byron's statements were, but there is no argument they were audible. It was easy to hear him say something, even if people might argue over exactly what he said.

There is also something visually remarkable about the 1.5 second pause, the pause that Kilgore failed to note, the pause which wasn't a pause, the pause in which Byron can be heard speaking by anyone clever enough to turn up the volume. When viewed with audio software, in my case Audacity, the amplitude of the waveform decreases continuously during Byron's side of the conversation, as if the recording device is moving away from the handset. You can see it in the image below.

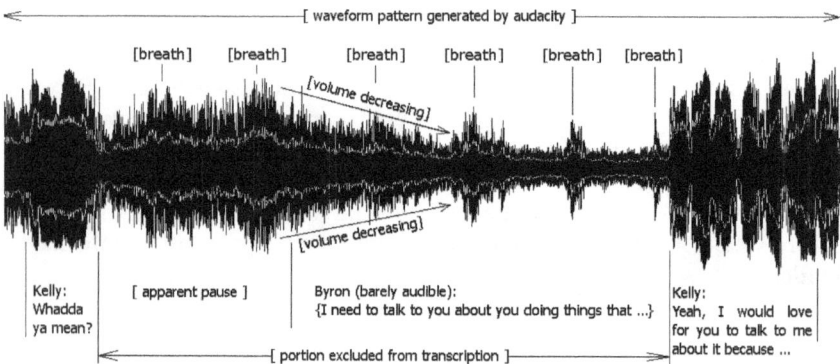

FIGURE 1: CRITICAL 6-SECOND SEGMENT OMITTED FROM TRANSCRIPTION OF JUNE 5, 2001 PHONE CALL

The bump at the left is Kelly saying "Whadda you mean?" The pause, the point where Byron is apparently speaking, runs from the end of the bump on the left to where Kelly says "Yeah. I would love for you to talk to me --" on the right. One can hear someone take six breaths while Kelly is not speaking. The breaths are the intermediate bumps, and are so labeled. The person breathing, not Byron for reasons soon to be obvious, is taking approximately sixty breaths per minute, four times the normal rate. Almost everything else you see is white noise. As I've noted before, it's a crappy recording.

Buried somewhere within the noise, among the breaths, one can barely hear Byron say "{I need to talk to you about you doing things that ...}."

❖

How is it that the recording system can hear Byron some of the time, but not hear him at times such as that displayed above? The recording system can hear Kelly's voice all of the time, so it's not as if the system is failing intermittently. It seems also as if Byron can hear Kelly all of the time. Of the three, only the recording system has trouble hearing, and it only has trouble hearing Byron, and only some of the time.

I have a possible scenario.

Assume Kelly, or a third party, removed the suction cup listening device from the handset, then held the listening device near the handset while Kelly was speaking, and moved it away from the handset at select times when Byron was speaking. That would explain why there is so much background noise throughout the call, why the background noise is so variable, why Kelly is almost always heard more clearly than Byron, and why Byron is intermittently inaudible.

If you study the image, you can easily envision the listening device moving further and further away from the handset. You can even see the breathing become quieter and quieter, at least to the listening device.

Since only the listening device would move in this scenario, Byron and Kelly would be able to hear one another as usual. Byron would of course be unaware that he was being recorded, much less being recorded selectively.

If any sheriff, prosecutor, judge, public defender, jury, or appellate court listened without skepticism, they would take no particular notice of pauses followed by answers to questions seemingly unasked. They would accept without challenge that Kelly's voice was always clear, while Byron's was variable. They would be uncurious about the persistent but variable background noises. No one would care. Everyone would simply presume Byron is guilty.

❖

Finally, there is one more piece of compelling evidence in the tape that Byron was willing, even eager to talk to Kelly. He agreed to meet with her at Loose Park, the next day, "the earlier the better." His words, not hers, not mine, his. He agreed to meet her though he had strep throat and a fever of 101 degrees or higher. Byron actually showed up at Loose Park, to talk, despite Missouri's insistence he was unwilling to talk.

It was Kelly who did not show. She was directed by the sheriff's office not to show. Though the State of Missouri claimed that Byron was unwilling to talk, it was in fact their star witness who avoided talking, at the insistence of the Sheriff's Office of Jackson County, Missouri.

Some of you may now finally concede that Byron was actually eager to talk, and some of you may now find his eagerness suspicious in and of itself. You may now believe that Byron's eagerness to talk is proof of his guilt. Therein lies the rub. For some of you, Byron would seem guilty if he didn't want to talk to Kelly, and he would seem guilty if he did want to talk to her. Either way, he would seem guilty.

It wasn't Byron's response that mattered. It was Kelly's accusation.

AFTERMATH: "SHOW"

So far, I haven't mentioned the part of the phone call that most nagged at me for so long. It wasn't the first seven lines. I hadn't even seen the first four lines until recently. It wasn't the beeps or the ringback tone. I was focusing on the words and paid little attention to extraneous noises. It wasn't even the "should" versus "shouldn't" issue. I had always, until recently, presumed Byron said "shouldn't." It just didn't matter to me.

What has nagged at me all this time is that Byron said nothing when Kelly asked him why he "felt the need to kill her." That's what's been bugging me. If Byron didn't kill Anastasia, why didn't he say something at that point?

I understand that absence of evidence is not evidence. I understand that I should presume a defendant innocent. I understand all that, but now that I am not currently a sworn juror, Byron's lack of response is a problem for me. I guess I'm weak.

It's finally time to suck it up and consider the most damning portion of the tape. There are startling surprises still to come.

In Kilgore's transcription, the damning portion of the conversation occurs within a single paragraph, uninterrupted by Byron, in which Kelly twice asks Byron why he killed Anastasia. The next thing Byron said, according to Kilgore's transcription is "We shouldn't talk about this."

Sounds bad, no doubt about it.

As you might expect by now, Kilgore bollixed this portion of the transcription as well. The first thing you might note if you were to compare Kilgore's transcript to the tape is that there are multiple pauses in Kelly's diatribe, one lasting nine seconds. The pauses are so frequent and of sufficient length that Kilgore transcribed one minute and twenty-seven seconds of tape into a single paragraph. Perhaps one might think that there was a two sided conversation taking place. I did.

I used the noise removal feature in Audacity to, well, remove the noise from those portions where Byron might be speaking. Sure enough, Byron was speaking. It was indeed a two-way conversation, not a long Kelly harangue as transcribed by Kilgore. Byron is barely audible, to be sure, and unintelligible, but I can definitely hear him speaking.

Once again, the waveform pattern suggests the listening device was being moved away from the mouthpiece when Byron spoke, as if Kelly did not want Byron's response recorded. The waveform patterns are in fact even more telling than the one presented previously. I present them below for the segment of the tape after Kelly says: "If you could seriously explain to me as to why you felt the need to show her, then that would really help me feel better about this whole fucking thing."

The first figure shows the waveform pattern before noise removal. It's obvious that the noise is diminishing throughout the nine seconds, as if the listening device is moving away from the handset. The second figure shows the same waveform pattern with noise removed from those nine seconds. What's left there are Byron's words, filtered, barely audible, and unintelligible. What Byron said was completely swamped by the noise.

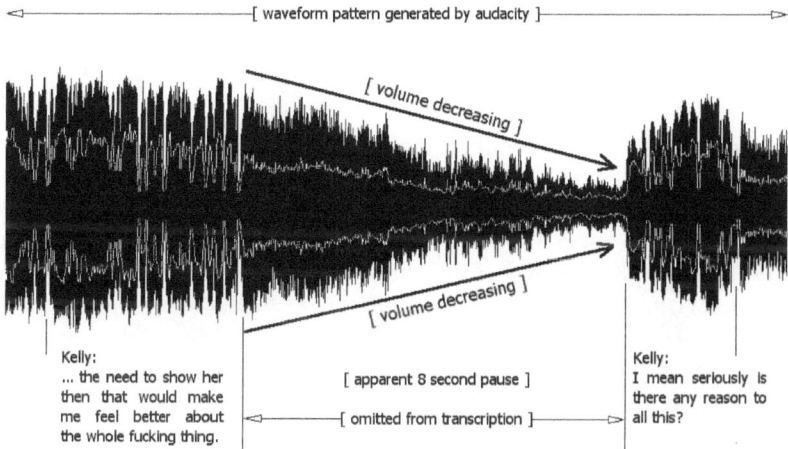

FIGURE 2: APPARENT 8-SECOND PAUSE OMITTED FROM TRANSCRIPTION OF JUNE 5, 2001 PHONE CALL

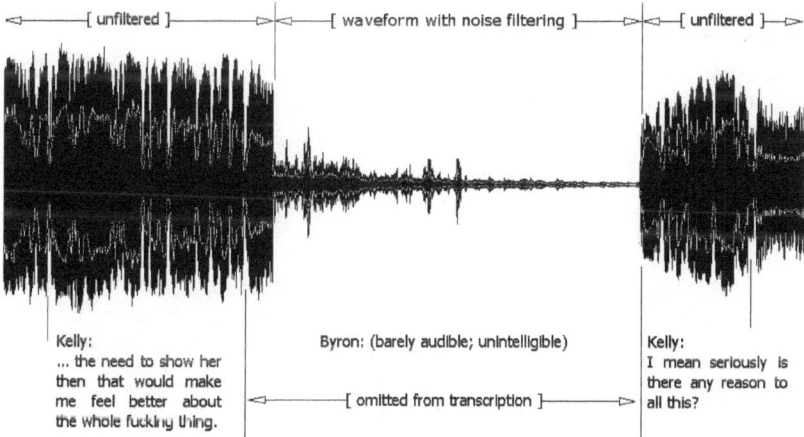

FIGURE 3: BYRON RESPONSE DISCOVERED AMIDST NOISE OF JUNE 5, 2001 PHONE CALL

I wish we could hear what Byron actually said. I wonder why we can't. Perhaps someone did not want us to.

If you're attentive, you will have noticed that I transcribed the money portion of Kelly's preceding sentence as "felt the need to show her." There's a good reason for that. That's what I hear on the tape. I don't hear "kill" as Kilgore writes. I hear "show." And it's not just me that hears "show." I prepared an audio clip of just that segment, slowed the tempo so that it was easier to hear, and sent it out for review. Of fifteen blind responses, thirteen people heard "show," two people heard "kill," and one person said it could be either one but thinks it's "show."

As it turns out, Kelly may not have asked Byron twice why he felt the need to kill Anastasia. At least one of those times, there is a very good possibility that she asked Byron why he felt the need to show Anastasia.

❖

As I considered the possibility that Kelly was manipulating what the recording device could hear, it occurred to me she could also control what Byron heard. All that would be necessary would be for Kelly to cover the mouthpiece with her hand when she wanted to say something that Byron would not hear. Kelly's end of the conversation would be heard clearly on the tape. Byron's end of the conversation would seem confused and evasive. If Kelly were really lucky, the person who transcribed the tape might actually leave out the pauses completely, making it seem as if Byron is completely unresponsive when Kelly is repeatedly accusing him of murder.

Confusing?

You bet. I'm guessing, however, that it would not be confusing had someone in authority been present when Kelly called Byron, if the State of Missouri had not left the fox to guard the hen house. We the jurors are left instead to rely on Kelly's trustworthiness if we are to conclude the tape is a tacit admission of Byron's guilt.

It angers me and I need a break. When I calm down, I'll return and continue the history of this sad and pathetic phone call travesty.

AFTERMATH: UNCONTROLLED

Way, way, way back on September 19, 2000, Kelly Moffett told the folks at the Jackson County Prosecutor's Office that she witnessed Byron Case shoot Anastasia WitbolsFeugen in the head with a shotgun. "She saw him with a shotgun . . . Byron went over to the victim and shot her in the head."

For 258 days, Byron Case remained a free man. No one at the Jackson County Prosecutor's Office filed charges against him. No one at the Jackson County Sheriff's office arrested him, or even interviewed him. On day 259, Kelly Moffett took control of the situation. She contacted Byron, "out of the blue." She asked him why he killed Anastasia. Byron's answers were incidental. The question was all that was needed. Kelly spun up the wheels of justice simply by asking the question.

On day 261, those wheels of justice began to grind. Sergeant Kilgore wrote and signed a "Probable Cause Statement." He made no mention of the phone call. Instead he wrote that "Ms. Moffett witnessed Byron Case shoot WitbolsFeugen in the face with a long barreled firearm." That doesn't seem to be quite accurate. Kelly told both the prosecutor's office and the sheriff's office that Byron shot Anastasia in the head with a shotgun. But when the wheels of justice are grinding, what's a misplaced cog here or there?

On day 261, same day, the County of Jackson, Missouri put out an arrest warrant for Byron C. Case. Bond was set at $200,000.

On day 261, same day, Detectives Scarbo and Edington of the Jackson County Drug Task Force joined the effort. From their report:

> [We] contacted cooperating witness (CW), Kelly Moffett, and her mother at the Jackson County Courthouse in Kansas City, Missouri. Those present for this contact were District Attorney Bob Beaird and Assistant District Attorney Crayon ... The Jackson County Prosecutor's office has asked the Jackson County Drug Task Force to assist in obtaining a controlled contact between the cooperating witness and the suspect, Byron C. Case.

Hmmm. A controlled contact. Very interesting. Very interesting, indeed.

It seems as if Kelly's "out of the blue" call was not quite satisfactory. Missouri had her statement. They had her "out of the blue" phone call. They had Sergeant Kilgore's nearly accurate "Probable Cause Statement." They had an arrest warrant with a $200,000 bond, but they weren't ready to make an arrest.

Nope. Not yet.

Instead, they recruited the folks who were adept at recording phone calls. They brought in the Jackson County Drug Task Force to make a "controlled contact" between the CW and the suspect. I'm guessing they did so because someone pointed out a flaw in their case. I'm guessing that someone is Theresa Crayon, who appears for the first time, best I can tell, in Detective Edington's report quoted above. Regardless of whomever might have recognized the problem, I'm envisioning the following conversation:

> We can't take this to court. Kelly's story is shaky as hell. We all know that. Now we're supposed to back up that story with a tape she made when none of us were there? Are you kidding me? If we have to face anyone other than Horton Lance, we're screwed. We need a controlled phone call and we need it quick. So get some guys who know what the hell they're doing, and get her to ask him again, on tape, when we're there. It doesn't make any difference what he says, we just need to be there when Kelly asks the question. Got it?

So they all sat around the prosecutor's office while Kelly tried to call Byron, but Byron didn't answer. Kelly told them it was probably because he couldn't see her caller ID. She wanted to call from her house. Ideally, she would be allowed privacy while she called, but the folks working for Jackson County had wised up at least a little bit. They wanted to be there when she placed the calls.

So the two detectives packed up everything and headed off to Kelly's house where, after many attempts, Kelly finally made contact with Byron while the authorities were present. So far, so good for Missouri. Kelly hadn't contacted Byron "out of the blue" like last time. This time she had made a controlled contact. There were two, not just one but two, detectives sitting right there to confirm no shenanigans were taking place when Kelly asked Byron why he killed Anastasia.

It would be wonderful from Missouri's standpoint if Byron admitted killing Anastasia, to be sure, but it would not be necessary. All Missouri really needed was for Kelly to ask the killer question followed by almost anything from Byron, anything other than "What the hell are you talking about?"

But Kelly didn't ask the killer question, not with the two detectives sitting there. Instead Kelly and Byron just did their "what, when, where" routine all over again. I could include the entire transcript, but that wouldn't be good for either of us. Okay, I'll provide a sample. "CW" in this transcription segment is the "cooperating witness". In other words, CW is Kelly.

> Case: So what's the problem? (Unintelligible) remember?
> CW: Wh, what?
> Case: Sometimes that isn't supposed to stick in your memory?
> CW: Well uh --
> Case: (Unintelligible) tied to it.
>
> CW: I guess. (Unintelligible) there's no way for you to meet up with me anytime?

Case:	What?
CW:	I said there's no way for you to meet up with me anytime?
Case:	When?
CW:	Just anytime.
Case:	(Unintelligible)
CW:	I said is there no way for you to?
Case.	I don't know. I just uh I'm sorry but the whole thing is a little bit on the weird side to me.
CW:	Why is that?
Case:	I mean like, I don't know.
CW:	Well whatever, can I just talk to you now?
Case:	On the phone?
CW:	Yes.
Case:	No.
CW:	Well then duh, that's what I want, I figured you'd say that, I feel the same way.

Okay, that's enough. You get the idea. It goes on like this for five plus pages, and there is no mention of either "kill" or "Anastasia" anywhere to be found. You've been through it before. At the end though, is something interesting, something professional. After Kelly and Byron end their conversation, Detective Edington spoke into the microphone and corroborated the call.

> This is Detective Eimee Edington with the Jackson County Drug Task Force. Today's date is 6-7 of 2001. Case number is 97-11829. This is a [sic] investigation involving a homicide. The following is a recorded conversation between cooperating witness, Kelly Moffett, and suspect, Byron C. Case, white male, 11-23-78. The cooperating witness placed a call to . . . Byron Case's residence, whereupon she made contact with Byron Case.

There we go. That's how it's done. That's a controlled contact. After the first phone call, there was no one from Jackson County speaking into the microphone because there was no one from Jackson County present. The first contact was a completely uncontrolled call, subject to manipulation and shenanigans. The second contact was a well controlled call during which Kelly never asked a single question nor made a single statement related to the crime being investigated.

I can envision the discussion which ensued after the second call.

> Nothing? Nothing at all? She never asked him about shooting Anastasia? You're kidding, right? Tell me you're kidding. Well this isn't going to cut it. Get those guys back out there and do it again. This time, get it right.

Day 262, next day, Detectives Scarbo and Edington were instructed to meet CW at "a pre-arranged location." They tried four times to contact Byron. Four times they got the answering machine. They gave up. Detective Edington spoke into the mike once again, as he did after the previous call, and they called it a day.

By the way, when Detective Edington made a transcription of the tape, he included items such as "(pause)" and "(Telephone rings)" and "(long beep)." It's great stuff. If Kilgore had been as diligent, we would probably not be here today.

Now back to the wheels of justice, grinding ever onward. Back to my vision of the ensuing conversation.

> Now that's just great. What are we going to do now? We've got a suicidal victim and a suicidal boyfriend. We've got a bullet hole that's half as big as it should be, and a time of death that's in the wrong day. We've got one witness who can't keep her story straight, and she doesn't know the difference between a shotgun and a BB gun, between getting shot in the nose at point blank range and shot in the back of the head from five feet away. Hell, she even claims she can see feet through solid car bodies. The defense has Anastasia's sister who says Kelly never called the house. They have witnesses that will say neither Byron nor Justin was drunk, stoned, crying, or upset like my witness claims. They even have an eyewitness who saw Anastasia get out of the car and walk away, for crissakes. And you give us this uncontrolled piece of crap tape. That's just great. The best we can hope for realistically is a jury who won't think too hard. Maybe we'll just tell them they shouldn't believe anything the defense says because Byron has a bigger motive to lie than anyone.
>
> Maybe they'll buy it.

AFTERMATH: HOT PURSUIT

Even the wheels of justice need to take a break every now and then, and so they did in this case. For two days.

The second controlled phone call to Byron took place on June 8, 2001. At that point, the law enforcement community in Jackson County, Missouri had everything they were going to have before arresting Byron Case. They had an eyewitness. Some might question why they waited 262 days, and counting, before acting on the claims of that eyewitness, but they had an eyewitness.

They had a tape in which Byron admitted killing Anastasia. Okay, maybe Byron had not actually admitted killing Anastasia, but he certainly never denied killing her. And, true, the tape wasn't well-controlled, by any stretch of the imagination, and may have some evidentiary problems, but the bottom line is they had his non-confession on tape.

They also had Sergeant Kilgore's Probable Cause Statement. It may have been a bit inflated, perhaps even falsified for those of you who are picky about such things, but they had Sergeant Kilgore's Probable Cause Statement.

They also had an arrest warrant with a $200,000 bond. Plus --

They had a controlled phone call with Byron to back up the previous uncontrolled phone call. Yes, it's true that Kelly never asked anything about Anastasia or about that terrible night, but they have a controlled phone call. As of day 262, they had pretty much everything they needed. It was time to get the murderer off the streets. And quickly.

Day 263. That was a Saturday. No arrest.

Day 264. That was a Sunday. No arrest.

Day 265. That was a Monday. June 11, 2001 to be exact. Monday worked better: no need for overtime, no interference with barbecues.

Detective DeValkenaere told us during the trial that he led the arrest team. As you may recall from our deliberations, I didn't care for Detective DeValkenaere as a witness. I didn't understand what his testimony had to do with Byron Case's guilt or innocence. I even suggested that his testimony was dramatized. More specifically, I believe I agreed with Jade, our fellow literary juror, when she said he was feeding us a bunch of crap. Having the ability to review police reports regarding the arrest gives us an opportunity to see if I stepped over the line.

Consider first the report of Sergeant Becker of the Jackson County Sheriff's Office. You have not heard of him yet in these pages. The State of Missouri and Horton Lance apparently concluded that Sergeant Becker knew nothing of interest or value to the jury. I quote below from his arrest report.

> Entry was made through the open front door while continuing to announce ourselves as police officers with a warrant. The suspect was located in a bedroom and taken into custody.

That's it. That's how Sergeant Becker describes Byron's arrest. So boring and mundane was his report that he was not asked to testify at the trial. Keep in mind this concise, uneventful description of Byron's arrest as we consider Detective DeValkenaere's description of the same event. First, I present the relevant portion from Detective DeValkenaere's police report, written soon after the arrest.

> Entry was made to the residence and I continued to yell 'Police.' As I moved toward the hallway that led to the bathroom and bedroom area of the residence a white male who resembled Case started to come out of the north bedroom. Upon seeing me, Case retreated into the bedroom, closed the door and was attempting to lock the door when I pushed it open. As I entered the room Case was in, Case stumbled backwards onto a bed. Case admitted his identity and was taken into custody without further incident.

That's somewhat more dramatic, but not inconsistent with Sergeant Becker's report.

Let's now consider Detective DeValkenaere's trial testimony, almost a year after the arrest. Let's skip down to the portion of his testimony where Byron attempted to escape and DeValkenaere had to "give chase." You remember that, don't you? DeValkenaere had to "give chase." I presume that was the only legal basis for his testimony. If Byron attempted to escape, it would indicate a guilty state of mind.

> I opened the screen door and moved to what will be a corner. At the corner, between the living room area and the hallway, that leads back to the bathroom and a couple of bedrooms. I took a position there as a position of cover while they cleared the kitchen area. The other officers cleared the kitchen area. From that position, I continued to yell, 'Police' and 'anybody inside come out.' About that time, Mr. Case came out of the north bedroom door on the north side. He started to turn toward me. He saw me. As soon as he saw me, he turned and ran back into that bedroom. I gave chase. And when I got to the door, just as he was trying to close it and trying to get it locked, I forced the door open. He used his body weight, I used my body weight to force against it, knocked him backward and took him into custody.

Does Detective DeValkenaere's trial testimony comport with his police report? I think not.

Did DeValkenaere dramatize his testimony? I believe so.

Did he perjure himself? I leave that for others to decide.

Assuming the police report is more accurate than the testimony, DeValkenaere did not take up a cover position outside Byron's room. He did not wait in that cover position while the others cleared the kitchen. He did not continue to yell "Police" and "anyone inside come on out" from that cover position. He could not have done so because he never took up that position. Instead, as is clear from his report, DeValkenaere first saw Byron as DeValkenaere "moved toward the hallway that led to the bedroom and bathroom area." That is less dramatic than taking up a cover position, but credit where credit is due. It may be truthful.

According to DeValkenaere's report, Byron never actually came out of his bedroom before seeing the police. Byron was only starting to come out of his bedroom. If Byron had not in fact come out of his bedroom, it would be impossible for him to have "turned and ran back into that bedroom," as DeValkenaere told the jurors, under oath. It's a small point. Perhaps.

Perhaps not. It was because Byron turned and ran back into the bedroom that DeValkenaere testified he "gave chase." There they are, the magic words. "Gave chase." DeValkenaere pursued a dangerous criminal attempting to escape justice, and the attempted escape gave legal grounds for DeValkenaere's testimony.

DeValkenaere's testimony started out more dramatically than did Sergeant Becker's report, but maybe DeValkenaere is just a more dramatic guy. Each of the three versions describe the same series of events: entry, identification, and arrest. The details, however, became more damning as DeValkenaere elaborated upon them during trial. At some point, his testimony seems to have turned from true crime to fiction.

If the wheels of justice are to grind ever onwards, except weekends, they must sometimes be lubricated with exaggerations and falsehoods.

AFTERMATH: SCREWED

There is a note on the bottom of Byron Case's Case Action Record. "T. Crayon advises that informant ID has been revealed to Δ. Because of threat to witnesses Δ is to be held w/o bond." It was written and signed by Judge Standridge. I know nothing about Judge Standridge other than his signature is impossible to read, he uses Greek symbols in his writing, and he takes Theresa Crayon at her word.

For those unfamiliar with Greek, Δ represents a capital Delta in the Greek alphabet. D is for defendant, so in the quote above Δ represents Byron Case.

Given the facility with which I mismanage special characters in my documents, I may have had more difficulty entering Δ into this book than Theresa Crayon had getting Byron's bond revoked. All she did was advise Judge Standridge that some unidentified person had at some unspecified time revealed to Byron that Kelly was an informant.

I'm pausing for a moment in the hope that this will raise multiple questions in your mind. It's an exercise of sorts, hoping to lure you into thinking as a skeptical juror.

Ready? Good. Here we go.

Who, you might ask, told Byron that Kelly was an informant, and when, you might ask, did this happen? The answer to the first question is a shocker. The answer to the second is disturbing.

As it turns out, Byron Case first learned that Kelly Moffett was acting as a police informant after his arrest and incarceration. You might therefore reasonably conclude that Byron's bond was revoked while he was in jail, before his mother had time to round up the $20,000 non-refundable deposit for the bond.

You would be seriously wrong. Byron's bond was revoked at least two hours before his arrest.

Byron Case was surprised by the sudden arrival of 13 officers from the Jackson County Sheriff's Office and the FBI. It took only seconds from initial knock, to yelling "police, come on out with your hands up," to the pursuit / stumble / whatever, to cuffing him. Byron had no idea what was going to happen beforehand, had no time to orient himself once it started, and had no hope (or intent) of resisting well-armed officers in tactical gear.

I believe the arrest was well-handled. By coupling overwhelming force with the element of surprise, the arrest team minimized the risk of harm to the officers, the suspect, and bystanders.

The arrest occurred at or near 1PM on June 11, 2001. Keep this in mind as you read from another of Sergeant Kilgore's reports.

> On 06-11-01, at approximately 1100 hrs., I received a telephone call from Mr. Spencer G. Colliate, the Director of Criminal Records in Kansas City Mo.
>
> At the time, Mr. Colliate asked me if I was aware the bond on the warrant for Byron Case had been changed. I told Mr. Colliate that I had received no information regarding the bond amount.
>
> Mr. Colliate stated Judge Standridge had been informed the witness' identity had been revealed to Case and for the witness safety he has ordered that Case be held without bond.
>
> I asked Mr. Colliate if he had a document signed by the Judge with this order and Mr. Colliate stated the Judge's order was written on the Case Action record. At my request, Mr. Colliate faxed me a copy of the Judge's order.

More than two hours _prior_ to arresting Byron Case, it appears as if Theresa Crayon managed to have Byron's bond revoked. She did so by telling Judge Standridge that Byron had learned Kelly was a police informant, though Byron was not to learn of that until after his arrest.

Crayon made no mention of how Byron might have learned of Kelly's role as an informant. It's unlikely law enforcement told him, since they relied on surprise and overwhelming force to take him into custody.

It's unlikely Kelly told Byron of her informant status, since the discovery in the case shows no further contact with Byron after the second, and only, controlled phone call to him.

It's unlikely Theresa Crayon or anyone from the prosecutor's office told Byron of Kelly's informant status. They too wanted to preserve the element of surprise. Also, there is no mention in the discovery papers of anyone contacting Byron after the second phone contact.

It's possible that no one informed Byron of Kelly's role as an informant until after he was in jail, just as Byron claims.

Do you understand now why I tell you repeatedly to be skeptical of everyone? They will lie to you. They will lie to judges. They will lie to the public. They will lie to themselves. It's all in the name of justice.

❖

Byron's incarceration turned out to be spectacularly effective in helping Theresa Crayon win what seemed to be a shaky case. Preparing a defense against the State is no easy task, even if you happen to be innocent. Preparing one from within the confines of the Jackson County jail is immeasurably more difficult. Preparing one while being unaware of manufactured evidence borders on the impossible.

Byron kept a journal while in the Jackson County jail. From that journal, we can continue tracking the history of the uncontrolled phone call and its falsified transcription. The journal shows that Byron was long kept unaware of the uncontrolled phone call and the egregiously erroneous transcription.

July 9th, day 29. Byron first meets with someone from the Public Defender's Office. "The lawyer I mentioned came to see me today bringing news of my case." No mention is made of the phone call. In fact, the lawyer Byron sees is not actually assigned to Byron's case. Byron remains effectively without counsel.

August 9th, day 60. Byron meets with his public defender, Jarrett Johnson, for the first time. "At last, my public defender came to speak with me this afternoon, giving me some reasons to be hopeful again. The motion for a bond hearing [to get the bond reinstated] will be submitted either tomorrow or Monday, which means the hearing will most likely be held on a Friday: either next week or the week after, but no later." No mention is made of the phone call.

August 15th, day 66. "I continue to hope beyond hope that I'll be free in time to welcome in what Bianca always called 'sweater weather,' and again I was assured of the favorable odds of that scenario by my lawyer, who said the judge would likely assign a bond of only $150,000." Byron obviously believes his family could raise the $15,000 non-refundable cash payment a bondsman would require before posting his $150,000 bond. His mother would take another mortgage on her house, but he would be out of jail while preparing his defense. He makes no mention of the tape.

August 21st, day 72. "Bittersweet news reached me today via Mum, who's becoming one of the only people I call anymore. The lawyer contacted her at work to let her know that ... my hearing was scheduled for Friday, September 7th, nearly three weeks from today. Ouch."

September 1st, day 83. Byron manages to place a phone call to his public defender. Byron first learns that his 5 June phone call to Kelly was recorded, and that the phone call will be used as evidence against him. He is told that the phone transcript will not be included in the 2000 pages of discovery the prosecution is about to provide. "Why is that relevant?" he writes. "Jarrett says they wouldn't have it if they didn't feel something said had been in some way incriminating. That bothers me because there wasn't anything said that even alluded to the night Anastasia was murdered, least of all anything which might have suggested that I killed her! Why can't I get a transcript? What's the big secret?"

September 5th, day 87. Byron finally receives the discovery. "At LONG last. Mr. Johnson brought me the epic work that is this case's discovery. Nine-hundred pages, all out of any degree of order, now need to be organized by me and subsequently read and annotated. It looks like I'll be busy for a long time." No mention of the tape or its transcription. There is, however, more hope expressed regarding the bond hearing. "Supposedly he's going to ask for $70,000, but the judge may choose to double that amount. Either way will be affordable assuming it's payable through the court. My head hurts just thinking about how long it's going to take to pay back the mortgage / credit company. Dog."

September 7th, day 89. Byron finally gets his bond hearing. It doesn't go well. "My stomach did summersaults when the judge ruled that I was to be given a $300,000 cash bond. He may as well have said 'bond refused' and left things the way they were. I can't fathom dealing out $30,000 (which would just be flushed into a bondsman, i.e. non refundable) to buy me back the next year of my life. . . . [T]he prosecution brought up Kelly's mom to say she's scared of me getting out and doing something to one of her daughters. The judge, doing his job, fell into the prosecutor's trap and decided I'm a danger to society / myself / whoever."

September 12th, day 94. "Sad to say, but Mum's going around and talking with mortgage companies to get the one with the lowest mortgage rates. The one she's found so far is a fat 12.9%er, which means monthly payments of over $300 a month for fifteen years. Yow. Scary thought." Byron's mother will be unable to raise the higher bond. Had the initial $200,000 bond not been revoked, she might have been able to raise the $20,000 fee for a bondsman. The delay and the increase put Byron's release out of reach. There is still no mention of hearing the tape or reading its transcription.

September 26th, day 108. Byron learns that he will be assigned a new public defender. Jarrett Johnson is leaving the PD's office for private practice. He writes in his journal. "Maybe I'll get lucky and someone a little more aggressive in the courtroom will find my discovery on their desk."

October 11th, day 123. Byron learns the name of his new public defender. "Shit. Shitshitshitshit. Um. . . when I first opened a line of communication with [a potential private attorney] he told me that if I couldn't get the money to hire him I shouldn't worry much due to the quality of Jackson County's public defenders. Of course there are some lawyers with more experience and such, but he told me they were all quite competent, except one. That attorney's name was Horton Lance and [he] said to me: 'If they assign him to your case, run like hell.' You get two guesses as to who my new attorney is."

December 17th, day 190. Byron has spoken to his new public defender only a few times in the last two months. "Oh, Horton Lance didn't come in. I'm calling him tomorrow to drop a little reminder that I am, in fact, still here."

January 18th, day 222. Byron reviews the discovery with his attorney for the first time. "My impression of Horton Lance gets better with every visit. This afternoon's two hour conversation with him was not only the most in depth (we were able to read parts of the discovery together for the first time) but at the end of it his previously flaccid handshake had become quite a bit more 'grippy.'" After 222 days in jail, Byron finally gets time with his public defender to discuss the case against him. Still there is no mention of hearing the tape or reading the transcript.

March 20th, day 283. Byron learns that Anastasia died of a contact wound to the nose. He is excited because he knows that Kelly alleged he was standing five feet from Anastasia when he shot her. "Some things of importance have happened with regard to my case, fortunately. Horton's talked with both Brahm [Kneisley] and Tara [McDowell] about possibly testifying in my behalf and he's subpoenaed the mechanic [Don Rand] who saw Anastasia get out of the car that night; depositions of Kelly and the Jackson County Deputy Medical Examiner [Chase Blanchard] have been done and copies have already reached me. ... I'm very lucky Kelly didn't consider the distance from shooter to victim when coming up with her story because if she somehow guessed right, or close to right, proving my innocence would probably be a lot tougher." Still Byron makes no mention of hearing the tape or reading the transcription.

April 4th, day 298. Byron mentions the recorded phone call for the first and last time in his journal. "It had been twenty-seven days since Horton Lance saw me or spoke with me ... [H]e left me several documents ... including ... the summary report from K.U. Med the day after she called me recording the conversation for the police, which shows I was running a very high fever and may have been delirious."

By day 298, Byron has finally seen Kilgore's transcription of the June 5 phone call. He has come to realize that the phone call is a problem. It's been nearly a year since the call, and he cannot recall it with sufficient clarity to challenge Kilgore's transcription. He's trying to understand how he could have failed to respond to Kelly's accusations that he killed Anastasia.

The trial is less than three weeks away. He has yet to hear the tape. In fact, he will never hear the tape until it is played for the jurors during trial. He is denied access to recording devices while he is in jail, even when speaking with his attorney. He will have no opportunity to listen to the tape, to compare it to the transcript, to correct Kilgore's transcription errors, to wonder about the beeps and ringback tones. He will certainly not have access to software that will allow him to filter the noise from the tape and learn that he actually did respond to Kelly. He will not be allowed to wonder why his voice had been silenced while Kelly's remained loud and clear.

During his three hundred days of incarceration, Byron lost the specific details of the seemingly insignificant phone conversation that would weigh so heavily on the jurors.

Few of us can remember the specifics of year-old calls, even if they were of supreme importance. When peppered with questions about the tape by someone who had been allowed to listen to the tape as frequently as desired, Byron could offer no explanation. He could only concede that if it was in the transcription, he must have said it; if it wasn't in the transcription, he must have said nothing.

The bond revocation worked wonders for the prosecution.

AFTERMATH: "EXCEPTIONAL"

At some point I can't identify, not long before the trial I believe, Theresa Crayon actually compared the transcript against the tape recording. We learn of that from the trial transcripts. The phone call was discussed on two different days when the attorneys argued pre-trial motions before the judge. On the first day, we find this statement by Crayon, rebutting a defense motion that the tapes be excluded because they are unreliable due to their poor quality.

> I do understand Mr. Lance's point. There are motions [portions] in there that are very muffled and you can't understand what's being said, but that is listed as inaudible. The transcripts don't try to put forth anything that you can't hear on the tapes with the aid of the transcript.

That's a ludicrous statement, accepted by Judge Atwell without question, unchallenged by Horton Lance. If you can't hear the tape without the aid of the transcript, you can't hear the tape. Reading does not improve hearing. It only biases what you think you hear. Crayon is admitting that inaudible portions of the tape have been transcribed as if they were audible. It's a stunning admission to introduce into the record.

Judge Atwell informed the attorneys he would listen to the tape overnight and compare it to the transcript. The next day, he reported his findings.

> I found the transcripts to be accurate, to be exceptionally accurate. ... When I heard it, obviously, I suspect it's because the recording device was on Ms. Moffett's phone I assume. Ms. Moffett's voice is very clear and distinct. Mr. Case's voice is not as clear, is much softer and harder to understand, although I was able, with the aid of the transcript, I was able to understand what he said.

Holy Hogwash!

Judge Atwell made the same legal and logical error as did Crayon. If he could only make out what was on the tapes by reading the transcript, he should not have declared the transcript valid, much less "exceptionally accurate." His conclusion is not simply wrong in a legal and logical sense. It is wrong in a factual sense. As we have seen, the transcript is demonstrably inaccurate based on those portions of the tape where Byron can be heard clearly.

Having ruled the tape comprehensible and the transcripts "exceptionally accurate," Judge Atwell proceeded to rule them admissible.

The transcripts themselves in the context of all the evidence, I
suspect, could be considered an admission against interests to Mr.
Case, although I don't find any smoking guns or anything that's
directly, I don't find any direct admissions. But the posture of what's
said by Mr. Case on these tapes in the context of all the evidence I
think theoretically would be an admission or at least might be
admissible once Ms. Moffett is examined to demonstrate contact she
has and concern she has.

Holy Prosecutor in a Robe!

Judge Atwell decides that while Byron made no direct admission, something
Byron said on the tapes might be an admission depending on Kelly's
"contact," whatever that is, and her "concern," whatever that may be. In
other words, it doesn't have anything to do with what Byron said, it has to
do with Kelly's contact and concern.

Now, having decided that the tape will be admitted depending on what
Kelly says in court, in other words having decided the tape will be admitted,
Atwell sets down the guidelines the prosecution must follow to build a
foundation for admitting the tape into evidence.

I believe the foundation is something like this. The person would
have to testify that this was a tape recording; that it was made on a
machine capable of recording voices; that the tape was unaltered;
and that the tape has been kept in some kind of chain of custody. Am
I pretty clear to that being the foundation?

To which Theresa Crayon replied:

Yeah. The only thing I would add to that, Judge, in the cases Mr.
Lance even cited, it shows the State is not required to show a hand-
to-hand custody; that the State must only prove reasonable
assurance that the evidence was not tampered with and we can do
that.

The reason I bring that up is because there was an attempt, as I have
explained to Mr. Lance, to enhance the tape so that the quality was a
bit better. So it was sent to a person down in Springfield who does
that sort of work, and it was sent back. And you've been presented
with those. It really didn't help. I mean, we are left with the same
thing we had before. They weren't able to enhance them.

So the tapes themselves had been moved from place to place, and we
do have the chain of custody document, but I would suggest that we
don't need to bring the person in from Springfield to testify about the
condition of the tapes and how he got them; et cetera; that, if we can
show they have not been tampered with, and we are prepared to
have Kelly Moffett listen to the whole thing, say if it's a fair and
accurate representation, it hasn't been adjusted, this is exactly what
we said when we said it was when the tape was made.

To which Judge Atwell said: "I suspect that gets over the hurdle," and then some other stuff.

To which Horton Lance, Byron's defense attorney I remind you, says:

> Judge, I don't have any additional requests. I think you bent over backwards with the work you're already doing.

Holy Inadequate Defense!

Judge Atwell tells the prosecution that they must show the tape is unaltered. The prosecution responds by telling the judge to his face the tape has indeed been altered. They call it "enhanced." They even tell him he's actually holding the altered, I mean enhanced, tape in his hand, but "Not to worry, Kelly will tell the jurors everything is on the up and up." Atwell says "Good enough for me." Then Lance says "Good enough for me too.""

❖

The trial went smoothly. . Theresa Crayon told the jurors they should not believe Byron Case because he was the defendant. Kelly failed to explain how a contact wound to the nose (with a ⅜"-diameter defect) could have been caused by a shotgun (with a 3/4" diameter slug) fired from behind at a distance of five feet. Byron stumbled though the questioning about the phone call recording he had never heard before. David Fry told the jurors that Kelly was a big fat liar, but they should believe her because she also told them about her drug abuse. Then jurors deliberated for two hours or so and unanimously decided the State had indeed proved its case beyond a reasonable doubt.

❖

When preparations were being made to play the tape for the jurors, Prosecutor Crayon had Kelly confirm that the transcript matched the tape.

Q: Ms. Moffett, you have heard this tape, is that right?
A: Yes.
Q: Is it very difficult to hear either you or Mr. Case?
A: Yes. It's difficult to hear him.
Q: And you were using the recording device that was on your phone, is that right?
A: Yeah. It was on the phone he provided for me.
Q: Right. So the phone was at your house?
A: Yes.
Q: And you come through very clearly, do you not?
A: Yes.
Q: And it's very difficult to hear Mr. Case, is that fair?
A: Yes, that's fair.
Q: But with the aid of the transcript, were you able to hear what he was saying with the transcript helping you along?
A: Oh yeah. It was the conversation.

AFTERMATH: WHO DONE IT?

It is a mistake for us as jurors to believe we can or must identify the real culprit before acquitting a defendant. Of all the people involved in a case, we as jurors are in the worst position to actually solve the crime.

We are purposely kept unaware of critical evidence. For example, neither you nor the actual jurors were made aware that Anastasia's father reported hearing a gunshot around midnight, while standing outside the gate of Mount Washington Cemetery. Nor did you or the actual jurors know, until now, that investigators were unable to locate Justin's eyeglasses, backpack, and a pair of his shoes after his suicide. Neither you nor the actual jurors knew that a local drug dealer reported to Sergeant Kilgore that Justin asked about buying a gun not long before Anastasia's death.

As you have already learned, the actual jurors were unaware that Anastasia was suicidal. They didn't know of the letter she left on Justin's computer stating she didn't want to live without him. They never heard that Betsy Owens could envision her daughter saying "Well, if you're going to leave me, kill me," or "I could see it being a suicide thing," or "I can see Stasi being the leader that she was, saying well I'll go first."

I learned of that evidence because I investigated the case well after the trial. That is allowed. You can investigate after a trial if you wish, after you are dismissed as a juror, but you may not, should not, must not perform any investigation during the trial.

Jurors would not have been allowed, for example, to research gunshot wounds, corneal cloudiness, or rigor mortis onset times, at least until the trial was over. The actual jurors, as you have learned, were not allowed to even make a careful comparison of the phone call audio recording and its transcription, much less subject the audio file to an acoustic analysis. More significantly, they weren't allowed to takes notes during trial testimony.

Because as jurors our knowledge is intentionally limited, and because we must not perform any investigation of our own, we have no realistic hope of actually solving the crime during deliberations. Disappointing as it may seem, it is not our job. We are to decide one thing, and one thing only: did the State prove beyond a reasonable doubt that the defendant committed the crime as charged.

"Well, if the defendant didn't do it, then who did?"

It's simply human to ask that question, at least to oneself. The question can become a crutch, though, for jurors who don't care for the defendant but fear the evidence falls short of proof beyond a reasonable doubt. These jurors may attempt to buttress the prosecution case by claiming the defendant must be guilty, since no one can figure out who else it could be.

No skeptical juror would ever step into that trap.

So, you may ask, if I'm not going to reveal who actually killed Anastasia, why did I title this chapter Who Done It? It's a good question. I'm glad you asked.

By using "Who Done It" as the chapter title, I'm not posing the question of who killed Anastasia WitbolsFeugen. I don't know, and as a juror I don't care.

I'm posing instead the question of who is responsible for the wrongful conviction of Byron Case.

Who did that?

And for that question, unfortunately, I have an answer.

The people responsible for the wrongful conviction of Byron Case are the same people responsible for the wrongful conviction of the recently exonerated Ted White, another victim of the Jackson County Prosecutor's office. They are the same people who wrongfully convicted the 248 people exonerated by the Innocence Project, the same people who have wrongfully imprisoned as many as fifty thousand of our fellow Americans.

The people responsible are you and I. We the people are responsible for the plight of the wrongfully convicted.

Those of us who enforce the law but cut corners, distort evidence and elaborate testimony, we are responsible.

Those of us who prosecute weak cases, withhold evidence, bend the truth, inflame rather than inform, and ask jurors to automatically disbelieve defendants, we must share in that responsibility.

Those of us who defend the accused but fail to defend with passion, we too are at fault.

Those of us who sit behind a bench, deny jurors the right to take notes, prohibit the re-reading of trial testimony, and otherwise deprive jurors of a clear recollection of the evidence, we too are to blame.

And those of us who deliberate a defendant's future behind a closed jury room door, yet fail to presume innocence and fail to burden the State with proof, we are responsible. We are to blame.

A jury summons is a clarion call straight from the U. S. Constitution, straight from our Bill of Rights. "In all criminal prosecutions, the accused shall enjoy the right to a speedy and public trial, by an impartial jury . . ."

As citizens, we have been tasked by our founding fathers to protect the innocent among us from our own government, to insure that those who govern do not go astray. We are the last line of defense in all matters criminal. We must stand true to our oath as jurors. We must not yield.

POSTLUDE

If you exit Lincoln Cemetery to the south and turn right on Truman Road, you will quickly encounter a stoplight. For three years, Kelly claimed that Anastasia got out of the car at that stoplight. Byron claims that to this day. Don Rand claims he saw Anastasia walking east that night. If you look in your rearview mirror, perhaps you'll see her in the ether.

If you look forward, you can't miss the I-435 overpass. Take the on ramp and head south. After ten miles or so, the interstate curves to your right. After the curving turn, take a glance to your left, to the south. There's yet another cemetery, Mount Moriah Cemetery. Anastasia is there now. Some of her ashes were scattered in Europe, but some of them are inurned there.

Russell and Clara Stover both rest there also, not far from Anastasia. They were the founders of Stover's Candy. They made and sold the original Eskimo Pie.

Dan Quisenberry rests there as well. He was a relief pitcher for the Kansas City Royals from 1979 to 1988. Five times he led the league in saves. Three times he was selected for the All Star team. I remember him. He threw side-armed, almost underhanded. One of his nicknames was The Australian because he pitched from down under.

Sixty miles north of Mt. Moriah Cemetery is the Crossroads Correctional Center. Byron Case is there today. He will be there tomorrow, and the next day, and the next, and the day after that. He will be there next week, next month, and next year. He is scheduled to be there every day for the rest of his life.

It brings to mind a quote by Dan Quisenberry, who now rests near Anastasia WitbolsFeugen. "I've seen the future and it's much like the present, only longer."

NOTES

I wish to acknowledge the role played in the development of this book by Lynn Allen, my wife. Lynn acted as both advisor and editor. She is responsible for the cover design concept. More significantly, she expanded the operation of our small company to include publishing, so that this work would see the light of day. Most significantly, she was by my side throughout the trial that prompted this book, the aftermath of that trial, and the creation of this book. Quite simply, without Lynn there would be no book.

I wish also to acknowledge the role played by Lauren Allen, my niece. Lauren too acted as both advisor and editor. Additionally, she assumed responsibility for page layout, and shoulders some of the marketing responsibilities. Significantly, her experience with voice-over work was key to my discovery of the hidden voices within the June 5, 2000 phone recording that is so significant to this case. As the only other full-fledged member of our Skeptical Juror team, she is co-authoring the third book in this series.

This book is unique both in its purpose and structure. We faced multiple literary challenges as we attempted simultaneously to enlighten our country's jury pool, preserve the integrity of the testimonial evidence, and create a viable literary product. After I completed the first draft, Lynn and Lauren were bold enough to inform me that my work was far from being ready for market. They were also kind enough to offer sincere encouragement for another effort, and wise enough to suggest changes that led to a vastly-improved, second-generation draft.

We provided the second-generation draft to a select group of early readers for additional comment and criticism. The group included family members, friends, colleagues, and acquaintances. The early readers represent the breadth of our country, geographically, occupationally, and politically. They reside from the west coast to the east coast. They hold conservative, liberal, and libertarian viewpoints. They work as lawyers, engineers, database designers, real estate agents, and pet-sitters. They also represent the retired community and the unemployed.

I wish to acknowledge the significant role they played in this book. Reading between the lines of their generous reviews, we could see the literary problems we had yet to solve. Their criticism and suggestions led to another rewrite, to a third generation of the book. It is the version you now hold in your hands.

In the cases where we have explicit permission to use the names of our early readers, they appear on the back cover of this book.

Finally, I wish to acknowledge Ed Lewis for the cover design of this book. We intend to use it as a format for those books that will follow in this series. You can find other examples of his work at www.edlewisdesign.com.

For complete, unabridged, unaltered trial transcripts, visit The Skeptical Juror web site: www.skepticaljuror.com

For case documents related to this trial, visit The Skeptical Juror web site.

For a digital recording of the 5 June 2000 phone call between Kelly Moffett and Byron Case, visit The Skeptical Juror web site.

I altered the Trial portion of this book, relative to the trial transcripts, in the following manner:

- Excluded opening statements by both prosecution and defense.

- Converted large portions of witness testimony to first person narrative.

- Removed false starts, repetition, and bad grammar from large portions of the witness testimony.

- Abridged the later, less significant portion of transcript for the June 5 phone call

- Excluded all trial testimony reference to the inconsequential June 7 phone call, the only controlled phone call, between Kelly and Byron.

- Excluded discussion of German ancestry and use of German language from the testimony of Evelyn Case.

- Excluded discussion regarding availability of Byron's car from Byron's testimony and that of his mother.

- Removed the testimony of David Hill, who measured the distance from Lincoln Cemetery to the location where Kelly told Kilgore he might search for the murder weapon.

- Removed the testimony of Tara McDowell, Abraham Kneisley's ex-girlfriend, who testified that Byron and Justin briefly dropped by her apartment after dropping Kelly off at the Moffett residence.

- Abridged many of the admonitions given by Judge Atwell to the jury prior to breaks.

- Removed Judge Atwell's reading of the jury instructions to the jury.

- Removed the closing arguments by both prosecution and defense.

With respect to the fictionalized Deliberations, I:

- removed reference to Counts 2, 3, and 4, thereby limiting the charges to murder in the first degree.
- renumbered the jury instructions accordingly.

With respect to the Aftermath, I include here a note regarding possible appeals based on new evidence of actual innocence:

On August 17, 2009, the U.S. Supreme Court decided the capital case of Troy Anthony Davis, 557 U.S. ___ (2009), instructing a district court to hear evidence of "actual innocence." The U.S. Supreme Court ordered the district court to "receive testimony and make findings of facts as to whether new evidence that could not have been obtained at the time of trial clearly establishes . . . innocence." As of the publication of this book, Davis' hearing has not occurred.

I used several quotes without citation. I credit them below.

From the Mary Tyler Moore show, I modified "A little song, a little dance, a little seltzer down your pants." That ditty was from the eulogy given Chuckles the Clown who died dressed as Peter Peanut when he was shucked by an elephant.

From Raymond Chandler's Philip Marlowe series, I adopted "He looked like he swallowed a bee."

From Monday Night Football, I adopted Al Michaels' line "Well, that was ill-conceived and poorly-executed." He threw out that one-time pithy description of a play that didn't work out particularly well.

I twice alluded to the large number of those wrongfully convicted. For discussion of those numbers, visit The Skeptical Juror web site at www.skepticaljuror.com.

EXPANDED CONTENTS: TESTIMONY

EXPANDED CONTENTS: DELIBERATION

EXPANDED CONTENTS: AFTERMATH

I dedicate this book to Lynn Marie Allen, my publisher, my partner, my wife, my friend, my love. Without you, this would not be possible.